PATENT LAW
IN A NUTSHELL

By

MARTIN J. ADELMAN
Theodore and James Pedas Family Professor of
Intellectual Property and Technology Law
George Washington University

RANDALL R. RADER
Circuit Judge
United States Court of Appeals
for the Federal Circuit
Professorial Lecturer in Law
George Washington University

GORDON P. KLANCNIK
Nixon & Vanderhye P.C.

THOMSON

WEST

Mat #18192160

© 2008 Thomson/West
  610 Opperman Drive
  St. Paul, MN 55123
  1–800–313–9378

Printed in the United States of America

ISBN: 978–0–314–25650–8

TEXT IS PRINTED ON 10% POST CONSUMER RECYCLED PAPER

DEDICATION

The authors thank Elizabeth Richardson and Aaron Johansen for their assistance in preparing this Nutshell. We also appreciate the dedication and diligence of the editors at Thomson/West, including Roxanne Birkel, Dennis Still, and Louis Higgins. Lastly, many thanks go to Michelle Walters, whose support was critical throughout this project.

*

OUTLINE

OUTLINE

*

XV

TABLE OF CASES

References are to Pages

A

B

C

D

E

F

G

H

I

L

M

N

O

P

Q

R

S

T

U

V

W

Y

Z

PATENT LAW
IN A NUTSHELL

*

CHAPTER 1

FOUNDATIONS OF PATENT LAW

I. FOUNDATIONS OF PATENT LAW

While historians occasionally refer to earlier precursors in Italy or Greece, the modern patent system began with an exception to the English 1624 Statute of Monopolies. Martin J. Adelman, Randall R. Rader, John R. Thomas & Harold C. Wegner, *Cases & Materials on Patent Law* 9 (2d ed. 2003) (ARTW). From that starting point, the various American colonies imported the patent tradition. Thus, the origins of U.S. patent law antedate the Republic itself. ARTW at 9–12. From those roots, scholars have set forth various justifications for the patent law regime.

Modern economic theorists, for instance, opine that patents promote an efficient use of scarce resources. In this case, the scarce resource is the technical knowledge that patent law promotes. A scarcity of knowledge about rats, fleas, and hygiene in 1342–5, for example, cost the lives of one-third of the inhabitants of Europe in the black plague epidemic. In modern terms, the plagues of AIDS or SARS illustrate that some forms of knowledge remain far too scarce.

Historians, on the other hand, attribute the rise of patent law to the antiquation of trade guilds. At the end of the feudal era, patents began to replace the trade secret scheme of the guilds as the optimal protection for intellectual property.

Natural law theory posits that the inventive labor entitles the innovator to enjoy exclusively the fruits of the new technology. Under this property-based theory, the discoverer earns a right to exclude others from use of the invention for a limited time. A corollary of this school of thought argues that patent law converts the conceptual and theoretical invention into property rights capable of valuation and trading in the market place. This aspect of patents, in turn, encourages the efficient conversion of those property rights into useful products and technology. Even more recent theories recognize patent law as a beneficial monopoly based on the public utility model. John F. Duffy, *Rethinking the Prospect Theory of Patents*, 71 U. CHI. L. REV. 439 (2004).

This brief overview will not discuss many less comprehensive rationales for patent law. For instance, academics have offered rent dissipation and races to invent as justifications for aspects of patent law. Mark F. Grady & Jay I. Alexander, *Patent Law and Rent Dissipation*, 78 VA. L. REV. 305 (1992); Robert P. Merges & Richard R. Nelson, *On the Complex Economics of Patent Scope*, 90 COLUM. L. REV. 839 (1990).

II. ECONOMICS (INCENTIVE TO INVENT)

The majority of modern patent literature emphasizes economic justifications. These rationales maintain that a patent system primarily creates an incentive to invent while minimizing free-riding. *See, e.g.*, Rebecca S. Eisenberg, *Patents and the Progress of Science: Exclusive Rights and Experimental Use*, 56 U. CHI. L. REV. 1017 (1989).

The patent system creates an incentive to invest in research, which, in turn, speeds the advance of technology. Often technological advances consume millions or even billions of dollars in research and development costs. Without some form of protection, free-riders would swiftly reverse-engineer and copy the innovator's technology. The innovator would lose its vast investment in an instant. In the short run, the public would receive the copied innovation at reduced costs. After all, the market would force free-rider(s) and the innovator to price the new good or service near the cost of production—in economic terms, at the marginal cost.

On the other hand, this free-riding would kill or diminish the incentive for future innovation. Because marginal prices for an inventive product or service would drop below the average cost (which includes both the marginal cost and the per-unit development cost), investors would have little economic incentive to fund expensive development projects. Without patent protections, a rational participant in the marketplace might avoid research investments and instead wait for others to develop a cure for cancer, then quickly copy it.

At the same time, a rational innovator would hide his advances as long as possible to boost his head-start advantage in the market. Even without patent rights, an innovator enjoys some benefit as the market's first mover. This head start, however, does not adequately protect inventions with vast re-search investments. Thus, inventors would protect their advances with trade secrets. In the rare event that trade secrets actually would work to impede reverse engineering, they would, in turn, make im-provements and further research more difficult and impede the advance of important, even life-saving, technology.

Assume, for example, that an inventor finds the cure for AIDS or SARS. No doubt that invention would represent years of effort and millions, if not billions, of dollars in research investments. Without patent protection, a copyist might easily reverse engineer that product within a few weeks. The inventor could never hope to recoup the costs of discovery.

Without a promise of protection, the rational in-vestor would seek more dependable investments. The patent system protects the investment by giv-ing the inventor control over the economic benefits from the technology for a limited time. Thus, the inventor may both recover research costs and accu-mulate capital for other projects.

Of course, consumers pay the differential between strict marginal pricing and accurate, investment-inducing pricing that compensates for research and development costs. Inevitably this price differential means that a smaller group of consumers may enjoy the product at the increased price during the limited period of exclusive rights. In a price-sensitive market, the higher price invariably reduces the demand for the good or service. This price elasticity restricts the use of inventions to those consumers willing (or able) to pay the exclusive-right price. Particularly in health care products (where the market is nearly inelastic), this economic reality creates a moral concern.

The limited period of exclusivity, however, substantially reduces those moral issues. Every invention before 1987 (assuming a 20–year exclusive right) is free after 2007. Thus each generation, in effect, funds a gift of technology to its children, asking only that their children do the same for their grandchildren. In essence, the patent system facilitates each generation's gift of inventive solutions to future generations. Thus, as each generation speeds life-saving or life-enhancing technology into use, the long-term benefits of early production of new technology outweigh the nominal costs of patents in the short term.

III. HISTORY: ANTIDOTE TO TRADE SECRETS (INCENTIVE TO DISCLOSE)

Historians often trace the rise of the patent system to the time when trade guilds began to fade as protectors of sensitive technology. As noted earlier, without a patent system, inventors would guard their advances as trade secrets. At the close of the feudal period, trade guilds required years of apprenticeship to earn access to proprietary secrets. These guilds restricted distribution of trade secrets to members of the guild. Although this practice prevented free-riding, the high barrier to entry (that is, completion of an apprenticeship) discouraged competition and impeded scientific advance. Only those within the guild had the incentive and know-how to make technological advances. Trade guilds, in essence, shrank the pool of potential inventors. The public patent grant removed those artificial barriers. In exchange for disclosure in the patent application, the inventor received a limited period of exclusive rights.

Even without trade guilds, trade secrets remain an option to protect innovations in the modern marketplace. Although secrecy may not protect inventions that are readily deciphered once in use, a widespread secrecy practice would impede advances in many technology fields. Patents, on the other hand, encourage rapid disclosure and give other innovators access to the most recent enhancements in technology. With this information available, each advance often spurs further improvements.

A race to disclose, however, can come at a cost. In particular, the profit incentive may concentrate scarce research resources on projects with the greatest economic rewards. For example, researchers may invest more in the search for curing universal heart-burn maladies than for curing a rare cancer. This academic complaint, however, ignores the economic realities of limited resources and mistrusts the market to efficiently allocate scarce research resources.

The race to disclose, furthermore, may complicate research by creating a patent thicket that increases the cost of research and development. While theoretically plausible, this so-called tragedy of the anti-commons, if it exists at all, is rare. In the first place, the patent system does not permit the scope of exclusive rights to exceed the scope of disclosure. This requirement, enforced by the enablement and obviousness doctrines, ensures that patents do not preempt more than they contribute to the useful arts. Accordingly, each patent delineates both its contribution and the prospect for further patentable improvements on the same technology. In other words, patents document the state of current technology and thus facilitate further research to extend the horizons of technology.

Moreover, the market generally licenses technology at a value commensurate with its contribution to the sciences. Thus, multiple minor patents in a crowded area of technology will generally be available for "rent or purchase" at very reasonable rates. Furthermore, competitors often thin-out the patent thicket by jointly cross-licensing—that is, "pooling"—patents covering various aspects of a technology area. Market forces thus can often reduce the tragedy of the anti-commons to an academic concern. Nonetheless in the crowded information technology industry with its heavy reliance on semiconductor and software technology, major corporations have argued that patent "trolls" (an undefined pejorative most often referring to a patentee seeking royalties without producing a product) use litigation strategies to obtain royalties beyond the economic contribution of the invention to the technology. Still, beyond anecdotal evidence, no authoritative and comprehensive study has yet documented that patents prevent technological advance by complicating research in a field preempted by multiple intellectual property rights.

IV. HISTORY: TECHNOLOGY TRANSFER

At the advent of the era of patents, a sovereign would often use the promise of an exclusive right to lure technology available in another nation into the sovereign's domain. Thus, the inventor-turned-entrepreneur could obtain an exclusive right by merely relocating innovative technology.

In the modern world, intellectual property is still a central component of international technology transfer policy. The 1995 treaty on the Trade Related Aspects of Intellectual Property (TRIPS) made membership in the World Trade Organization (WTO) conditional on adoption of intellectual property institutions. At that point, every nation had an incentive to adopt a patent system that meets basic international standards. Functional patent-granting and patent-enforcing institutions became every nation's ticket to enjoy minimal tariffs and other WTO trade benefits. In simple terms, protecting advanced technology became the means of acquiring advanced technology.

Even before TRIPS, however, patent protection influenced technology transfer. Most developed nations have had some form of patent protection for decades, if not centuries. Developing nations, on the other hand, generally lack robust patent systems. In many cases, patent owners no doubt declined to transfer their technology to nations without adequate enforcement. Thus, national patent policy and institutions have consistently influenced technology transfer.

Of course, even without an inventor's consent, copyists may nonetheless acquire access to patented technology available in other parts of the world. In one sense, the inventor is no worse off, because he presumably was not counting on remuneration from countries where he would hold no rights. On the other hand, nations without a vigorous patent system, at a minimum, discourage legitimate research investments and technology transfer within their borders. Often an inadequate patent system may also create incentives for a nation's own inventors, with their ability to develop a technology that may lift the economy of their entire nation, to do their work where it will be protected. Any potential for this kind of "brain drain" may have the long-term consequence of transferring technology even before its development.

V. NATURAL RIGHTS (ENTITLEMENT THEORY)

Patents are a form of property. 35 U.S.C. § 261, in fact, provides that "patents shall have the attributes of personal property." As a species of property, patents share the philosophical origins of real property. Under John Locke's fundamental justification for property rights, a divine being created the world as a universal common in which individuals possess an equal right. *See* John Locke, THE SECOND TREATISE OF GOVERNMENT ¶ 27 (1690), in TWO TREATISES OF GOVERNMENT (Peter Laslett ed. 1960). Within that universal common, each individual personally owns the products of his labor. In a related theory, Georg Wilhelm Friedrich Hegel proffered that property results not from the fruit of one's labor but from the exercise of free will. *See* HEGEL'S PHILOSOPHY OF RIGHT (T.M. Knox trans. 1952). In other words, the interaction of human will with the corporeal world creates enduring objects, or property. These objects, a natural part of their creator's personality, deserve protection from unauthorized use.

Under either Locke's labor theory or Hegel's moral rights theory, invented knowledge belongs to its creator or discoverer. But these labor-based rights are not limitless: an individual cannot take from the universal common without leaving enough for others to use and enjoy. To some degree, knowledge as a form of private property is counterintuitive. Most cultures view knowledge as something to be freely shared. On the other hand, technical knowledge, often the product of expensive research ventures, must be generated. Patent rights provide the requisite "fuel of interest," in the words of Abraham Lincoln, to stimulate inventive labor or the "fire of genius."

Entitlement theories also show that patents serve the larger economic service of converting inchoate knowledge into useful technology for public consumption. In other words, the incentives of patent law do some of their best work after invention, disclosure, and issuance of a patent. At that point, the patent system enables an inventor to raise capital to market and manufacture the invention.

Private ownership of those valuable property rights can generate capital and incentives to convert the concepts into usable products. In other words, invention only starts the process of creating useful technology. The further work or conversion to useful products, manufacturing, and distribution also requires capital. Patents can generate that investment. In addition, patents solve the inventor's dilemma by creating a way to obtain development capital without compromising the idea. The owner of the idea, additionally, must use the knowledge efficiently or the market will transfer that ownership to better uses. In simple terms, private is more efficient than collective ownership.

A modern corollary of this principle, the prospect theory, suggests that patents promote efficient use of a scarce resource like knowledge. Edmund W. Kitch, *The Nature and Function of the Patent System*, 20 J.L. & Econ. 265 (1977). The prospect theory opines that the owner/inventor can efficiently direct future research to refine and improve the new technology.

VI. PATENTS AND PUBLIC UTILITY THEORY

Many economists criticize the patent system for eliminating the "surplus" otherwise enjoyed by the consumer. In other words, the consumer would get the benefit of lower prices without patents recapturing the costs of research and development. The usual economic proposal to retain the consumer surplus emphasizes rewards in lieu of patents. A leading scholar, Professor Duffy, has recently made a frontal assault on this chorus by pointing out that there is a similar loss of consumer surplus in the field of public utilities—an example where economists almost universally praise the benefits of pricing above marginal cost. John F. Duffy, *Rethinking the Prospect Theory of Patents*, 71 U. CHI. L. REV. 439 (2004). Under this response, public utilities, like electricity generation, have very low marginal costs once the infrastructure of dams and power lines are in place. These utilities, however, require a monopoly to both promote efficiency in generation and distribution and to recover over time the vast investment in infrastructure. Similarly patents engender a beneficial monopoly that allows the innovator to recover research and development costs over the life of the patent. In other words, the international patent system is more efficient than an international reward system (which the governments of the world are not likely to create or administer anyway).

VII. CONCLUSION

In spite of some defects, the patent system is one of the greatest inventions of Western civilization. With manageable costs of administration, the system stimulates inventive activity that facilitates economic expansion while simultaneously encouraging conversion of theoretical science into useful technology. Finally, the system achieves moral benefits by its limited terms with each generation providing a gift of innovation to its successors.

CHAPTER 2

PATENT ACQUISITION

I. THE UNITED STATES PATENT AND TRADEMARK OFFICE

A. Examination

As the administrative agency in charge of granting patents, the United States Patent and Trademark Office—typically abbreviated as USPTO, PTO, or simply Patent Office—examines all patent applications to ensure compliance with substantive and procedural requirements.[1] In particular, § 131 requires the Patent Office to examine patent applications:

> The Director shall cause an examination to be made of the application and the alleged new invention; and if on such examination it appears that the applicant is entitled to a patent under the law, the Director shall issue a patent therefor.

To fulfill this statutory requirement, the Patent Office will examine patent applications on a first-come-first-served basis, absent compelling or unusu-

---

1. To fund its operations, the Patent Office charges fees for performing various functions, including those related to examining applications. *See* 35 U.S.C. § 41; 37 C.F.R. §§ 1.16–1.28. In fact, the revenue collected from these fees in recent history frequently has exceeded the amount Congress appropriates to the Patent Office.

al circumstances requiring accelerated examination. During this examination process, the Patent Office will examine the application for compliance with formal requirements as well as perform a search for prior art. Should the application fail to conform with either procedural or substantive requirements, § 132(a) provides:

> Whenever, on examination, any claim for a patent is rejected, or any objection or requirement made, the Director shall notify the applicant thereof, stating the reasons for such rejection, or objection or requirement, together with such information and references as may be useful in judging of the propriety of continuing the prosecution of his application; and if after receiving such notice, the applicant persists in his claim for a patent, with or without amendment, the application shall be reexamined. No amendment shall introduce new matter into the disclosure of the invention.

Upon rejection or objection, the Patent Office issues an Office Action setting forth the inadequacies of the patent application. 37 C.F.R. § 1.104. Ordinarily, an applicant will have three months to respond to an Office Action (in unusual circumstances, just one month). The applicant may extend this period up to a total of 6 months. 35 U.S.C. § 133. Within the prescribed time, the applicant responds and argues in a Reply or an Amendment— the nomenclature depends on whether the applicant contests the action or amends the application in light of the rejection or objection—that the rejection or objection was either factually or legally improper.

37 C.F.R. §§ 1.111 & 1.121. This back-and-forth will continue until the Patent Office allows the application or issues a Final Office Action under 37 C.F.R. § 1.113, at which point, the applicant must either appeal the rejected claims or request continued examination (or, of course, abandon the application).

The Patent Office thus plays an important gatekeeping function. Stated otherwise, the PTO facilitates an efficient and trustworthy patent system by preventing the issuance of undeserving patents. Without rigorous examination, so-called "scarecrow" patents would raise costs of doing business, either in extracting preventable royalty payments or forcing litigation to invalidate worthless patents. During examination, the Patent Office applies the substantive requirements of patent law: eligibility, utility, novelty, nonobviousness, adequate disclosure, and definiteness. Importantly, even if a patent issues, the mere fact of issuance does not preclude future challenges based on these substantive requirements. An affected party has recourse through litigation or through limited post-grant procedures at the Patent Office.

The following chart outlines the pre-examination, examination, and post-examination procedures relating to prosecuting and obtaining a United States patent. The chart shows a generally predictable flow to prosecution, even if the specific path of an individual case's prosecution may vary. Two common paths towards a patent grant are marked by solid lines; other possibilities are marked with dashed lines. One solid line shows an allowance issued directly by the examiner. The other leads to an appeal to the Board of Patent Appeals and Interferences, which may affirm, reject, or modify the examiner's rejections. As will be appreciated, this chart does not summarize all potential permutations. For example, post-grant proceedings, like reexamination and reissue are not shown. Similarly, petitions and pre-grant publications are not shown. Nevertheless, it provides a good overview of typical prosecution before the United States Patent and Trademark Office.

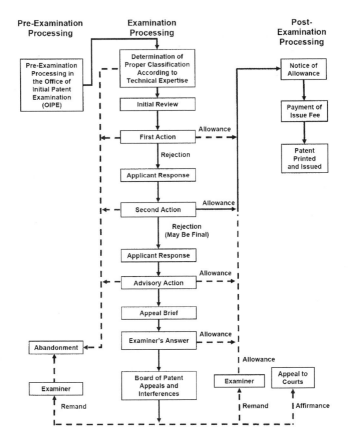

B. Historical Development

The evolution of the Patent Office parallels the convolution of the patent system as a whole. The Constitution sets forth the primary authority for enacting these laws: "The Congress shall have Power ... To promote the Progress of Science and useful Arts, by securing for limited Times to Authors and Inventors the exclusive Right to their respective Writings and Discoveries." U.S. CONST. Art. I, § 8, cl. 8. Like other grants of power in the Constitution, this clause merely gives Congress the power to shape the substantive and procedural requirements of patents. *See, e.g.*, *In re Bergy*, 596 F.2d 952 (CCPA 1979).

Swiftly utilizing this power, Congress enacted the first Patent Act in 1790, which authorized the first three examiners—the Secretary of State, the Secretary of War, and the Attorney General—to grant patents. Patent Act of 1790, 1 Stat. 109 (Apr. 10, 1790). Congress soon realized that the many competing responsibilities of these cabinet members prevented substantive examination of patent applications. Therefore, the next iteration of the Patent Act eliminated the three-person board in favor of a pure registration system. Patent Act of 1793, 2 Stat. 318 (Feb. 21, 1793). Even though the Department of State maintained a registry of all patents under this act, patents received no substantive examination. Litigation was the sole means of detecting and invalidating unpatentable subject matter.

This registration system proved inefficient. Under the 1793 Act, two parties could even acquire patents on the same invention, which may have been actually unpatentable for both of them when a court finally litigated validity issues. In 1836, the next Patent Act reinstated an examination system. Patent Act of 1836, 5 Stat. 117 (Jul. 4, 1836). This act created a Patent Office, albeit within the Department of State, and set forth procedural and substantive requirements for patentability. The 1870 Act followed with important changes establishing the modern practice of peripheral claims to define the outer bounds of the invention. Before 1870, central claiming described inventions in more general terms. In any event, judicial interpretation of the 1836 and 1870 Acts resulted in the common law origins of many doctrines familiar to current patent practitioners, including nonobviousness, enablement, and experimental use.

Aside from the creation of the Court of Claims and Patent Appeals (CCPA), which was granted jurisdiction over appeals from the Patent Office in 1929, statutory patent law remained largely untouched until the seminal Patent Act of 1952. This monumental achievement both codified much of the common law and also reoriented the law in important areas such as obviousness and functional claiming.

The modern obviousness requirement remains the crowning achievement of the 1952 Act. Before 1952, the judiciary struggled to articulate a neutral, objective standard to distinguish genuine "inventions" from mere minor technological improvements. Moreover, the advent of the antitrust era cast an unfavorable light on the patent "monopolies." *Transparent-Wrap Mach. Corp. v. Stokes & Smith Co.*, 329 U.S. 637, 644 (1947) (calling a patent a "legalized monopoly"); The Sherman Act, 15 U.S.C. § 2 (1890). The Supreme Court began requiring a "flash of creative genius" to prove an invention worthy of a patent. *See, e.g., Cuno Eng'g.*

Corp. v. Automatic Devices Corp., 314 U.S. 84, 91 (1941). This inherently subjective test for nonobviousness relied on an after-the-fact assessment of the invention's ability to evoke a "gee-whiz" reaction. The fabled Judge Learned Hand protested openly that this test was "as fugitive, impalpable, wayward, and vague a phantom as exists in the whole paraphernalia of legal concepts." *Harries v. Air King Prods. Co.*, 183 F.2d 158, 162 (2d Cir. 1950).

As discussed in Chapter 8, the modern test for obviousness that appeared in 1952 is objective, resting on factual considerations evaluated through the prism of a hypothetical person of ordinary skill in the technical art of the invention. This advance in the legal art of evaluating inventive contributions transformed patent acquisition (also called prosecution) as well as litigation.

Even after the 1952 Act, however, the Supreme Court could not articulate and apply a uniform test for inventiveness. *Anderson's-Black Rock, Inc. v. Pavement Salvage Co.*, 396 U.S. 57 (1969); *Sakraida v. Ag Pro, Inc.*, 425 U.S. 273 (1976). Without uniformity, some circuits followed the nonobviousness requirement in the 1952 Act; others continued to apply the "phantom" tests of synergism or flash of genius. Compare *Republic Indus., Inc. v. Schlage Lock Co.*, 592 F.2d 963 (7th Cir. 1979) and *Rengo Co. v. Molins Mach. Co.*, 657 F.2d 535 (3d Cir. 1981) with *Fred Whitaker Co. v. E.T. Barwick Indus., Inc.*, 551 F.2d 622 (5th Cir. 1977) and *Am. Seating Co. v. Nat'l Seating Co.*, 586 F.2d 611 (6th Cir. 1978). The vast differences amongst hospitable and inhospitable courts of appeals generated widespread forum shopping and undercut predictability in patent law. This unseemly situation contributed to Congress's decision in 1982 to create the United States Court of Appeals for the Federal Circuit. This new circuit consolidated all patent appeals from district courts across the country in a single court with exclusive subject matter jurisdiction over patent appeals from district courts and the Patent Office.

The Federal Circuit promptly adopted the decisions of its predecessor court, the CCPA, as precedent. *South Corp. v. United States*, 690 F.2d 1368 (Fed. Cir. 1982). While the Federal Circuit has 12 active judges, appeals are typically heard and decided by a 3–judge panel. On occasion, though, the full court will sit *en banc*, either to overrule precedent, *Newell Cos. v. Kenney Mfg. Co.*, 864 F.2d 757 (Fed. Cir. 1988) (*en banc*), or to settle important issues of law. *See, e.g.*, *Cybor Corp. v. FAS Techs., Inc.*, 138 F.3d 1448 (Fed. Cir. 1998) (*en banc*). The creation of the Federal Circuit disrupted the long-time system that distributed appeals amongst the various circuits according to geographic jurisdiction, regardless of subject matter. Congress and patent lawyers hoped that this dramatic disruption would bring certainty, uniformity, and predictability to the law. For the most part, the Federal Circuit has met these expectations. Some critics contend, however, that the court's decisions vary depending on the judges on any particular panel, thus undermining predictability. R. Polk Wagner & Lee Petherbridge, *Is the Federal Circuit Succeeding?: An Empirical*

Assessment of Judicial Performance, 152 U. PENN. L. REV. 1105 (2004).

From 1952 to 1999, the basic structure of the patent system remained largely untouched, but a few Patent Act amendments in this era deserve mention. Most notably, the 1995 amendments changed the statutory term of a patent from 17 years from the date of grant to 20 years from the date of filing. Uruguay Round Agreements Act, Pub. L. No. 103–465, 108 Stat. 4809 (1994). In 1980, Congress gave universities and other inventors patent rights in inventions developed with federal funds. Bayh–Dole Act, Pub. L. No. 96–517, 94 Stat. 3019 (1980). In 1984, Congress gave generic drug manufacturers permission to develop and test their products before expiration of patent rights. Drug Price Competition and Patent Term Restoration Act of 1984, Pub. L. No. 98–417, 98 Stat. 1585 (1984) (Hatch–Waxman Act). In 1988, Congress created remedies for importation and exportation of patented goods or goods made by patented processes. Process Patents Amendments Act of 1988, Pub. L. No. 100–418, § 9001–17, 102 Stat. 1107.

In 1999, for the first time, changes in the Patent Act seemed to reflect the value of harmonizing U.S. law with intellectual property standards around the world. American Inventors Protection Act, Pub. L. No. 106–113, 113 Stat. 1501 (1999). The most noteworthy changes accommodate U.S. law with European and Japanese standards, including a first user defense to infringement, the publication of pending applications 18 months from the priority date, and *inter partes* reexaminations of issued patents. The publication of pending applications marks a significant departure from the prior policy of maintaining the secrecy of pending applications, which dated back to the Patent Act of 1790. Moreover, *inter partes* reexamination, which provides an alternative to challenging a patent's validity in court, marks the first step towards an administrative opposition system.

C. Organization

Like any massive institution, the Patent Office has a well-organized structure to ensure efficient examination of patent applications as well as other functions. With respect to examining applications, the Office of Initial Patent Examination receives patent applications, labels them with unique application numbers, and forwards them along for examination (so long as they are complete enough for examination). The Patent Office divides applications among about a half-dozen Technology Centers, each of which is dedicated to a different general technical area. These Technology Centers comprise Work Groups, which are further subdivided into Art Units. As a rule, the Art Units, each of which comprises multiple primary and assistant examiners, have great expertise with—and repeated exposure to—applications pertaining to similar subject matter. As the front-line representatives for the interests of the Patent Office (and thus the public), the primary and assistant examiners review patent applications and issue official actions.

II. PROSECUTION PROCEDURES

Three sources provide the procedures governing the prosecution of a patent: the Patent Act as codified in 35 U.S.C. § 1 *et seq.*, administrative rules as set forth in 37 C.F.R. § 1.1 *et seq.*, and the Manual of Patent Examining Procedure (MPEP). Although the MPEP is a publication of the Patent Office, it does not set out binding law, even if courts sometimes cite its provisions as persuasive authority. *Compare In re Recreative Techs.*, 83 F.3d 1394 (Fed. Cir. 1996) *with Litton Sys., Inc. v. Whirlpool Corp.*, 728 F.2d 1423 (Fed. Cir. 1984). Patent examiners and applicants routinely rely upon the MPEP during prosecution.

A. Application Types

Under 35 U.S.C. § 111, an application falls into one of two mutually exclusive categories: a provisional application under subsection (b) or a nonprovisional application under subsection (a). Aside from originally filed applications, nonprovisional applications include continuing applications, such as divisional, continuation, and continuation-in-part applications. More recently, an applicant may request continued examination of an application subject to a final rejection; this procedure mimics the filing of a continuation application.

1. Provisional Applications

As its name suggests, a provisional application is a temporary placeholder for a more substantive application to follow. This form of application thus has streamlined requirements. In particular, a pro-

visional application has a disclosure that complies
with the requirements of § 112, first paragraph,
and a drawing (if necessary to understand the disclosed subject matter). Notably, a provisional application need not include any claim. 35 U.S.C.
§ 111(b)(2). The provisional does not undergo substantive examination. Rather the Patent Office
merely records and stores it. Unless the applicant
converts it into a nonprovisional application within
12 months, the Patent Office will deem it abandoned.

The provisional application serves the purpose of
setting a priority date for the disclosed subject
matter. In other words, a nonprovisional application
claiming an invention described in a provisional
application receives the benefit of the earlier filing
date. *See, e.g.*, *New Railhead Mfg., L.L.C. v. Ver-
meer Mfg. Co.*, 298 F.3d 1290 (Fed. Cir. 2002).
Because a provisional application is a temporary
placeholder, it cannot claim priority to any earlier
application. Perhaps more importantly, the provisional application, because not examined, does not
reduce the term of any patent that arises from its
initial filing. In other words, the filing of a provisional application does not trigger the start of a
patent's 20–year term.

2. Nonprovisional Applications

The Patent Office substantively examines each
nonprovisional application. The filing of these applications triggers the running of the patent term.
These applications must contain a specification with

a disclosure, at least one claim, a drawing (if necessary to understand the disclosed and claimed subject matter), and an oath by an applicant. 35 U.S.C. § 111(a)(2). Even if initially missing the oath or any requisite fees, the filing date of the application is the date of receipt of the specification and drawings (if any). Although not mandatory, 37 C.F.R. § 1.77 strongly recommends a particular arrangement for the contents of the specification. In part, a specification generally has a background of the invention, a brief summary of the invention, a brief description of the drawings, a detailed description of the invention, at least one claim, and an abstract of the disclosure.

3. Continuing Applications

Aside from claiming priority to a provisional application, a patent application may claim priority to another nonprovisional application. As a matter of convenience, patents claiming priority are said to be "related," and genealogical terms, such as "parent," "grandparent," "child," "sibling," and so on, are typically used to denote the ancestry of a patent family. The descendent applications, which include continuations, continuations-in-part (CIP), and divisional applications, fall under the general heading of continuing applications. These continuing applications generally provide the benefit of preserving the original filing and priority date while prolonging the prosecution process. To get this benefit, the subsequent application must contain claims with subject matter sufficiently supported or described in the prior application to satisfy § 112, first paragraph, share at least one inventor with the prior application, originate (be filed) while the prior application is still pending, and expressly reference the prior application. *See* 35 U.S.C. § 120; 37 C.F.R. §§ 1.53(b) & 1.78(a).

The Federal Circuit has explained the differences between these continuing applications:

"Continuation" and "divisional" applications are alike in that they are both continuing applications based on the same disclosure as an earlier application. They differ, however, in what they claim. A "continuation" application claims the same invention claimed in an earlier application, although there may be some variation in the scope of the subject matter claimed. A "divisional" application, on the other hand, is one carved out of an earlier application which disclosed and claimed more than one independent invention, the result being that the divisional application claims only one or more, but not all, of the independent inventions of the earlier application. A "CIP" application is a continuing application containing a portion or all of the disclosure of an earlier application together with added matter not present in that earlier application.

Transco Prods. Inc. v. Performance Contracting, Inc., 38 F.3d 551, 555–56 (Fed. Cir. 1994) (citations omitted). By noting that a CIP application contains new matter, the court implicitly acknowledged that it may have more than one priority date. Indeed, any subject matter not expressly or inherently disclosed in the parent application is not entitled to the benefit of that parent's filing date. *See, e.g.*, *Litton Sys., Inc. v. Whirlpool Corp.*, 728 F.2d 1423 (Fed. Cir. 1984).

a) Restriction Requirements and Divisionals

The Patent Office creates a divisional application with a "restriction requirement" under § 121. This statutory provision, in part, states:

> If two or more independent and distinct inventions are claimed in one application, the Director may require the application to be restricted to one of the inventions. If the other invention is made the subject of a divisional application which complies with the requirements of section 120 of this title it shall be entitled to the benefit of the filing date of the original application.... The validity of a patent shall not be questioned for failure of the Director to require the application to be restricted to one invention.

35 U.S.C. § 121. This provision authorizes the Patent Office to separate out claims directed to distinct inventions into separate applications.

The Patent Office employs restriction requirements to prevent applicants from circumventing the fee structure by prosecuting multiple separate inventions in a single application. Restriction requirements also increase the efficiency of examination by sending different inventions to Art Units more experienced in examining the separate inventions. These purely procedural requirements do not affect a patent's validity.

The statute, moreover, cryptically provides:

A patent issuing on an application with respect to which a requirement for restriction under this section has been made, or on an application filed as a result of such a requirement, shall not be used as a reference either in the Patent and Trademark Office or in the courts against a divisional application or against the original application or any patent issued on either of them, if the divisional application is filed before the issuance of the patent on the other application.

35 U.S.C. § 121. This sentence alludes to a potential problem related to double patenting, which is discussed in Chapter 11. In particular, this sentence shields claims withdrawn in response to a restriction requirement from a double patenting rejection in light of the initial application. *See, e.g., Geneva Pharms., Inc. v. GlaxoSmithKline PLC*, 349 F.3d 1373 (Fed. Cir. 2003). Indeed, so long as the "independent and distinct inventions" remain separated in subsequent continuing applications—referred to as "consonance" between originally restricted claims and their respective descendents—the applicant retains a statutory shield against invalidity for double patenting. If the applicant breaks consonance or if the Patent Office does not issue a restriction requirement unambiguously, the statutory shield disappears.

b) Requests for Continued Examination

An applicant may file a request for continued examination (RCE) under 37 C.F.R. § 1.114 to further prosecute a pending application under a final rejection (or where prosecution is otherwise closed.) A request for continued examination must include a submission, such as an information disclosure statement that lists additional references for consideration by the Patent Office, an amendment to any portion of the specification, or new evidence in support of patentability. In the event of an outstanding Office Action, the request for continued examination must address each ground of rejection and objection in that Office Action. 37 C.F.R. § 1.114(c). In other words, an applicant must make an effort to advance prosecution.

c) Presumptive Limits on Continuations, CIPs, and RCEs

In an effort to address perceived problems relating to the potential for abusive tactics in filing continuations and CIPs, the Patent Office promulgated rules setting forth presumptive limits on the number of continuations and CIPs in a patent family. See 72 Fed. Reg. 46,716 (Aug. 21, 2007). Under the revised rules, an applicant may file two continuations or CIPs in addition to one RCE in a single patent family without any explanation or justification. But any subsequent continuations, CIPs, or RCEs may only be filed if the application provides an adequate justification. The justification must include a petition explaining why the amendment, argument, or evidence could not have been previously submitted.

If an applicant files a divisional application in response to a restriction requirement, the new rules similarly allow only two continuations or CIPs in addition to one RCE in the divisional application family (which does not include any ancestors to the divisional application). Again, any subsequent continuations, CIPs, or RCEs may be filed if accompanied by an adequate justification.

B. Publication Rule

Until changed as the last century ended, the Patent Act protected the secrecy of all patent applications. To harmonize U.S. practice with international standards, the Patent Act now orders publication of most applications 18 months after their earliest filing date. In accordance with the most notable exception, if the subject matter claimed in the application is not the subject of a foreign application filed in accordance with an international agreement (like the Paris Convention or the Patent Cooperation Treaty), an applicant may request at the time of filing the application that the Patent Office refrain from publishing the application. 35 U.S.C. § 122.

In exchange for eliminating the secrecy of the pending application, the Patent Act provides provisional rights in limited circumstances. A patent applicant may obtain a reasonable royalty from infringers counted from the date of Patent Office publication, so long as two conditions are met: the published application must contain claims substantially identical to the claims in the patent maturing from that application and the patentee must have given actual notice of the published application to the infringer. 35 U.S.C. § 154(d). Because most patent applications are amended during prosecution, these provisional rights have nominal value.

C. Interferences

Aside from *ex parte* prosecution of a patent application, the Patent Office examines pending applications in an *inter partes* setting where a patent or patent application claims the same invention as, that is, "interferes" with, a pending application. A so-called interference—a deceptively intricate administrative proceeding governed by 35 U.S.C. §§ 135 & 102(g) and 37 C.F.R. § 1.601 *et seq.*—determines which applicant (or patentee) has priority over the invention. The statute provides that an interference occurs when "an application is made for a patent which ... would interfere with any pending application, or with any unexpired patent." 35 U.S.C. § 135. The Patent Office may declare an interference between two conflicting applications without any prompting by (or even knowledge of) either applicant. Alternatively, a patent applicant may provoke an interference upon discovering a newly issued patent or published pending application that claims the same invention. Importantly, a party who anticipates losing the priority contest may nonetheless prevent the winner from obtaining a patent by successfully arguing that the subject matter is not patentable. Chapter 7 examines interferences in greater detail.

D. Petition and Appeal Rights

Upon a final rejection or objection, an applicant may either appeal, in the case of a rejection, to the Board of Patent Appeals and Interferences under 35 U.S.C. § 134 or petition, in the case of an objection, the Commissioner of Patents under 37 C.F.R. § 1.181. The CCPA distinguished these separate courses:

> Decisions of the examiner directly relating to the rejection of claims are subject to appeal. These questions generally deal with the merits of the invention, involving factual determinations and the legal conclusions drawn therefrom regarding the application disclosure, the claims and the prior art. The examiner's rulings dealing with procedural matters, such as whether an affidavit or amendment is untimely, and formal requirements, such as whether a new application title will be required, are reviewable upon petition.

In re Searles, 422 F.2d 431, 435 (CCPA 1970). The Board hears all internal appeals, including interferences. This administrative body consists primarily of administrative patent judges who are typically former examiners with both scientific and legal credentials. 35 U.S.C. § 6. Three administrative patent judges hear each appeal. The entire Board may rehear any case decided by a three-judge panel. The Board delivers opinions supported by "substantial evidence"—that is, evidence that a reasonable person would accept as adequate to support a conclusion. *See, e.g.*, *In re Gartside*, 203 F.3d 1305

(Fed. Cir. 2000). Notably, the Board is not wholly independent from the Patent Office:

> Even though Board members serve an essential function, they are but examiner-employees of the PTO, and the ultimate authority regarding the granting of a patent lies with the Commissioner ... The Board is merely the highest level of the Examining Corps, and like all other members of the Examining Corps, the Board operates subject to the Commissioner's overall ultimate authority and responsibility.

In re Alappat, 33 F.3d 1526, 1535 (Fed. Cir. 1994) (*en banc*) (footnotes omitted).

As this passage suggests, a patent applicant who unsuccessfully appeals to the Board of Patent Appeals and Interferences may seek judicial review. Most often, an applicant will appeal to the Court of Appeals for the Federal Circuit under 35 U.S.C. § 141. Alternatively, an applicant may file a civil action in district court under 35 U.S.C. §§ 145 or 146. This second route, although less common due to the additional expense and time, contains an advantage: the applicant may introduce additional evidence (or the same evidence in a separate form, such as live testimony) beyond the Patent Office record. *See Mazzari v. Rogan*, 323 F.3d 1000 (Fed. Cir. 2003).

Furthermore, a patent applicant who unsuccessfully petitions the Commissioner may seek judicial review. These challenges, which occur rarely, invoke a number of different statutes, including the Administrative Procedure Act, 5 U.S.C. § 701 *et seq.*, the All Writs Act, 28 U.S.C. § 1651, or a civil suit under § 1338(a) against the highest-ranking Patent Office official. The Federal Circuit hears appeals from these suits as well as from actions under § 145 or § 146.

III. POST–GRANT PROCEDURES

Once the Patent Office issues a patent, the agency does not revisit that patent grant except in limited circumstances. The statute restricts these post-grant actions to three circumstances: issuing certificates of correction that fix typographical or minor mistakes, examining reissue applications to fix substantive errors, and reexamining the validity of a patent in light of additional references or arguments.

A. Certificates of Correction

If the Patent Office makes an error in printing a patent, a patentee may request the Patent Office to correct the mistake, so long as the mistake is evident in the publicly available prosecution history file. 35 U.S.C. § 254. This commonsense provision permits a blameless patentee to undo the Patent Office's inadvertent mistakes at no additional cost. Even if the patentee is partially responsible for the error, he may nevertheless petition to correct the mistake:

> Whenever a mistake of a clerical or typographical nature, or of minor character, which was not the fault of the Patent and Trademark Office, appears in a patent and a showing has been made that such mistake occurred in good faith, the Director may, upon payment of the required fee, issue a certificate of correction, if the correction does not involve such changes in the patent as

would constitute new matter or would require reexamination.

35 U.S.C. § 255.

This statutory provision contains a few salient points. First, the provision only permits corrections of a typographical or minor character; a patentee may not make substantive changes to a patent with a certificate of correction. A patentee thus may not add new matter or make changes that would require reexamination. A patentee may seek correction only "where it is clearly evident from the specification, drawings, and prosecution history how the error should appropriately be corrected." *Superior Fireplace Co. v. Majestic Prods. Co.*, 270 F.3d 1358, 1373 (Fed. Cir. 2001). Second, the mistake must have occurred in good faith; a patentee may not mislead the Patent Office during prosecution to obtain allowance then later attempt to correct that deception through a certificate of correction. Finally, the provision contains a sentence that makes a certificate of correction only effective against subsequently filed litigations; it does not have retroactive effect with respect to litigation pending at the time the certificate of correction issues. *Southwest Software, Inc. v. Harlequin Inc.*, 226 F.3d 1280 (Fed. Cir. 2000).

Notably, a patentee may enforce a patent containing insignificant errors without first petitioning the Patent Office for a certificate of correction. Indeed, a court has inherent authority to correct minor errors through, for example, claim construction, so long as "the correction is not subject to reasonable debate based on consideration of the claim language and the specification and the prosecution history does not suggest a different interpretation of the claims." *Novo Indus., L.P. v. Micro Molds Corp.*, 350 F.3d 1348, 1354 (Fed Cir. 2003).

B. Reissue

1. Error Correction

Unlike the minor corrections permitted by a certificate of correction, reissue permits significant revisions affecting the scope, validity, and even enforceability of an issued patent. In part, the Patent Act provides:

> Whenever any patent is, through error without any deceptive intention, deemed wholly or partly inoperative or invalid, by reason of a defective specification or drawing, or by reason of the patentee claiming more or less than he had a right to claim in the patent, the Director shall, on the surrender of such patent and the payment of the fee required by law, reissue the patent for the invention disclosed in the original patent, and in accordance with a new and amended application, for the unexpired part of the term of the original patent. No new matter shall be introduced into the application for reissue.

35 U.S.C. § 251. To qualify for reissue, a patentee must thus declare that, without deceptive intent, the patent is wholly or partly inoperative or invalid either due to a defective specification or due to the failure of a patentee to claim more or less than he had a right to claim. *See* 37 C.F.R. § 1.175.

Reissue focuses on two separate errors: an error in the patent and error in conduct that caused the error in the patent. *Hewlett-Packard Co. v. Bausch & Lomb Inc.*, 882 F.2d 1556 (Fed. Cir. 1989). In

Hewlett-Packard, the court ruled that a reissue patent that added claims of narrower scope than the original claims was invalid. Without deciding that a failure to include narrower claims is correctable through a reissue application, the court held that the reissue oath did not assert an error in conduct. In particular, the court held that the prosecuting attorney's affidavits mischaracterized the circumstances that caused the error in patent claim scope. In other circumstances, though, the court has explained that an "attorney's failure to appreciate the full scope of the invention is one of the most common sources of defects in patents." *In re Wilder*, 736 F.2d 1516, 1519 (Fed. Cir. 1984). Indeed, the *Wilder* court further stated that the "fact that the error could have been discovered at the time of prosecution with a more thorough patentability search or with improved communication between the inventors and the attorney does not, by itself, preclude a patent owner from correcting defects through reissue." *Id.*

Once the Patent Office accepts the patentee's reissue application, the prosecution starts anew with the typical back-and-forth of Office Actions and responses. 37 C.F.R. § 1.176. Indeed, an applicant may even file continuing applications, such as divisional applications, as necessary. *See In re Graff*, 111 F.3d 874 (Fed. Cir. 1997). Because the first paragraph of § 251 includes the express prohibition that "[n]o new matter shall be introduced into the application for reissue," however, the patentee cannot file a continuation-in-part claiming priority to the reissue application. If the Patent Office reissues the patent, the amended claims will have only prospective application while reissue claims that are substantially identical to the original claims will have both retrospective and prospective application. 35 U.S.C. § 252, first paragraph. Reissue proceedings, furthermore, are open to the public.[2] Anyone may request to inspect the application and related papers under 37 C.F.R. § 1.11(b). Even without requesting the file, any interested third party may protest a reissue application by citing prior art to the Patent Office under 37 C.F.R. § 1.291.

As the statute implies, a patentee may seek to broaden the scope of the claimed subject matter. The patentee, however, may only do so within a relatively short period of time after the patent issues: "No reissued patent shall be granted enlarging the scope of the claims of the original patent unless applied for within two years from the grant of the original patent." 35 U.S.C. § 251, fourth paragraph. This two-year window enables a patentee to claim subject matter within the scope of the patent that was erroneously omitted from the original version of the patent.

2. Intervening Rights

Because the public is entitled to reasonably rely upon the scope of an issued patent and because that patent might undergo revision during reissue proceedings, the Patent Act provides for limited rights to the originally claimed subject matter. 35 U.S.C. § 252, second paragraph. In particular, the statute provides for absolute intervening rights and equita-

2. The Patent Office maintains a website called the Patent Application Information Retrieval system (PAIR) that hosts documents relating to all public communications to and from the Office.

ble intervening rights. *See, e.g.*, *Shockley v. Arcan, Inc.*, 248 F.3d 1349 (Fed. Cir. 2001).

Absolute intervening rights permit a would-be infringer to continue the infringing activity so long as that activity began before the grant of reissue, unless, of course, the activity would have infringed the original patent anyway. Absolute intervening rights are automatic and, thus, do not require judicial intervention. Equitable intervening rights, on the other hand, permit a court to provide for continuing, otherwise infringing activity when "substantial preparation was made before the grant of reissue ... to the extent and under such terms as the court deems equitable for the protection of investments made or business commenced before the grant of the reissue." 35 U.S.C. § 252, second paragraph. Thus, a party must have made substantial investments before the reissue. As with absolute intervening rights, there are no equitable intervening rights if the infringing activity fell within the scope of the original claims. Although appearing infrequently in the case law, both types of intervening rights are likely available in all reissued patents, even those that narrow the scope of the claims.

3. Recapture

If a patentee intends on correcting the failure to recognize or appreciate the full scope of an invention by seeking broader claims within two years, the law contains an important policy-based safeguard beyond intervening rights. Indeed, not all errors are correctable. The "reissue statute was not enacted as a panacea for all patent prosecution problems, nor as a grant to the patentee of a second opportunity to prosecute *de novo* his original application." *In re Weiler*, 790 F.2d 1576, 1582 (Fed. Cir. 1986). For instance, the patentee may not use reissue to erase a clear intent to exclude certain subject matter from the scope of the claimed invention. This recapture rule typically "bars the patentee from acquiring, through reissue, claims that are of the *same* or of *broader scope* than those claims that were canceled from the original application." *Ball Corp. v. United States*, 729 F.2d 1429, 1436 (Fed. Cir. 1984) (emphasis original).

A basic framework governs the recapture rule:

if the reissue claim is broader in some aspects, but narrower in others, then: (a) if the reissue claim is as broad as or broader in an aspect germane to a prior art rejection, but narrower in another aspect completely unrelated to the rejection, the recapture rule bars the claim; (b) if the reissue claim is narrower in an aspect germane to prior art rejection, and broader in an aspect unrelated to the rejection, the recapture rule does not bar the claim, but other rejections are possible.

In re Clement, 131 F.3d 1464, 1470 (Fed. Cir. 1997). The recapture rule, however, may also apply in instances beyond incorporating canceled subject matter into the scope of a reissue claim. In particular, a patentee may not attempt to delete limitations that he emphasized during the prosecution, even if those limitations may not have been essential to the patentability of the original claims. *Hester Indus., Inc. v. Stein, Inc.*, 142 F.3d 1472 (Fed. Cir. 1998).

C. **Reexamination**

Unlike certificates of correction and reissue, reexamination does not involve correcting an error in the patent. Rather, reexamination is an administrative proceeding that—just as its name suggests—involves a secondary examination of patented subject matter. Reexam, in theory, provides an alternative to judicial resolution of validity in a faster, less costly manner. The statute, however, only permits a reexamination when the Patent Office determines, either on its own or at the request of the patentee or third party, that there is a "substantial new question of patentability" based solely on prior art patents and printed publications. Under the current statutes, furthermore, the "existence of a substantial new question of patentability is not precluded by the fact that a patent or printed publication was previously cited by or to the Office or considered by the Office." *See* 35 U.S.C. §§ 303(a) & 312(a). In the relatively short period since its inception only a few decades ago, reexamination has expanded from a purely *ex parte* scheme to include an *inter partes* proceeding more akin to civil litigation, though still before the Patent Office.

1. *Ex Parte*

Any individual—a competitor, a patentee, a licensee, or any other third-party—may file a request for *ex parte* reexamination of a patent by citing prior art patents or printed publications to the Patent Office along with a statement of their relevance to at least one the claim of the patent. 35 U.S.C. §§ 301 & 302. Once the Patent Office orders reexamination, the statute provides that the prosecution of a reexamination application follows the same procedures as the prosecution of any other application. Indeed, the statute expressly authorizes a patentee "to propose any amendment to his patent and a new claim or claims thereto, in order to distinguish the invention as claimed from the prior art cited ... or in response to a decision adverse to patentability of a claim of a patent." 35 U.S.C. § 305. This recourse does not give a patentee free reign to amend unrelated aspects of the claims; any amendment must concern some aspect related to the reexamination proceedings. *See In re Freeman*, 30 F.3d 1459 (Fed. Cir. 1994).

Aside from limiting the available universe of amendments, the statute further states: "No proposed amended or new claim enlarging the scope of a claim of the patent will be permitted in a reexamination proceeding." 35 U.S.C. § 305. This means that claim scope after amendment cannot exceed the broadest claim scope of the issued patent. That is, an amended claim cannot include any subject matter not within the scope of any unamended claim, even if the amended claim is narrower in other aspects. Unsurprisingly, this involves a dual claim construction then comparison of the initial claims and amended claims. *See, e.g., Hockerson-Halberstadt, Inc. v. Converse Inc.*, 183 F.3d 1369 (Fed. Cir. 1999). If there is any broadening scope—even changing "at least" to "at least approximately"—the broadened claim does not revert to its unamended form. Instead, the claim is invalid. *Quantum Corp. v. Rodime, PLC*, 65 F.3d 1577 (Fed. Cir. 1995).

Moreover, even a narrowing amendment may limit a patentee's ability to enforce a patent surviving reexamination. Under 35 U.S.C. § 307(b), the statute provides for intervening rights identical to those for reissue patents. This section, like § 252, provides at least some protection to a person who would not have been liable for infringing the initial claims, even if liable for infringing the reexamined claims. *See Bloom Eng'g Co. v. N. Am. Mfg. Co.*, 129 F.3d 1247 (Fed. Cir. 1997).

2. *Inter Partes*

One of the criticisms of *ex parte* reexamination stemmed from the absence of an adversary rebutting the arguments of patentability proffered by the patentee. Even after initiating the proceedings, an interested party would be relegated to the sidelines and prohibited from participation. To alleviate this problem, the statute now provides for limited *inter partes* reexamination, which permits a third-party requestor to participate in the reexamination. 35 U.S.C. §§ 311–318. This optional alternative to *ex parte* reexamination is, in effect, a limited opposition system. Although scarcely used—only a couple dozen have been filed each year—*inter partes* reexamination may become an attractive surrogate for expensive and protracted litigation.

IV. CONCLUSION: THE WORLD'S MOST LIBERAL SYSTEM

The United States has the most liberal system in the world for obtaining patents. For instance, it permits inventors to broaden their claims using the reissue process in the first two years after grant and to achieve essentially the same result with a continuing application perhaps for the life of the continuation. In general, other major patent systems such as those in Europe and Japan do not permit inventors to broaden their claims after grant. The details of the prosecution of patent applications in other major systems such as at the European Patent Office and the Japanese Patent Office are generally similar to USPTO practices.

CHAPTER 3

PATENT ELIGIBILITY

I. INTRODUCTION

This chapter examines patent "eligibility," which is a threshold issue before examining other requirements of "patentability," such as whether the claimed invention is useful, novel, nonobvious, adequately described, and properly claimed. Although many discoveries are eligible for patenting, some subject matter cannot be patented even if it meets the other requirements. To a large extent, the mutually exclusive categories of eligible and noneligible subject matter are well defined. At least in the United States, almost every invention with a practical, concrete, or tangible application, however nominal, is eligible for patenting.

The historic common law standard for determining eligibility—"manner of new manufacture"—flows from the words of the famous Statute of Monopolies. The United States broke away from the common law tradition in 1790, followed by Canada in the nineteenth century. This U.S. approach defines eligibility positively. The European Patent Office takes a different approach and defines what cannot be patented rather than what can be patented.

A. The Constitution

The Constitution's patent and copyright clause grants Congress the authority to enact laws that "promote the progress of science and useful arts." U.S. CONST. Art. I, § 8, cl. 8. Because this constitutional requirement provides a minimal constraint, the general rule is that all useful subject matter is eligible for patenting. The Supreme Court has carved-out some common-sense exceptions to that general rule: "laws of nature, natural phenomena, and abstract ideas." *Diamond v. Diehr*, 450 U.S. 175, 185 (1980). Thus, abstract principles or natural phenomena by themselves are not eligible for patenting. Under the abstract ideas exclusion, non-applied mathematics and physical, chemical, or biological theories do not qualify for patenting. Although undoubtedly worthy of investigation and discovery, this kind of ethereal subject matter standing alone does not evince a practical application. Eligible subject matter must be useful, practical, or tangible.

B. Section 101

Beginning with the Patent Act of 1790, eligible subject matter has always included physical items. *See* Patent Act of 1790, 1 Stat. 109, 110 (Apr. 10, 1790) (setting forth the eligible subject matter as "any useful art, manufacture, engine, machine, or device, or any improvement therein"). In subsequent enactments, however, the categories expanded to include explicitly processes—formerly included as an "art"—and compositions of matter. Section 101 of the Patent Act currently recites: "Whoever invents or discovers any new and useful process, machine, manufacture, or composition of matter, or any new and useful improvement thereof, may obtain a patent therefor, subject to the conditions and requirements of this title."

Thus, the statute sets forth in positive terms four general categories of patent-eligible subject matter—processes, machines, manufactures, and compositions of matter. A new and useful process refers to the use of any "process, machine, manufacture, composition of matter, or material." 35 U.S.C. § 100(b). For example, a patent-eligible process can be a treatment of certain materials to achieve a desired result. *Cochrane v. Deener*, 94 U.S. 780 (1877). A new and useful machine refers to "a concrete thing, consisting of parts, or of certain devices and combination of devices." *Burr v. Duryee*, 68 U.S. 531, 570 (1864). A new and useful manufacture refers to "the production of articles for use from raw or prepared materials by giving to these materials new forms, qualities, properties, or combinations, whether by hand-labor or by machinery." *Diamond v. Chakrabarty*, 447 U.S. 303, 308 (1980) (quoting *Am. Fruit Growers, Inc. v. Brogdex Co.*, 283 U.S. 1, 11 (1931)). And lastly, a new and useful composition of matter refers to "all compositions of two or more substances and . . . all composite articles, whether they be the results of chemical union, or of mechanical mixture, or whether they be gases, fluids, powders or solids." *Id.* (quoting *Shell Dev. Co. v. Watson*, 149 F. Supp. 279, 280 (D.D.C. 1957)). Although the statute divides eligible subject matter into four categories, these categories are not mutually exclusive. An inventor may claim an invention as subject matter falling in more than one category. *Bandag, Inc. v. Al Bolser's Tire Stores, Inc.*, 750 F.2d 903 (Fed. Cir. 1984).

II. PROCESSES

A. Process Versus Product Claims

As mentioned above, the four statutory categories eligible for patenting are processes, machines, manufactured objects, and compositions of matter. While the latter three categories are physical and relatively easy to deem tangible, processes present more difficulties. In fact, processes are the only category that the Patent Act attempts to define, albeit somewhat reflexively: "The term 'process' means process, art or method, and includes a new use of a known process, machine, manufacture, composition of matter, or material." 35 U.S.C. § 100(b). While not removing all ambiguity, this definition at least strongly suggests that most processes are eligible for patenting. Though more conceptually difficult, processes are eligible unless falling within the excluded categories (laws of nature, natural phenomena, and abstract ideas). Thus, processes must engage or produce something tangible. Indeed, the statutory definition clarifies that the use of physical entities qualifies as eligible.

For example, a metallic alloy is eligible as a physical composition of matter. A man-made process for forging that alloy on an industrial scale would similarly be eligible, as would a process for using that alloy in the body of a car. In short, any process related to the use or production of that alloy is eligible.

B. Computer-Related Methods

The most important modern patent issue involving processes examines processes incorporated into an electronic device, like a computer or other machine. Courts have struggled to understand the tangible aspects of hardware and software. Early in the computer age, software processes, for instance, often received treatment in courts as just ethereal algorithms. The United States has since reached the conclusion that these processes are indeed eligible for patenting, so long as the claims are formatted properly. In Europe, "computer programs as such" are not patent eligible.

At its simplest, computer software performs a process that manipulates data in a computer. Although hardware is the physical substrate on which software exists, hardware and software are interchangeable. That is, every process can exist as either software or hardware. This dual nature causes problems. A computer program containing a theory-based algorithm residing in software seems to be analogous to an ineligible abstract idea, but that same computer program with the same algorithm residing in hardware is analogous to an eligible machine or article of manufacture.

In the very earliest days of computer technology, the Supreme Court struggled with this dichotomous relationship in *Gottschalk v. Benson*, 409 U.S. 63 (1972). In *Benson*, the claimed method related to a conversion of numbers from a pure binary format to a binary-coded decimal. While computers typically understand and encode numbers in binary format, human beings prefer viewing numbers in the familiar decimal format. Thus, the invention seems to have a real application and value. Nonetheless, the Court held that the claims recited subject matter ineligible for patenting. The Court, in particular, followed a body of case law that imposed a "physical transformation" requirement. Because the claimed binary transformation in this case was easily accomplished by "head and hand," the Court held that the claimed method was merely an abstract mathematical formula. Perhaps the nascency of the computer technology and a failure to foresee its importance influenced the Court's opinion. Or perhaps a failure to understand that a computer-related method could exist as hardware, a physical object, influenced the opinion. Finally the Court may have simply overlooked some of the claims because claim 8, as opposed to claim 13, claimed a method of using a reentrant shift register, a fairly standard electronic component.

In any event, the Court's opinion is laced with self-impeaching reasoning. For instance, the Court states, "It is conceded that one may not patent an idea." 409 U.S. at 71. To the contrary, all patents are ideas. The Supreme Court either confused patent law with copyright law or meant to say "one may not patent an *abstract* idea." At another point, the Court opined, "The mathematical formula involved here has no substantial practical application except in connection with a digital computer. . . ." *Id.* The Court seems to belittle the invention as limited to improving a mere digital computer, which may, of course, qualify as the most revolutionary advance of the twentieth century.

Whatever its basis, the Court's unfavorable treatment of computer-related claims came to an end nearly a decade later in *Diamond v. Diehr*, 450 U.S. 175 (1981). In *Diehr*, the claims recited a method for operating a rubber-molding press that incorporated a well-known scientific principle, the Arrhenius equation, for calculating the reaction time of polymers. Distinguishing *Benson*, the Court characterized the claims as a process of curing synthetic rubber, not a mathematical formula. Specifically, the Court focused on the claims as a whole with an emphasis on limitations that recited a physical transformation. If the Arrhenius equation were a theory applicable only to polymeric reactions, the Supreme Court's logic would be suspect. In that circumstance, the use of the equation and the physical transformation would be redundant. The equation would only apply to a machine for curing polymers like rubber. In truth, however, the Arrhenius equation derives from generalized thermodynamics and predicts the rate of chemical reactions beyond just polymerization.

In any event, *Diehr* realigned the law of *patent* eligibility to more accurately reflect the breadth of the Patent Act. In *Diehr*, the Supreme Court precluded an analysis that subtracts patent ineligible components from the claim before measuring patentability. In other words, a claim may qualify as patentable when the inventive advance in the claim is the part that standing alone would not be patent eligible. Thus, even though Sir Isaac Newton's laws of mechanics would be abstract and ineligible, their application to make new machines or technical processes would qualify as patentable because the claim as a whole would be nonobvious.

For example, in 1994 the Federal Circuit decided *In re Alappat*, 33 F.3d 1526 (Fed. Cir. 1994) (*en banc*). In *Alappat*, the court examined means-plus-function claims (means-plus-function claims are discussed in Chapter 10) directed to an apparatus that displayed a smooth waveform in an oscilloscope, a device for displaying certain electrical characteristics like current, voltage, etc. The court determined that although directed to a machine—one of the four enumerated categories—the claims could possibly be directed to ineligible subject matter because they incorporate a mathematical algorithm. Disregarding that argument, however, the court held that the subject matter was indeed patentable, partially because the software that implemented the algorithm affected the operation of a tangible machine. (Recall that software and hardware are interchangeable.) *Alappat* presaged the later decision of *State Street Bank & Trust Co. v. Signature Financial Group, Inc.*, 149 F.3d 1368 (Fed. Cir. 1998).

Although sometimes (often pejoratively) referred to as the case that opened the floodgates to patenting business methods, *State Street Bank* is best understood as the case that explicitly confirmed the patent eligibility of computer-implemented inventions. In *State Street Bank*, the Federal Circuit examined the patent eligibility of a computer system to reallocate investment income to maximize tax benefits. Instead of engaging in an analysis of transformation or algorithm characterizations, the court returned to basic statutory construction. The invention recited a statutory process that qualified for patenting unless it fell within one of the three prohibited categories (laws of nature, natural phenomena, and abstract ideas). The only possible exclusion for a mathematical algorithm or a computer process is abstractness. An invention is not abstract if useful. The claimed invention had a practical utility and therefore was not abstract.

In this direct analysis, the court refocused the eligibility inquiry onto the essential characteristics of the subject matter, namely whether the subject matter has practical utility. Because a machine programmed with the claimed financial system undeniably produced a useful, concrete, and tangible result, the claims were eligible for patenting.

C. Business Method Patents

Beyond limiting the ineligible subject matter as a merely abstract mathematical algorithm, the court took the opportunity to lay the "ill-conceived" business-method exception to rest. The court noted that the alleged exception had no support in the legal precedents of the Federal Circuit or its predecessors.

Despite providing some dicta on the subject, the *State Street Bank* court could not rule on the eligibility of method claims. Within a few months, though that question was definitively answered in *AT&T Corp. v. Excel Communications, Inc.*, 172 F.3d 1352 (Fed. Cir. 1999). In that case, the only claims at issue were process claims directed to a method of inserting data into a long distance call record to facilitate billing—solely an exchange of information, not a physical transformation. The court held that they recited eligible subject matter. These complementary decisions of *State Street Bank* and *AT & T* effectively terminated all challenges to the patent eligibility of so-called business methods.

Many people think of business methods as computer-implemented—one of the most notorious is Amazon.com's "one-click" patent, U.S. Patent No. 5,960,411 (issued Sept. 28, 1999). But does this mean that all business-related ideas are eligible for patenting? For example, could the airline that first conceived of a hub-and-spoke system for shuttling passengers across the country have patented it? It surely is not a law of nature or a natural phenomenon. But is it an abstract idea? Probably not—it applies a system that improves the cost-effectiveness of travel (have you ever seen birds congregate at specified points to exchange passengers?). Of course, the major hurdles for business methods are likely to be the statutory requirements for patentability, like novelty and nonobviousness.

D.   Methods of Medical Treatment

A method of medical treatment is unquestionably patent eligible in the United States. Almost invariably such methods have a practical—and beneficial–result. Accordingly surgical methods are eligible for patents. For example, U.S. Patent No. 6,761,724 (issued July 13, 2004) claims methods for inserting a medical device into the subretinal region of an eye. Methods of diagnosing a disease are similarly patent-eligible. As an example, U.S. Patent No. 4,940,658 (issued July 10, 1990) claims methods for detecting a cobalamin or folate deficiency, which if untreated could cause a serious illness, such as vascular disease, cognitive dysfunction, birth defect and cancer. Likewise, methods of treating a disease using a particular dosing regimen are patent-eligible. Again, U.S. Patent No. 5,994,329 (issued Nov. 30, 1999) claims methods of treating and preventing osteoporosis by administering a compound according to a specific dosing regimen.

Even though these medical-related methods are eligible for patenting, physicians objected to the patenting of surgical procedures as such. They raised a chorus of concern about potential threats to public health in the event of an injunction on a medical procedure, about potential effects on ethical obligations of physicians to publicize medical advances, about potential increases in the cost of health care, about potential interferences with peer-reviewed medical procedures, and about potential invasions of privacy during enforcement of a medical method patent. In response, Congress added paragraph (c) to 35 U.S.C. § 287, a section of the Patent Act related to remedies (discussed in Chapter 15), and eliminated any remedy, including injunction, damages, and attorney fees, due to a medical practitioner's performance of a medical activity. Specifically, section 287(c) defines "medical activity" as "the performance of a medical or surgical procedure on a body," excluding "(i) the use of a patented machine, manufacture, or composition of matter in violation of such patent, (ii) the practice of a patented use of a composition of matter in violation of such patent, or (iii) the practice of a process in violation of a biotechnology patent." In essence, medical practitioners may infringe a patent claiming a medical activity as such without impunity, which effectively removes many medical methods from patent protection.

Other countries apply far more restrictive reservations regarding the propriety of patenting methods of medical treatment. For example, both Article 1709 of NAFTA and Article 27 of the TRIPS agreement permit the exclusion of diagnostic, therapeutic and surgical methods for the treatment of humans or animals from the subject matter eligible for patenting. The European Patent Convention takes advantage of that option, and contains Article 52(4), which states:

> Methods for treatment of the human or animal body by surgery or therapy and diagnostic methods practiced on the human or animal body shall not be regarded as inventions which are susceptible of industrial application within the meaning

of paragraph 1. This provision shall not apply to products, in particular substances or compositions, for use in any of these methods.

Despite that provision, Article 54(5) permits patenting of a medical use of a compound not previously used as a medicament by torturing the meaning of prior art: "The provisions of paragraphs 1 to 4 [relating to novelty] shall not exclude the patentability of any substance or composition, comprised in the state of the art, for use in a method referred to in Article 52, paragraph 4, provided that its use for any method referred to in that paragraph is not comprised in the state of the art." In other words an old compound is not to be treated as old. Furthermore, a so-called "Swiss claim," which recites the use of a compound in the *manufacture* of a medicament for the treatment of a disease, circumvents the prohibition on claiming a method for treating a disease using that compound, so-called "second medical indications."

Thus exclusions on medical methods have led creative lawyers to circumvent the exceptions. Ironically at least in the European Patent Office, a first medical use claim of an old compound gives the inventor all pharmaceutical uses for that known compound whereas the United States provides protection only for the medical indication disclosed by the inventor.

E. Compositions of Matter/Biotechnology

Compositions of matter, one of the four enumerated categories explicitly set forth in the statute, did not create problems related to patent eligibility

until the era of genetic engineering and biotechnology. These technologies permit manipulation of
genes in a living organism, which allows for the
creation of novel organisms which express advanta-
geous characteristics, such as pest-resistant crops,
or production of complex biological compounds,
such as proteins. For example, genetic engineering
produced the "oncomouse," a type of mouse susceptible to cancer that facilitates research on those
dreaded diseases. However, unlike the tortuous
path taken towards settling the eligibility of computer-related inventions, the Supreme Court quickly put an end to the question of the eligibility of
living organisms in *Diamond v. Chakrabarty*, 447
U.S. 303 (1980).

In that case, the patent claimed a bacterium
genetically modified to enable it to consume oil. The
Court treated the issue as a narrow question of
statutory interpretation: whether the claimed organism fell into either the manufacture or composition of matter categories of section 101. On that
point, the Court determined that the modified bacterium did not appear in nature. The new organism
was a product of human ingenuity. Accordingly, it
was patent-eligible subject matter. Even though the
case only decided that the organism itself was patent eligible, it provided a strong signal that all
aspects of biotechnology would be eligible for patenting.

While the *Chakrabarty* decision facilitated the
patenting of any genetically modified organism in
the U.S., the Supreme Court of Canada interpreted

the exact same statutory eligibility language to reach the opposite conclusion for the oncomouse invention. That court held that the genetically engineered oncomouse was neither a "manufacture" nor a "composition of matter." *Harvard College v. Canada*, 2002 SCC 76. This decision diverged from the worldwide consensus on the patentability of life forms. Even the Council of the European Union and the European Parliament finally adopted the *Directive on the Legal Protection of Biotechnological Inventions* (the *Biotech Directive*) on July 6, 1998 to provide broad protection of life forms within the European Community.

Even though *Chakrabarty* firmly established the eligibility of man-made, living subject matter, the Supreme Court revisited a related issue to determine whether a man-made plant was eligible for patenting under section 101 of the Patent Act in addition to protection under either the Plant Protection Act or the Plant Variety Protection Act in *J.E.M. Ag Supply, Inc. v. Pioneer Hi–Bred International, Inc.*, 534 U.S. 124 (2001). Again focusing on the expansive language of section 101, the Court ruled that an engineered plant qualifies as patent-eligible subject matter. In essence, the Court held that more than one statute may supply protection to plant inventions.

Once again, however, the patent eligibility for many biotechnological inventions may depend on the form of the claims. A claim, standing alone, to an amino acid sequence would raise the concern that the sequence does appear in nature. Accordingly, a careful patent drafter will claim the "isolated" or "purified" version of the gene. After all, the genetic sequence is not likely found in an isolated or purified state in nature.

III. TRIPS

Article 27 of the TRIPS Agreement, an agreement that has been entered into by most of the countries of the world, defines subject matter eligible for patenting:

> 1. Subject to the provisions of paragraphs 2 and 3, patents shall be available for any inventions, whether products or processes, in all fields of technology, provided that they are new, involve an inventive step and are capable of industrial application.[3] Subject to paragraph 4 of Article 65, paragraph 8 of Article 70 and paragraph 3 of this Article, patents shall be available and patent rights enjoyable without discrimination as to the place of invention, the field of technology and whether products are imported or locally produced.

This vital international treaty makes any invention capable of an industrial application (which may be reminiscent of *State Street Bank*'s utility-based reasoning) subject matter eligible for patenting. Member countries, however, retain the discretion to exclude certain subject matter specified in paragraphs 2 and 3:

3. For the purposes of this Article, the terms "inventive step" and "capable of industrial application" may be deemed by a Member to be synonymous with the terms "non-obvious" and "useful" respectively.

2. Members may exclude from patentability inventions, the prevention within their territory of the commercial exploitation of which is necessary to protect ordre public or morality, including to protect human, animal or plant life or health or to avoid serious prejudice to the environment, provided that such exclusion is not made merely because the exploitation is prohibited by their law.

3. Members may also exclude from patentability:

(a) diagnostic, therapeutic and surgical methods for the treatment of humans or animals;

(b) plants and animals other than micro-organisms, and essentially biological processes for the production of plants or animals other than non-biological and microbiological processes. However, Members shall provide for the protection of plant varieties either by patents or by an effective *sui generis* system or by any combination thereof. The provisions of this subparagraph shall be reviewed four years after the date of entry into force of the WTO Agreement.

Many countries experience difficulties in defining the scope of these exceptions. Perhaps the best course to provide proper incentives for investment and research might be to maintain a broad scope for patent eligibility and instead vigorously scrutinize applications under the requirements for patentability—novelty, inventive step, enablement, and so forth.

CHAPTER 4

UTILITY

I. INTRODUCTION

A. Section 101

In addition to the categories of patent eligible subject matter, 35 U.S.C. § 101 sets forth the "useful" requirement for patent protection. Section 101 states:

> Whoever invents or discovers any new and useful process, machine, manufacture, or composition of matter, or any new and useful improvement thereof, may obtain a patent therefor, subject to the conditions and requirements of this title.

This requirement might seem to contradict common sense. After all, a rational inventor would not invest in research and development and then pour more resources into prosecuting or enforcing a patent if the invention has no use. Indeed, even if an irrational inventor undertook those expenses, enforcing an exclusive right to useless subject matter would bring no damages. Thus, it is no surprise that this statutory requirement has not often proven important in patent case law. When utility does appear in litigation or policy disputes, it usually betokens some agenda other than preventing inventors from acquiring and enforcing useless patents on useless technology.

Use of an invention does play an important role in patent jurisprudence, but not in the sense of the ultimate usefulness of the innovation, which, as suggested above, is a requirement enforced more by market realities than by judicial intervention. The use provision of significance appears in 35 U.S.C. § 112, paragraph 1. This provision (discussed in Chapter 9) ensures that each patent contains sufficient description to enable one of ordinary skill in the art to make and use the invention. This statutory provision presumes, of course, that every invention worthy of a patent has some describable use.

Nonetheless, because the statute uses the word "useful" in section 101, this requirement has presented a few questions. For instance, how useful must a new invention be? Must an invention improve on existing technology or merely serve some practical purpose? Should the invention's social, economic, or environmental impact affect patentability? And, of more importance than any of the other questions, should utility replace obviousness as a primary measure of patentability for biotechnological inventions?

B. Historical Development of the Doctrine

The venerable Justice Story inaugurated the commentary on utility. Apparently recognizing the self-enforcing character of utility, he sought a purpose for the requirement that restricted the patentability of nefarious or immoral inventions:

All that the law requires is, that the invention should not be frivolous or injurious to the well-being, good policy, or sound morals of society. The word "useful," therefore, is incorporated into the act in contradistinction to mischievous or immoral. For instance, a new invention to poison people, or to promote debauchery, or to facilitate private assassination, is not a patentable invention. But if the invention steers wide of these objections, whether it be more or less useful is a circumstance very material to the interests of the patentee, but of no importance to the public. If it be not extensively useful, it will silently sink into contempt and disregard.

Lowell v. Lewis, 15 F. Cas. 1018, 1019 (No. 8568) (C.C.D. Mass. 1817). Justice Story's remarks acknowledge that the patent system does not require that an invention improve on prior art. Thus the utility doctrine does not inaugurate a subjective search for "better" uses. Instead, as first articulated by Justice Story, utility generally lets the market decide if an invention carries "importance to the public" or "sink[s] into contempt and disregard." With the market policing usefulness in the sense of economic worthiness and the obviousness requirement policing usefulness in the sense of worthiness for a patent, Justice Story finds moral concerns the only role remaining for the statutory "usefulness" requirement.

For this reason, utility produced little case law until the rise of biotechnology. The leading treatise on patent law at the end of the nineteenth century

had little to say about the usefulness requirement.
This treatise reached for some general language
that utility means more than "a mere curiosity, a
scientific process exciting wonder yet not producing
physical results, or [a] frivolous or trifling article
not aiding in the progress nor increasing the possession of the human race." 1 W. Robinson, TREATISE
ON THE LAW OF PATENTS FOR USEFUL INVENTIONS 463
(1890).

II. THREE TYPES OF UTILITY

At various times, utility has taken on three separate purposes. These purposes fall into three separate categories: beneficial, general, and specific. The
first category, beneficial utility, arose from Justice
Story's recitation. Based on the Justice's reasoning,
nineteenth century courts would invalidate patents
on inventions considered immoral, such as gambling
devices. *See, e.g., Brewer v. Lichtenstein*, 278 F. 512
(7th Cir. 1922); *Schultze v. Holtz*, 82 F. 448 (N.D.
Cal. 1897); *Nat'l Automatic Device Co. v. Lloyd*, 40
F. 89 (N.D. Ill. 1889). With little to justify patent
law as a moral arbiter, this fleeting impulse has
long since disappeared. Novel and nonobvious gambling devices are indeed patentable, regardless of
subjective moral considerations. *WMS Gaming, Inc.
v. Int'l Game Tech.*, 184 F.3d 1339 (Fed. Cir. 1999);
In re Murphy, 200 USPQ 801 (BPAI 1977).

Another iteration of beneficial utility has received
some modern attention, specifically, use of patented
devices to deceive consumers. As noted, this consideration fell within early applications of beneficial

utility. *See Rickard v. Du Bon*, 103 F. 868 (2d Cir. 1900); *Scott & Williams, Inc. v. Aristo Hosiery Co.*, 7 F.2d 1003 (2d Cir. 1925). The Federal Circuit, however, has held that even deceptive devices do not lack utility.

In *Juicy Whip, Inc. v. Orange Bang, Inc.*, 185 F.3d 1364 (Fed. Cir. 1999), the patentee asserted infringement of a patent on a device that dispensed beverages. In particular, the invention mixed a beverage from separate ingredients after the consumer ordered a drink. This last-second mixing kept drinks more germ-free. The invention, however, also displayed a large globe with a luscious-appearing liquid sloshing about to attract customers. Of course, the display liquid was not the beverage actually dispensed to the buyer. The aspects of the invention that displayed a liquid solely for visual appeal raised the issue of consumer deception. The Federal Circuit did not evaluate these moral concerns. In rejecting the out-dated formulation of utility, the court stated:

> The fact that one product can be altered to make it look like another is in itself a specific benefit sufficient to satisfy the statutory requirement of utility.

> It is not at all unusual for a product to be designed to appear to viewers to be something it is not. For example, cubic zirconium is designed to simulate a diamond, imitation gold leaf is designed to imitate real gold leaf, synthetic fabrics are designed to simulate expensive natural fab-

rics, and imitation leather is designed to look like real leather. In each case, the invention of the product or process that makes such imitation possible has "utility" within the meaning of the patent statute, and indeed there are numerous patents directed toward making one product imitate another.

Id. at 1367. The court then explained that the patent laws do not serve to prevent deceptive trade practices. Accordingly, deceptive or fraudulent inventions do not *per se* lack utility. Beneficial utility simply does not apply any more in patent cases.

The next rare category of usefulness, general utility, requires that the invention actually work. This aspect of usefulness does not mean that the invention must work as well as expected or even function better than the prior art. Rather, general utility is more fundamental: does the invention purport to violate scientific truths? For example, a perpetual motion machine (or any device allegedly creating more energy than it consumes) lacks general utility because it violates the laws of thermodynamics. *See, e.g.*, *Newman v. Quigg*, 877 F.2d 1575 (Fed. Cir. 1989).

The third category, specific utility, requires that the invention work for its intended purpose. Most subject matter clearly satisfies this requirement–a new fastener, for example, by its very nature fastens one thing to another. Specific utility, however, is the branch of usefulness that has become significant in the modern world of chemical and biotechnological inventions. These types of inventions are often developed long before research can discover their specific purpose or purposes. An amino acid sequence of a protein, for instance, does not inherently designate its biological activity. Indeed, an inventor may develop a new chemical composition or biotechnological sequence without a definitive grasp of its potential uses. Often the inventor can only guess about those potential uses based on similar compositions or sequences already in use.

A. Chemistry and Biotechnology

A Supreme Court case inaugurated the heightened scrutiny of chemical inventions under the guise of specific utility. *Brenner v. Manson*, 383 U.S. 519 (1966). The technology at issue in that case related to steroids, a class of compounds having a backbone of carbon rings. The positioning of particular atoms on these rings dictates the use and application of a specific steroid. In *Brenner*, the Supreme Court invalidated a process patent, because the patentee did not know the specific purpose of the chemical entities resulting from the process. The Court explained:

The basic quid pro quo contemplated by the Constitution and the Congress for granting a patent monopoly is the benefit derived by the public from an invention with substantial utility. Unless and until a process is refined and developed to this point—where specific benefit exists in currently available form—there is insufficient justification for permitting an applicant to engross what may prove to be a broad field.

* * *

This is not to say that we mean to disparage the importance of contributions to the fund of scientific information short of the invention of something "useful," or that we are blind to the prospect that what now seems without "use" may tomorrow command the grateful attention of the public. But a patent is not a hunting license. It is not a reward for the search, but compensation for its successful conclusion.

Brenner, 383 U.S. at 534–36 (footnotes omitted). The Court's holding is particularly harsh, because a utility had been disclosed to the public by another inventor prior to Manson's filing date. Because the useful property was certainly inherent in the compound, perhaps a more correct reading of *Brenner*, consistent with much of its language, is that a failure to disclose utility renders the subject matter unpatentable under § 112, paragraph 1, not § 101. Nonetheless, the Supreme Court refocused the utility requirement on some showing in the specification of a benefit to the public.

The Federal Circuit, no doubt recognizing the difficulty of a judicial assessment of benefit to the public when even science itself often does not recognize an inherent benefit for years, attempted to narrow the application of the Supreme Court's reasoning. Calling on other precedents, the Federal Circuit opined that an invention need not be more effective than prior art devices: "Finding that an invention is an 'improvement' is not a prerequisite to patentability. It is possible for an invention to be less effective than existing devices but nevertheless meet the statutory criteria for patentability." *Custom Accessories, Inc. v. Jeffrey–Allan Indus., Inc.*, 807 F.2d 955, 960 n.12 (Fed. Cir. 1986). *In re Brana*, 51 F.3d 1560 (Fed. Cir. 1995), epitomized the Federal Circuit's attempt to narrow the application of *Brenner*. In that case, the Federal Circuit considered a specification's description of the utility of certain antitumor compounds. The court upheld as adequate a designation of some *specific* biological activity, even if not conclusively proven safe and efficacious in humans. The court explained: "Usefulness in patent law, and in particular in the context of pharmaceutical inventions, necessarily includes the expectation of further research and development. The stage at which an invention in this field becomes useful is well before it is ready to be administered to humans." *Id.* at 1568.

B. Modern Biotech Guidelines

Brana did not put an end to the *Brenner* rejuvenation of the utility requirement. Instead, the Patent and Trademark Office found a use for *Brenner* utility when it promulgated guidelines for biotechnological inventions. Under these guidelines, "[i]f at any time during the examination, it becomes readily apparent that the claimed invention has a well-established utility, do not impose a rejection based on lack of utility. An invention has a well-established utility if (i) a person of ordinary skill in the art would immediately appreciate why the invention is useful based on the characteristics of the invention (e.g., properties or applications of a product or process), and (ii) the utility is specific, substantial, and credible." Manual of Patent Examining Procedure § 2107.

Applying these guidelines, the PTO rejected a claim to a gene fragment—an "expressed sequence tag" (EST)—within a variety of corn with natural herbicidal properties for lack of a recitation of a "substantial" utility. Although the applicant protested that it had disclosed several uses, including use of the fragment as a probe to identify the valuable genetic properties of the new corn variety, the Federal Circuit upheld the rejection and the PTO guidelines:

> Essentially, the claimed ESTs act as no more than research intermediates that may help scientists to isolate the particular underlying protein-encoding genes and conduct further experimentation on those genes. The overall goal of such experimentation is presumably to understand the maize genome—the functions of the underlying genes, the identity of the encoded proteins, the role those proteins play during anthesis, whether polymorphisms exist, the identity of promoters that trigger protein expression, whether protein expression may be controlled, etc. Accordingly, the claimed ESTs are, in words of the Supreme Court, mere "objects of use-testing," to wit, objects upon which scientific research could be per-

formed with no assurance that anything useful will be discovered in the end.

In re Fisher, 421 F.3d 1365, 1373 (Fed. Cir. 2005) (citation omitted). The Federal Circuit relied prominently on *Brenner* in reaching this result.

These PTO utility guidelines reject inventions (in this case a biotechnological research tool) that purportedly contribute "insubstantially" to the advance of technology. Unfortunately the utility requirement is ill suited to that task because it lacks any standard for assessing the state of the prior art and the contributions of the claimed advance. The proper tool for assessing the "substantiality" and "credibility" of inventive contributions is the obviousness requirement of 35 U.S.C. § 103. Thus, the guidelines and the *Fisher* case that upholds them are best understood as compensating for the easily-met standard of obviousness for biotechnological inventions. *See In re Deuel*, 51 F.3d 1552 (Fed. Cir. 1995). Nonetheless the PTO guidelines, upheld at least initially by the Federal Circuit, promise to complete the *Brenner* revival of the utility doctrine.

III. INDUSTRIAL APPLICATION

Many of the world's patent systems have a requirement of industrial application rather than utility. Both Europe and Japan require industrial application as a prerequisite for patentability. The importance of this requirement varies depending on other features of the patent system.

CHAPTER 5

ANTICIPATION

I. INTRODUCTION

Novelty, the most fundamental characteristic of patentability, ensures that an inventor has truly created something new. An inventor has invented nothing if the "new creation" already exists elsewhere. In patent parlance, to gain a patent, knowledge in the prior art cannot anticipate the claimed subject matter. Thus, this basic rule protects the public domain of technical knowledge. Novelty prevents anyone from obtaining an exclusive right to technology already in the public domain.

This rule also achieves the policy objective of promoting efficient research. Novelty encourages an inventor to investigate extant, known solutions before undertaking expensive research—libraries before laboratories, investigation before investment. Otherwise, an inventor might just reinvent the wheel.

The novelty rule requires that a single prior art reference contain, expressly or inherently, each and every feature of the claimed invention. Application of this rule, in turn, requires a definition of prior art. Thus, the statutory provisions governing novelty also are the sections that set forth the types of prior knowledge—that is, prior art—that will preclude a patent. These statutory categories of prior art generally provide reliable and verifiable descriptions of the state of public knowledge.

Anticipation requires two discrete steps. First, the test assesses the current state of public knowledge. This step requires identification of the information available in the statutory categories that define the prior art. The Patent Act gives a different geographical reach to the various prior art categories. For instance, patents or printed publications anywhere in the world qualify as prior art references. Unwritten historical information also qualifies as prior art—for example, a public use or sale of the claimed subject matter—but the statute limits these less verifiable sources of prior art to the United States.

After identifying the most relevant prior art, the test examines each of those references individually to find, if possible, each and every aspect of the claimed invention. The test for anticipation is austere: each and every element of the claimed invention must appear expressly or inherently in that single reference.

II. IDENTIFICATION OF PRIOR ART UNDER THE U.S. FIRST–TO–INVENT REGIME

Although a patentable invention must certainly be new, the statutory intricacies of novelty and other patent-barring events are among the more dense and complex in patent law. The governing provision, § 102, states:

A person shall be entitled to a patent unless—

(a) the invention was known or used by others in this country, or patented or described in a printed publication in this or a foreign country, before the invention thereof by the applicant for patent, or

(b) the invention was patented or described in a printed publication in this or a foreign country or in public use or on sale in this country, more than one year prior to the date of the application for patent in the United States, or

(c) he has abandoned the invention, or

(d) the invention was first patented or caused to be patented, or was the subject of an inventor's certificate, by the applicant or his legal representatives or assigns in a foreign country prior to the date of the application for patent in this country on an application for patent or inventor's certificate filed more than twelve months before the filing of the application in the United States, or

(e) The invention was described in—

(1) an application for patent, published under section 122(b), by another filed in the United States before the invention by the applicant for patent, except that an international application filed under the treaty defined in section 351(a) shall have the effect under this subsection of a national application published under section 122(b) only if the international application designating the United States was published under

Article 21(2)(a) of such treaty in the English language; or

(2) a patent granted on an application for patent by another filed in the United States before the invention by the applicant for patent, except that a patent shall not be deemed filed in the United States for the purposes of this subsection based on the filing of an international application filed under the treaty defined in section 351(a); or

(f) he did not himself invent the subject matter sought to be patented, or

(g)(1) during the course of an interference conducted under section 135 or section 291, another inventor involved therein establishes, to the extent permitted in section 104, that before such person's invention thereof the invention was made by such other inventor and not abandoned, suppressed, or concealed, or

(2) before such person's invention thereof, the invention was made in this country by another inventor who had not abandoned, suppressed, or concealed it. In determining priority of invention under this subsection, there shall be considered not only the respective dates of conception and reduction to practice of the invention, but also the reasonable diligence of one who was first to conceive and last to reduce to practice, from a time prior to conception by the other.

For ease of understanding, this dense section creates two different "unless" categories or subsections that bar patentability and also define prior art. The novelty subsections—(a), (e), (f), and (g)–collectively preclude any patent on preexisting knowledge. These categories become "prior art" if they occur before the date of the claimed invention. The barring subsections—(b), (c), and (d)—have a different cut-off, namely the date of application. This priority cut-off is also called the "critical date." These barring provisions—particularly the very important subsection (b)—operate much like the prior art provisions of first-to-file patent systems except that the critical date is one year before the actual U.S. filing date rather than before the Paris Convention filing date. The date of invention, of course, usually differs from the date of application. In some cases, however, the law can operate to merge the invention date and the application date.

The novelty sections award a patent to the first inventor of a technology, regardless of a later inventor who nonetheless filed an earlier application claiming the same subject matter. These provisions form the basis of the first-to-invent priority system unique to the United States. When multiple persons claim the right to a patent on a given technology, the United States (alone!) allows inventors who file the second (or third or ...) application for the subject matter to prove their inventive acts occurred before those of the earlier filer.

Every other patent system in the world has rejected the United States' approach, choosing instead the efficiency and ease of a first-to-file priority system. This priority system awards the patent to the first applicant, even if another actually invented the technology first. Although simple to administer, this rule, according to proponents of the U.S. rule, lacks fairness. In any event, protection of an invention in an international market requires careful attention to the differences between the United States' first-to-invent system and the world's first-to-file system.

The statutory bars collectively prevent the patenting of subject matter in certain circumstances, all of which depend on events prior to the filing date (not the invention date). In particular, the statutory bars of § 102(b), such as publications or sales, arise one year before the filing date—the so-called "critical date." During this time, the inventor may assess the merits of filing a patent application or carefully prepare an application. Thus, inventors who publish an article in a scientific journal know that they have one year to prepare an application on that inventive material. Once again, however, this grace period does not operate in a vacuum. Inventors must remember that events other than their own publications can create prior art. Thus, other publications, public uses by other parties, or offers to sell by other parties more than a year before the actual U.S. filing date are prior art. Such an occurrence might seem unlikely. On the contrary, the competitive atmosphere of the rush to invent a cure for a cancer or AIDS, with many of the leading researchers attending the same conferences, makes inventive coincidence nearly a norm. Therefore, even with the benefit of a one-year grace period, inventors have a strong incentive to file as soon as possible. Moreover, first-to-file systems in the rest of the world make the virtues of early filing very clear for foreign patent protection.

The statutory bars in §§ 102(c) and (d) preclude patenting of inventions that have been abandoned to the public or claimed in a foreign application filed more than a year before the domestic filing date. All of the statutory bars carry the attributes of a statute of limitations on a first inventor's entitlement to a patent. Chapter 6 examines the statutory bars in greater detail.

A.   Novelty Under § 102(a)

The novelty requirement ensures that the inventive subject matter is, in fact, new. The most important novelty provision, § 102(a), sets forth four patent-defeating events: (i) the purported invention was already known by others, (ii) the purported invention was already used by others, (iii) the purported invention was already patented, or (iv) the purported invention was already described in a printed publication. Again, the first two categories only apply to domestic events. The other two have no such geographic limitation. The apparent simplicity of the terms "patented," "printed publication," and "in this country" mask counter-intuitive subtleties.

A prior patent on the same invention, at least in the United States, is easy enough to determine with a search of issued patents. The "patented" category, however, extends to every foreign country. Some foreign intellectual property regimes offer unique forms of intellectual property protection that do not correspond perfectly with a domestic patent. For example, in *In re Carlson*, 983 F.2d 1032 (Fed. Cir. 1992), the Federal Circuit determined that a design protected by a German Geschmacksmuster qualified as "patented." A Geschmacksmuster requires only registration of a design and lacks any substantive examination process (somewhat similar to copyright protection). The Federal Circuit emphasized the public availability of these German registrations in designating them as prior art. Even though only a local office in Germany provided access to the information and the notice of publication in the Bundesanzeiger did not contain a copy of the registered design, the court placed the Geschmacksmuster within the scope of § 102(a) prior art.

Similarly, a description of the claimed invention in a journal article disseminated in printed hardcopy obviously serves as a printed publication. A description in an electronic document or other communication medium, on the other hand, might seem to lack the reliability of a "printed publication." Nevertheless, these electronic storage, retrieval, and dissemination devices qualify as printed publications. *In re Wyer*, 655 F.2d 221 (CCPA 1981).

Courts have often referred to public access as the touchstone for qualification as prior art. Assessing this touchstone, however, defies bright-line rules. For example, in *In re Hall*, 781 F.2d 897 (Fed. Cir.

1986), the prior art reference was a doctoral thesis for a graduate student at Freiburg University in Germany. Although a printed publication, the court, as expected, invoked public accessibility as the deciding factor. In measuring public access, the court held that a single, cataloged thesis in only one library provides sufficient access to the publication's teachings to reasonably diligent persons of ordinary skill in the art. Thus, an indexed or distributed publication apparently qualifies as sufficiently accessible to the interested public, but other indicia of availability may also suffice. *In re Klopfenstein*, 380 F.3d 1345 (Fed. Cir. 2004); *Bruckelmyer v. Ground Heaters, Inc.*, 445 F.3d 1374 (Fed. Cir. 2006).

Oftentimes, the description of an invention in a patent or patent application serves as a printed publication. The United States Patent and Trademark Office publishes all patents upon issuance, but most patent applications appear in published form 18 months after their filing date. Foreign patent offices typically publish all applications 18 months after filing. Accordingly, upon publication, even the pre-grant publication will serve as prior art.

The entire disclosure within the specification of an issued patent, regardless of the scope of the claims, becomes prior art. In other words, the prior art in a patent is not limited by the applicant's choice to claim less subject matter. For most intents and purposes, therefore, the "printed publication" category subsumes the "patented" category of § 102(a).

Lastly, the geographic location of the knowledge or use by someone other than the inventor can be readily and easily determined in most cases. In the modern world, however, research within multinational companies may pose some difficulty in assessing the locus of uses and knowledge. For example, in *Ex Parte Thomson*, 24 USPQ2d 1618 (BPAI 1992), the Board sustained a rejection based on references that alone would not have permitted a person of ordinary skill in the art to make and use the subject matter, because the claimed subject matter was commercially available in a foreign country, Australia. Accordingly, the Board allowed a foreign use to supplement the disclosure in domestic printed publications. In other words, extraterritorial evidence helped show that a printed publication in the United States contained sufficient disclosure (enabled) to anticipate the claimed subject matter. *Cf. In re Elsner*, 381 F.3d 1125 (Fed. Cir. 2004).

B. Secret Prior Art

The fundamental attribute of prior art is its ability to reflect the state of knowledge in the public domain (remember that § 102 encourages library research ahead of laboratory research and that public accessibility is the touchstone). This fundamental attribute, however, contains limited exceptions in §§ 102(e), (f), and (g). Compelled by the first-to-invent system in the United States, these sections together define secret prior art—a necessary but disfavored category.

The secret information defined in § 102(e) may fit the designation of "inevitable" prior art. Prior art principles must accord protection to secret applications for patents. The Supreme Court firmly established this category of prior art in *Alexander Milburn Co. v. Davis–Bournonville Co.*, 270 U.S. 390 (1926). In that case, the Court held that disclosed (even if unclaimed) subject matter in an issued patent is prior art as of its filing date, not its issue date. The second paragraph of § 102(e) codified this case. More recently added, the first paragraph works similarly: an issued patent that describes subject matter in a published patent application is prior art as of the filing date of the application. The statute refers to the Patent Cooperation Treaty, which is partially codified at § 351(a). Section 102(e)(1) provides that a PCT application designating the United States and published in English are prior art on its filing date, while § 102(e)(2) prohibits using the filing dates of other PCT applications (which will serve as printed publications on their dates of publication). The rule in § 102(e)(2) stems from *In re Hilmer*, 359 F.2d 859 (CCPA 1966). In *Hilmer*, the CCPA blatantly attempted to narrow the category of secret prior art. The Patent Cooperation Treaty is discussed in Chapter 16.

The secret prior art of § 102(f) bars a patent on another's invention. Under this provision, an applicant cannot claim subject matter derived from someone else, the true inventor. *See Pannu v. Iolab Corp.*, 155 F.3d 1344 (Fed. Cir. 1998). The final category of secret prior art, § 102(g), prohibits the patenting of subject matter previously invented by another. This statutory provision not only provides for interferences, which are administrative procedures governing a priority fight involving at least one pending application, but also provides for invalidating patents based on prior invention in certain circumstances. The brevity of § 102(g) belies its complexity. This section receives its own separate explanation in Chapter 7.

III. ANTICIPATION

Although parsing the text of § 102 can present challenges, the actual test for anticipation is straightforward and strict: each and every element of the claimed subject matter must be disclosed inherently or expressly in a single, enabling reference. Anticipation presents the mirror image of infringement: "That which infringes if later anticipates if earlier." *Polaroid Corp. v. Eastman Kodak Co.*, 789 F.2d 1556, 1573 (Fed. Cir. 1986) (citing *Peters v. Active Mfg. Co.*, 129 U.S. 530 (1889)).

A. Each and Every Element

Undoubtedly, the identification of each and every element of the claimed subject matter turns on the proper construction of the claims themselves. As discussed in later chapters, the claims define the scope of the invention. The interesting case of *Titanium Metals Corp. v. Banner*, 778 F.2d 775 (Fed. Cir. 1985), shows the importance of the claims to all aspects of patent law, including anticipation. In addition, this case shows that the discovery of a new property in an old device or composition does not entitle the discoverer to a new patent on the prior art. In *Titanium Metals*, the patent at issue generally related to a titanium-nickel-molybdenum alloy and recited three claims:

1.   A titanium base alloy consisting essentially by weight of about 0.6% to 0.9% nickel, 0.2% to 0.4% molybdenum, up to 0.2% maximum iron, balance titanium, said alloy being characterized by good corrosion resistance in hot brine environments.

2.   A titanium base alloy as set forth in claim 1 having up to 0.1% iron, balance titanium.

3.   A titanium base alloy as set forth in claim 1 having up to 0.8% nickel, 0.3% molybdenum, up to 0.1% maximum iron, balance titanium.

The patent applicant stressed that these compositions resisted corrosion in hot brine environments. The most relevant piece of prior art was a minor three-page article in the Russian language showing data generated by various titanium-nickel-molybdenum alloys. One dot on one of many graphs in the Russian article showed a titanium base alloy containing 0.25% molybdenum by weight and 0.75% nickel by weight—a composition clearly falling within the percentages recited in claims 1 and 2. By the way, the dot is the third dot from the left on the graph marked Figure 1c. The article did not, however, disclose superior resistance to corrosion in hot brine environments. Nevertheless, the court held that the Russian article anticipated claims 1 and 2, because the alloy was not new, even if the applicants for the patent discovered properties of the alloy (corrosion resistance) unspecified by the article. Of course, this result would not have prevented the applicant from acquiring a method patent on the use of the old alloy for corrosion resistance. *Perricone v. Medicis Pharm. Corp.*, 432 F.3d 1368 (Fed. Cir. 2005).

Titanium Metals also sets forth an important anticipation rule: a reference that discloses a single composition anticipates a broader range containing the single composition. That is, a disclosure of a single species anticipates a claimed genus. The inverse, however, is not necessarily true. Prior disclosure of a genus does not automatically anticipate a single species within that genus. The rule is different because the claimed species within a prior art genus may have properties not shared by the rest of the class. This genus/species problem arises most often with chemical compounds.

The test for anticipation is sometimes called the four-corners test. If the claimed subject matter can be found within the ambit of a single prior art reference, the subject matter is anticipated. This inquiry does not combine references (though one or more additional references may be consulted to flesh out the disclosed subject matter by evidencing the inherent knowledge or understanding of ordinarily skilled artisans without, however, supplying an otherwise missing element). Similarly, this inquiry does not consider elements analogous to the disclosure of a reference.

B. Enablement Requirement

The test for sufficient disclosure of each and every element within a single reference is enablement. The disclosure must contain sufficient disclosure to enable one of skill in the art to make (or in this case, identify) each and every element of the claimed subject matter. This echoes the enablement rule in Chapter 9, even though an anticipatory reference need not teach how to use the subject matter. *See Rasmusson v. SmithKline Beecham Corp.*, 413 F.3d 1318 (Fed. Cir. 2005). For example, in *Titanium Metals*, the Russian article did not disclose a method to make the claimed alloy. Nonetheless the article showed that manufacture of the alloy was well within the knowledge of one of ordinary skill in the art. In fact, even the patent applicant's expert admitted that, given the disclosure of the Russian article, he knew multiple methods of preparing the alloys. Thus, the article contained sufficient enabling disclosure of each and every element and thus qualified as an anticipatory reference.

C. Inherency

The most difficult portion of the test for anticipation relates to inherency. The prior art may disclose inherently, rather than expressly, some aspect or all of the claimed subject matter. Under this rule, the prior art disclosure must *necessarily* include the inherent (unexpressed) subject matter. That is, the inherent subject matter must not be occasionally present or accidentally present; the inherent subject matter must be inevitable from the prior art reference's disclosure. *Tilghman v. Proctor*, 102 U.S. 707 (1880). Probabilities and possibilities do not suffice.

Inherent disclosure requires resort to extrinsic evidence, meaning evidence beyond the four corners of the prior art reference. Therefore, the inherency rule poses a question about the kinds of extrinsic evidence that suffice for inherent disclosure. As a general matter, inherency requires recognition by one of ordinary skill in the art that the disclosure contains the nonexpress subject matter. This rule does not, however, temporally fix the types of evidence to show inherent disclosure. For example, technology may progress and previously unknown (or even unknowable) features and properties of the prior art may become apparent. Yet, if necessarily present, the unknown element inherently anticipates. Thus, the inherent subject matter need not be recognized at the time of the anticipatory reference or even before the date of invention or filing. *EMI Group of N. Am., Inc. v. Cypress Semiconductor Corp.*, 268 F.3d 1342 (Fed. Cir. 2001).

The case of *Schering Corp. v. Geneva Pharmaceuticals, Inc.*, 339 F.3d 1373 (Fed. Cir. 2003), illustrates this complex doctrine of inherent anticipation. The prior art was a non-drowsy antihistamine compound, loratadine or CLARITIN®. When a patient ingested loratadine, the body changed it, or metabolized it, into a metabolite, DCL or CLARINEX®. The patent claimed this metabolite. Researchers did not identify or isolate the metabolite outside a patient's body until several years later. Nonetheless, the loratadine reference anticipated the application for the metabolite, even though the earlier patent on loratadine made no mention of metabolites. The Federal Circuit, however, noted that the metabolite was necessarily present upon ingestion of loratadine. Therefore the metabolite was inherent in the ingestion of the prior art compound and anticipated by that earlier reference. In other words, the prior art inherently anticipated the new metabolite compound even though no one recognized or knew of the metabolite until years later. The court also noted, however, that the prior reference would not anticipate a careful claim to an isolated and purified metabolite outside the body. The isolated and purified form of DCL outside the body was a worthy invention when properly claimed.

D. Anticipation vs. Obviousness

A final note of comparison and caution: novelty, of course, is the rarer of the two primary conditions for patentability based on prior art. The more common condition, nonobviousness, does not mandate absolute newness. Instead, nonobviousness carves out an area of unpatentable subject matter around preexisting knowledge. Although their functions are very similar, novelty and nonobviousness are quite distinct, despite the rote incantation that "anticipation is the epitome of obviousness." *Jones v. Hardy*, 727 F.2d 1524, 1529 (Fed. Cir. 1984). Novelty is judged by a single reference; obviousness, on the other hand, is judged by any number of references. Thus, as Chapter 8 discusses later, obviousness requires the collective knowledge in the prior art to contain a motivation to combine individual pieces of knowledge to derive the claimed subject matter.

This axiomatic distinction, at times, becomes blurred. For example, a second reference may aid in determining novelty when it more fully explicates a feature inherent in the primary reference. Similarly, subject matter may be unpatentable in view of a single reference where it would have been obvious at the time of the invention to modify the teachings of the single reference to arrive at the claimed invention, so long as a person of ordinary skill in the art would have followed common-sensical reasoning in making the modification.

Even though novelty and nonobviousness are separate statutory requirements, the provisions that guide a novelty inquiry provide evidence of the knowledge at the time of the invention, which in turn guides a nonobviousness inquiry. That is, the prior art used to judge obviousness arises from the novelty provisions.

CHAPTER 6

STATUTORY BARS

I. INTRODUCTION

Embedded in 35 U.S.C. § 102 are provisions that create statutory bars, namely subsections (b), (c), and (d). Of these, section 102(b) provides the most common, yet most difficult to grasp, bar. This section bars a patent for any invention "in public use or on sale in this country, more than one year prior to the date of the application for patent in the United States." In other words, if one can show that the invention was used publicly or offered for sale by anyone, including the inventor, in the United States more than one year before the application was filed, that invention cannot receive a patent.

These statutory bars encourage timely filing and disclosure of an invention. Under section 102(b), an inventor must file within one year of any public use of, or offer to sell, the invention. Due to its importance, the date corresponding to one year before the filing of the patent application is called the "critical date." Statutorily barred activities, such as publishing an invention in a scientific journal or offering it for sale, even one day before the critical date negates patentability.

The one-year delay between publication or commercialization provides an inventor with a "grace period." This grace period gives the inventor one year after a publication or first sale to perfect the invention or prepare a patent application. An inventor can typically control the critical date by choosing when to publicize or commercialize an invention. Of course, a third party may also trigger the one-year period, thus catching an unwary inventor off guard. Accordingly, despite the grace period, an astute inventor will file an application as quickly as possible.

The justification for the statutory bars becomes apparent by comparing the first-to-invent patent system employed in the United States and the first-to-file patent system employed by the rest of the world. Under a first-to-file system, an inventor who files a patent application for a particular invention first obtains the patent, even if someone else previously invented the technology. This system, of course, encourages a race to the patent office. In the United States, on the other hand, the first inventor obtains the patent, even if someone else filed a patent application earlier on the same invention. This system, of course, tolerates or even encourages an inventor to delay filing a patent application. Thus, to ensure an inventor does not delay disclosure and defeat the objectives of the patent system, the Act includes statutory bars.

A hypothetical clarifies the rationale for the statutory bars in the Patent Act. Assume for a moment that an inventor creates a pill that grows new cartilage. This invention, as may often occur, has unanticipated side-effects, such as growing cartilage where it is not needed (protruding noses and drooping earlobes). In a pure first-to-invent system, the inventor would wait until a third party independently created the same invention and corrected the side-effects. Then, the initial inventor would step in and claim the exclusive right. In the process, the inventor might gain the benefits of the third party's work. Even without the side-effects wrinkle in the hypothetical, an inventor would have an incentive to let someone else undertake the expense of manufacturing and marketing the invention before stepping in to claim an exclusive right to the technology and a share of the profit.

In another scenario, without these statutory bars, an inventor could publicize and commercialize an invention for years, reaping monetary benefits and intangible goodwill and yet all the while waiting until a competitor attempted to enter the market before filing a patent application. This strategy would allow an inventor to prolong the term of the exclusive right indefinitely if no competitor penetrated the market. Under a pure first-to-invent system, nothing would discourage an inventor from keeping the invention secret and filing a patent only when a competitor enters the same market.

The statutory bars, however, prevent these strategies and encourage inventors, under peril of losing all their rights as inventors, to file and disclose their invention earlier rather than later. The United States patent system thus, is not really a pure first-to-invent system. Rather, the first inventor obtains the patent, even if someone else files a patent application earlier claiming the same invention, unless the inventor or anyone else publicizes or commercializes the invention more than one year before the first inventor's filing date.

A grace period between publication and filing can also serve important objectives in a first-to-file system. In a first-to-file regime, an inventor can lose all patent rights by inadvertently disclosing the invention before filing. Thus, an inventor who publishes the invention at a scientific convention has created prior art against his own later filing of a patent application. A grace period prevents this kind of forfeiture and offers the inventor an opportunity to prepare an application after initial publication.

The operation of the bar and grace period in § 102(b) produces a further surprising benefit: it ameliorates the differences between the world first-to-file systems and the U.S. first-to-invent system. The difference could be vast because the world defines "prior" art based on the filing date. The U.S. generally uses the date of invention to determine the art that qualifies as "prior" for validity determinations. Under § 102(b), however, this difference narrows because any art in existence more than a year before the filing date will be "prior" art under both systems. Because § 102(b) makes everything more than a year before filing "prior" art, the world and U.S. systems in fact almost always recognize and rely upon the same references when considering validity. In effect the U.S. system operates much like a first-to-file system in most instances.

The legal implications of the "public use" and "on-sale" statutory bars depend on the character of the barring activities. Thus, the barring activities in section 102(b) fall into two categories: activities performed by the applicant and activities performed by a (usually unknown) third party. Those activities further divide into three different subcategories: informing, noninforming, and secret activities. Accordingly, a third party's secret use may differ in implications from an inventor's own noninforming use, and so forth.

In all cases, however, the "critical date" is essential to application of the statutory bars. As mentioned above, the critical date is the date one year before the filing of the patent application that triggers the start of the grace period.

II. Public Use

Section 102(b) precludes a patent for any invention in public use in this country more than one year before its filing date.

A. Definitions

The first—and most obvious—inquiry asks when a use is considered "public." Public use under 35 U.S.C. § 102(b) includes any use of the claimed invention by an applicant in a public setting as well as any use by a person other than the applicant who is under no limitation, restriction or obligation of secrecy to the inventor. Thus, the "public" nature of a use or disclosure depends on the informing, noninforming, and secret categories. Informing uses reveal the very nature of the invention. Mere disclosure puts the public in possession of the invention. For example, mere disclosure of a new material for a tennis racquet frame or a new stringing pattern would place those inventions in the possession of the observing public.

Noninforming uses do not reveal the nature of the invention. Thus, the public can have and even enjoy the benefits of the invention without observing its inventive features. Inventive processes may often supply benefits to the public that are not readily discernible. For example, a new water purification process may benefit the public without any public awareness of the inventive features.

Similarly, secret uses do not reveal the nature of the invention. Secret uses differ from noninforming uses only in the intent of the inventor or possessor of the invention. With a secret use, the inventor adopts a deliberate policy of keeping the invention as a trade secret and refusing to disclose it to the public.

B. Activities of the Applicant

An applicant, of course, may erect a statutory bar against his own application. An applicant's own informing, noninforming and secret uses all bar the patentability of an invention so long as the use occurred more than one-year before the critical date.

1. Informing

Informing activities are those uses that reveal the very nature of the invention and, thus, put the public in possession of the invention. An informing use by the inventor will create a bar to a patent, so long as the use occurred more than one year prior to the critical date. For example, in *Pennock v. Dialogue*, 27 U.S. 1 (1829), a patentee sold substantial amounts of patented hose to several hose companies for public use in fighting fires. The invention claimed a process for making hose by joining the sections together to resist pressure at the joints. Upon use or careful observation, the public would gain possession of the invention. The patentee instituted a lawsuit against an accused infringer, who defended by asserting that the patent-in-suit was invalid because the patentee allowed others to use the invention in public for over seven years before filing a patent application.

Justice Story aptly described the flaws in a pure first-to-invent system, where a patentee's own activity would not result in a bar:

If an inventor should be permitted to hold back from the knowledge of the public the secrets of his invention; if he should for a long period of years, retain the monopoly, and make and sell his invention publicly and thus gather the whole profits of it, relying upon his superior skill and knowledge of the structure; and then, and then only, when the danger of competition should force him to procure the exclusive right, he should be allowed to take out a patent, and thus exclude the public from any farther use than what should be derived under it during his fourteen years; it would materially retard the progress of science and the useful arts, and give a premium to those who should be least prompt to communicate their discoveries.

Pennock, 27 U.S. at 19.

In other words, inventors should not be able to place their inventions in the public domain and then when someone else decides to make use of the invention, file an application for patent in an attempt to exclude the third party from using the invention. Rather the Patent Act permits only a single year during which an inventor may perfect the invention before filing. In *Pennock*, the Supreme Court concluded that because the inventor put the invention into public use more than seven years before filing a patent application, the patent was invalid.

2. Noninforming

Noninforming activities are those that do not reveal the nature of the invention and, thus, do not put the public in possession of the invention. Noninforming uses by the inventor bar the invention so long as the use occurred more than one-year prior to the filing date.

The United States Supreme Court first dealt with a noninforming use in *Egbert v. Lippmann*, 104 U.S. 333 (1881). In *Egbert*, Samuel Barnes invented an improved corset spring after hearing complaints from a friend that her corset springs continually broke. In 1855 and 1858, Barnes gave her a pair of the improved corset springs, which she wore over a long period of time. In 1863, Joseph Sturgis visited Barnes and received an explanation of how the corset springs worked. Subsequently, in 1866, Barnes filed a patent application for the improvement, which matured into a patent.

The Supreme Court, in deciding whether the single, "private," invisible and therefore noninforming use, was public, enunciated three important principles. First, a single use may be "public." Second, the public to whom the inventor reveals the invention can be a single person. The number of persons privy to the use does not make it public or private. Disclosure to a single person without any obligation of confidentiality can constitute a public use. Finally, the Court explained that an invisible use may still be public. A part embedded deep in a machine and beyond view may still be in public use.

In applying these principles, the Court found sufficient evidence to indicate that Barnes had made a public use of the invention at least two years before the date of filing. (In 1881, when *Egbert* was decided, the grace period lasted two years, which Congress reduced to one year in 1939.) The Court emphasized that Barnes had given the corset springs to his friend, without any restriction on their use, and that she had worn them for several years before he filed his application. Moreover, the Court found that he had waited eleven years before filing a patent application. Thus, he enjoyed the full use of his invention for many years before seeking a patent. Accordingly, he could not retrieve rights to the springs from the public. Nonetheless, all was not lost; his intimate friend became Mrs. Barnes.

3. Secret

Like noninforming uses, secret activities do not reveal the nature of the invention and, thus, do not put the public in possession of the invention. Secret uses differ from the noninforming uses only in the intent of the inventor to avoid the patent system by keeping the invention as a trade secret.

For example, in *Metallizing Engineering Co. v. Kenyon Bearing & Auto Parts Co.*, 153 F.2d 516 (2d Cir. 1946), the Second Circuit held that a secret exploitation of an invention by an inventor constitutes a "public use" under section 102(b). In *Metallizing Engineering*, the patentee created a novel process for metallizing that he employed in his facility, but maintained as a trade secret. Only the finished products were sold, but the products themselves gave no indication of the secret process. The patentee had not himself disclosed the method until he filed for a patent application. For more than one year prior to his application, the inventor used the process secretly in his facility.

Judge Learned Hand held that the secret method still erects a public use bar. Therefore, the inventor forfeited all rights to a patent by selling a product made with the inventive method more than one year before the inventor's filing date. It was irrelevant that the consumers did not know that their purchase was the product of a secret inventive method.

C. Activities of Third Parties

Like the activities by an applicant, the activities of a third party can create statutory bars precluding an inventor from procuring a patent to his invention. Similar to uses by the inventor, informing and noninforming uses by a third party bar the patentability of an invention so long as the use occurred more than one year before the critical date. Secret uses by a third party, however, do not trigger a statutory bar.

1. Informing

Informing uses by third parties invoke the statutory bar even though the third party initiates the use without the knowledge of the inventor. The informing use gives the public the expectation that the invention is in the public domain, regardless of the identity of the user.

For instance, in *Electric Storage Battery Co. v. Shimadzu*, 307 U.S. 5 (1939), Shimadzu invented a method of forming a lead powder with increased reactivity. The defendant in this case, Electric Storage Battery, defended by asserting that it had used a machine that involved both the claimed methods and claimed apparatus more than two years prior to Shimadzu's filing of a United States application for patent.

The Court held that the defendant's use of the machine, which was open to the employees of the plant where it was used and was not shielded or kept secret, invalidated the patents at issue. That is, an informing use of the patented invention by a third party before the critical date invalidated the asserted patents.

2. Noninforming

A noninforming use by a third party may also create a statutory bar prohibiting the issuance of a patent. In *Abbott Laboratories v. Geneva Pharmaceuticals, Inc.*, 182 F.3d 1315 (Fed. Cir. 1999), the Federal Circuit decided that a sale by a third party of a composition that, unbeknownst to the third party, contained the patented compound invoked the statutory bar.

Abbott invented and marketed a hypertension medicine that was a Form IV anhydrate of a chemical compound. A third party, Byron Chemical, sold a small amount of the patented Form IV prior to the critical date. At the time of the sales, Byron did not even know that the composition it sold included traces of Form IV. Three years after the sale and one year after the filing date of the patent application, Abbott discovered that Byron's sale included the Form IV anhydrate. One year later the defendant whom Abbott had sued for infringement discovered this fact as well.

The Federal Circuit held that the Form IV anhydrate was on-sale despite the patentee's assertion that the sale was insufficient because no one in the public knew that the compound had been sold in that form. In other words, even though the public had no reason to believe that it had received the invention, the court held that the noninforming sale invoked the statutory bar to Abbott's patent.

3. Secret

A secret use by a third party, on the other hand, does not invoke a bar to patentability for an inventor. In *W.L. Gore & Associates, Inc. v. Garlock, Inc.*, 721 F.2d 1540 (Fed. Cir. 1983), the technology at issue related to polytetrafluorethylene, commonly known as PTFE or TEFLON®. To make PTFE required stretching the basic composition. Unfortunately PTFE broke fairly easily when it was stretched, even when stretched very slowly. Contrary to the prevailing wisdom in the art, the patentee learned to make PTFE by stretching it very quickly. Thus he filed a patent application claiming the process and the composition.

In the 1960s, John Cropper of New Zealand developed and constructed a machine for stretching PTFE quickly to make a special tape. In 1968, Cropper sold his machine to Budd, a company in the United States. Budd began selling the tape, but kept the machine and process a trade secret.

The Federal Circuit concluded that the sale of the tape was not sufficient to disclose the method of producing it. The public would not learn the claimed process by examining the tape, but of course, the same is true of noninforming uses. The key to this case is that the third party, in this case

Budd, should not enjoy the right to invoke the protections of the Patent Act to invalidate Gore's invention when it had deliberately chosen to avoid the disclosure requirements of the Act. Otherwise Budd could profit from keeping the new technology as a trade secret and then continue to enjoy that advantage by blocking Gore's application for patent protection. The court, therefore, held that Budd's secret use could not invalidate Gore's patent. Perhaps for this reason, the public today often refers to PTFE as "GORE–TEX®," not "BUDD–TEX."

III. ON SALE

A. Definitions

The on-sale bar prevents inventors from commercially exploiting a discovery after it is ready to be patented for more than a year before filing a patent application. The Patent Act thus provides an inventor a one-year grace period during which the inventor may sell or offer for sale the invention.

The threshold inquiry in an on-sale bar case is often whether the product or process is complete and ready for sale. Inventions rarely, if ever, spring fully operational out of the head of their creator. Rather the inventive process typically progresses from day to day towards a solution of a problem. During this development phase, events may transpire that place a new technology in the public domain. For example, a company may separate the engineering department from the marketing department or sales department, yet request that the marketers determine demand for a product while the engineers continue development. Courts, and particularly the Federal Circuit, struggled with different factual situations to set forth a test to determine when the invention is sufficiently complete to invoke the on-sale bar. Compare *UMC Elecs. Co. v. United States*, 816 F.2d 647, 656 (Fed. Cir. 1987) (stating that "without question, the challenger has the burden of proving that there was a definite sale or offer to sell more than one year before the application for the subject patent, and that the subject matter of the sale or offer to sell fully anticipated the claimed invention or would have rendered the claimed invention obvious by its addition to the prior art") with *Seal-Flex, Inc. v. Athletic Track & Court Construction*, 98 F.3d 1318, 1322 (Fed. Cir. 1996) (stating that "the issue is not how much development had already been done, but whether the invention was in fact complete and was known to work for its intended purpose").

In *Pfaff v. Wells Electronics, Inc.*, 525 U.S. 55 (1998), the Supreme Court finally ventured to resolve the confusion with a two-part test for the on-sale bar. First, the invention must be the subject of a commercial offer for sale. Second, the invention must be ready for patenting at the time of that offer. The two parts of the Supreme Court's test are considered in detail below.

B. Two-Part Test

1. Commercial Offer for Sale

The first element in the on-sale bar test turns on whether the invention was the subject of a commercial offer for sale. A commercial offer for sale is typically measured by general rules of contract law, that is, an offer must be sufficiently firm and definite to permit immediate acceptance to form a binding contract (assuming consideration supports both ends of the bargain). *Group One, Ltd. v. Hallmark Cards, Inc.*, 254 F.3d 1041 (Fed. Cir. 2001).

In *Pfaff*, for example, the Supreme Court was asked to determine whether certain activity by the inventor of a simple mechanical invention, a semiconductor chip socket, was sufficient to invoke the on-sale bar. The inventor had shown drawings to a customer and subsequently received an order for the invention from the customer. The Court held that the inventor's acceptance of the purchase order evinced a commercial offer before the critical date. The on-sale bar does not require an actual sale. A sufficiently definite offer that *could* be accepted (even if not actually accepted) will suffice to invoke the bar. Indeed, even a single unrestricted offer for sale precludes patentability.

2. Ready for Patenting

The second element in the on-sale bar test discerns whether the invention is ready for patenting. The ready for patenting standard does not require that the inventor reduce the invention to practice (e.g., by performing experiments or otherwise showing that it will actually work for its intended purpose). Of course, a reduction to practice shows that the invention is ready for patenting. Nonetheless an invention can be ready for patenting before the final tests and trials that reduce the invention to practice. For instance, an invention may be ready for patenting by proof that the inventor had prepared drawings or other descriptions of the invention that were sufficiently specific to enable a person skilled in the art to practice the invention. In other words, the enablement test governs the "ready for patenting" requirement. *Scaltech, Inc. v. Retec/Tetra, L.L.C.*, 269 F.3d 1321 (Fed. Cir. 2001).

In *Pfaff*, for example, the inventor sent engineering drawings to a manufacturer to begin making the invention. Thus, these drawings satisfied the second portion of the test because the drawings enabled the manufacturer to make the invention as claimed. Because the invention was the subject of a commercial offer for sale and because it was ready for patenting before the critical date, the Supreme Court held that the inventor was precluded from receiving a patent for the invention.

IV. EXPERIMENTAL USE NEGATION

A. Exception Versus Negation

The experimental use negation operates to expand the grace period laid out in section 102(b). As a negation instead of an exception, experimental use is not an independent test. That is, the experimental use negation is merely the application of the standard statutory bar test but without a concomitant indication or suggestion that the pre-critical date use was public or that the offer for sale was commercial. In *Pfaff*, the Supreme Court reaffirmed the experimental use (or sale) negation to the section 102(b) bars, stating that "an inventor who seeks to perfect his discovery may conduct extensive testing without losing his right to obtain a patent for his invention—even if such testing occurs in the public eye. The law has long recognized the distinction between inventions put to experimental use and products sold commercially." 525 U.S. at 64.

The Court expressly reaffirmed the primary precedent for experimental uses, *City of Elizabeth v. American Nicholson Pavement Co.*, 97 U.S. 126 (1878), and stated: "In 1878, we explained why patentability may turn on an inventor's use of his product." 525 U.S. at 64. The Supreme Court first established the experimental use negation doctrine in *City of Elizabeth*. This nineteenth century case featured an inventive wooden pavement for a road. The inventor put the claimed wooden pavement surface on a road in Boston, Massachusetts, more than six years before filing a patent application. After receiving the patent, the inventor sued Elizabeth, New Jersey, for infringement.

The accused infringer defended by asserting that the inventor violated the public use bar precluding patentability because the inventor did not file an application for a patent within two years of laying the road for the public to use. While acknowledging that the inventor used the invention in public, the Court could not agree that the inventor's use was public. Rather the Supreme Court fashioned a doctrine allowing an inventor (including a person acting under his directions or orders) to perfect the inventive subject matter through experimentation, even openly, without using it publicly under the bar rules. The Court reasoned that, although the inventor laid his road in a public area where the public gained some benefit from it, he laid the road in order to test the features rather than to abandon his invention or donate it to the public. In addition, the inventor installed the road at his own expense, with the consent of the owner of the road, and he carefully monitored the conditions of the roadway.

The Court relied heavily on the inventor's witness, a toll-collector, who worked near the experimental road. The witness testified that the inventor visited the road almost daily and that he asked questions about the response of drivers passing over the road. Further, he testified that the inventor examined the pavement closely each time, walking over the road and striking it with his cane. This evidence convinced the Court that the inventor used the road not publicly but experimentally to test its usefulness and durability.

A century later, the Federal Circuit emphasizes the singular nature of the experimental use negation to the public use bar:

[I]t is incorrect to impose on the patent owner, as the trial court in this case did, the burden of proving that a "public use" was "experimental." These are not two separable issues. It is incorrect to ask: "Was it public use?" and then, "Was it experimental?" Rather, the court is faced with a single issue: Was it public use under § 102(b)?

TP Labs., Inc. v. Prof'l Positioners, Inc., 724 F.2d 965, 971 (Fed. Cir. 1984). Thus, the same facts should be examined when evaluating public use as well as the experimental use negation to the public use bar.

B. Sales of the Invention

The experimental use negation likewise applies in the on-sale bar context. An inventor may sell an invention for experimental purposes without running afoul of the on-sale bar doctrine in certain circumstances. For example, in *Manville Sales Corp. v. Paramount Systems, Inc.*, 917 F.2d 544 (Fed. Cir. 1990), the Federal Circuit examined an inventor's sale of his highway lighting system to the State of Wyoming. The Court determined that the sale was experimental and not commercial.

The court found that the inventor did nothing to lead the public to believe that the new lighting system was in the public domain. Instead, the inventor conveyed to a state official that Wyoming's use in this single, remote location was experimental. Indeed the inventor also marked the invention as experimental. Moreover, of particular importance, the inventor marked the design drawing as confidential. Finally even the rest stop chosen for the experimental sale was closed to the public during testing.

The court, furthermore, found that the inventor did not do anything to extend the term of his patent by commercially exploiting the invention. Rather, he retained ownership of the invention throughout the testing, only subsequently receiving compensation for the invention. In addition, he did not initiate a sales campaign until after he determined that the invention worked for its intended purpose. Therefore, the court concluded that the inventor did not have any basis for believing that the invention would work in all weather conditions until after he had actually tested it and, accordingly, he had "no proven invention to disclose." 917 F.2d at 550.

V. PATENTS AND PRINTED PUBLICATIONS

Under another provision of 35 U.S.C. § 102(b), a patent is anticipated if "the invention was patented or described in a printed publication in this or a foreign country . . . more than one year prior to the date of the application for patent in the United States." This provision of section 102(b) thus makes the United States first-to-invent system analogous to a first-to-file system for any invention patented or described in a printed publication more than one year before the filing date of the application for patent. That is, section 102(b) triggers the running of a statute of limitations of sorts when an invention is disclosed in a printed publication anywhere in the world. *In re Foster*, 343 F.2d 980 (CCPA 1965).

The difficulty in this section lies in determining what constitutes a printed publication. For example, in *In re Hall*, 781 F.2d 897 (Fed. Cir. 1986), the Federal Circuit was faced with the question of whether a doctoral thesis that was published more than one year before the critical dated was sufficient to invoke the printed publication bar even though the publication was in a foreign language and resided solely at Freiburg University in Germany.

The court held that the German thesis was indeed sufficient to bar the issuance of a patent to the invention, explaining that " 'public accessibility' has been called the touchstone in determining whether a reference constitutes a 'printed publication' bar . . . . " 781 F.2d at 899. The court further stated that the "proponent of the publication bar must show that prior to the critical date the reference was sufficiently accessible, at least to the public interested in the art, so that such a one by examining the reference could make the claimed invention without further research or experimentation." *Id.* Because the doctoral thesis was accessible through indexing and cataloging, the court held that the publication was a valid prior art reference and refused to allow the patent to issue. *See also Bruckelmyer v. Ground Heaters, Inc.*, 445 F.3d 1374 (Fed. Cir. 2006).

VI. OTHER STATUTORY BARS

Beyond section 102(b), sections 102(c) and 102(d) also erect bars to patentability.

A. Abandonment

Under 35 U.S.C. § 102(c), an inventor is not entitled to a patent for an invention if he abandoned the invention. For example, in *Kendall v. Winsor*, 62 U.S. 322 (1858), Winsor filed suit based on a patent for a harness-making machine. The defendants claimed that Winsor had informed the defendants that he did not want to obtain a patent, but rather preferred to retain the technology as a trade secret. Accordingly, the defendants asserted that he had abandoned the invention. The jury, however, disagreed and concluded that the patentee had not in fact abandoned the patented technology.

In *Kendall*, the Court explained that "[i]t is the unquestionable right of every inventor to confer gratuitously the benefits of his ingenuity upon the public, and this he may do either by express declaration or by conduct equally significant with language. . . ." 62 U.S. at 329. The Court then provided three examples of inventor abandonment: acquiescing to others' use of the invention, forfeiting rights by a willfully or negligently postponing protection of the invention, and attempting to keep the improvement as a trade secret until another introduces it. The latter two of these three scenarios are largely redundant over other patent-defeating sections, that is, sections 102(b) and 102(g). Accordingly, abandonment typically applies only where the inventor consciously and intentionally dedicates the invention to the public. Notably, only the inventor may abandon his invention. That is, a third party may not effect an abandonment by surreptitiously pirating the invention and communicating it to the public. 62 U.S. at 330–31.

B. Delay

Under 35 U.S.C. § 102(d), an inventor is not entitled to a patent for an invention if "the invention was first patented or caused to be patented, or was the subject of an inventors' certificate, by the applicant or his legal representatives or assigns in a foreign country prior to the date of the application for patent in this country on an application for patent or inventors' certificate filed more than twelve months before the filing of the application in the United States." That is, applicants may confront a bar if they file for patent protection in a foreign country more than a year prior to the filing date of their U.S. patent application and the foreign application matured into a patent before the U.S. filing date. *Bayer AG v. Schein Pharms., Inc.*, 301 F.3d 1306 (Fed. Cir. 2002).

For example, in *In re Kathawala*, 9 F.3d 942 (Fed. Cir. 1993), the inventor filed patent applications in the United States, Greece, and Spain. The United States application was filed on April 11, 1985, more than one year after the Greek and Spanish applications were filed on November 21, 1983. In addition, the Greek application issued as a patent on October 2, 1984, and the Spanish application issued on January 21, 1985, both prior to the United States filing date. The Federal Circuit upheld the bar. Because the inventor had the opportunity to file an application for patent in the United States prior to the critical date and before the issuance of the foreign patents, but instead delayed filing, the court held that the inventor was not entitled to a patent in the United States. Under the special circumstances described by § 102(d) the one-year period is eliminated from § 102(b).

CHAPTER 7

NOVELTY: PRIOR INVENTION

I. INTRODUCTION

As introduced in Chapter 5, this chapter discusses the novelty requirements set forth in § 102, specifically paragraphs (a), (e), (f), and (g). These paragraphs all concern ways to ascertain whether the subject matter has already been invented. Section 102(a) straightforwardly states the essential first-to-invent rule that is fundamental to novelty in the United States. In particular, an inventor is entitled to a patent unless "the invention was known or used by others in this country, or patented or described in a printed publication in this or a foreign country, before the invention thereof by the applicant for patent." Section 102(a) thus sets forth that a public disclosure will preclude a later patent for the same subject matter. The four categories—knowledge by another in the United States, use by another in the United States, patented, or described in a printed publication—are examined in greater detail in Chapter 5.

Section 102(e) relates to a special category of secret, nonpublic disclosure that nonetheless precludes a patent for the disclosed subject matter, namely an earlier patent application. To preempt a later patent application on the same subject matter under this section, the earlier application must have appeared publicly as a published application or as an issued patent.

Section 102(f) prevents a putative inventor from patenting subject matter that he did not truly invent. In other words, an imposter may not receive a patent for subject matter derived from another's work. In a real sense, this non-derivation requirement is different from the prior art generating provisions of §§ 102(a), (e) and (g). Nonetheless its emphasis on novelty correlates sufficiently with those other paragraphs to warrant joint consideration.

Perhaps the most critical and complex category of secret prior art, § 102(g), generally prevents the patenting of subject matter already invented by another. Section 102(g) contains two paragraphs. The first paragraph provides the statutory basis for an interference—an administrative proceeding determining which of two pending patent applications (or which of a pending application and an issued patent) represents the work of the first inventor. In other words, an interference determines inventive priority before the Patent Office. The second paragraph provides the statutory basis to invalidate a patent based on another's prior invention of the same subject matter. The relatively terse statutory language belies the complexity of determining priority or validity based on prior invention.

In contrast to Chapter 6 discussing statutory bars, the novelty requirements in this chapter are not universally applicable across the world. In fact, these rules are entirely unique to the United States' first-to-invent system. If this country ever adopts a first-to-file system, a frequent legislative proposal and topic for debate, this chapter of the Patent Act would fade into obsolescence. Accordingly, these provisions both add complexity to domestic patent law and increase the transaction costs of worldwide patenting.

II. PRIOR INVENTION UNDER SECTION 102(a)

A. "Known or Used"

One of the earliest U.S. patent cases set forth the first-to-invent requirement in § 102(a). In *Woodcock v. Parker*, 30 F. Cas. 491 (D. Mass. 1813), the court explained that only the first and original inventor receives a patent, even if a second person independently invented the same subject matter. In fact, once the subject matter becomes public, it does not even matter that the first inventor abandoned it, making the second inventor the person who actually produced a benefit for society. To repeat the central principle, the event that defeats novelty is the prior invention, not simply the prior disclosure of inventive subject matter. After *Woodcock*, the statute began explicitly prohibiting the award of a patent to subject matter "known or used" before the applicant's date of invention (as opposed to the applicant's filing date).

Even though the important date is the date of invention, an applicant is not generally required to identify that precise date. Rather, for ease of administration, the inventor typically relies on his filing date and only specifies an earlier invention date when prior art arises that necessitates the specificity. Thus, if an examiner discovers prior art that anticipates the claimed subject matter under § 102(a), the applicant may then file an affidavit under 37 C.F.R. § 1.131—an eponymically named Rule 131 affidavit—that shows an invention date before the anticipatory reference.

Chapter 5 goes over the territorial limitations of knowledge or use by others in § 102(a) as well as the meaning of "patented or described in a printed publication." This examination of the phrase "known or used by others" thus completes the discussion of § 102(a). Notably, unlike the "public use" bar of § 102(b), this phrase limits the patent-defeating knowledge to persons other than the inventor. In other words, inventors cannot create prior art against themselves under U.S. law. Inventors can, of course, publish, exploit, or sell their work and thus create a statutory bar under § 102(b), but their undisclosed work does not otherwise become prior art that disqualifies their own later inventions under § 102(a).

In any event, another's prior use or knowledge of the subject matter does not defeat a later patent application if that prior use was kept secret, that is, never made public. *Gillman v. Stern*, 114 F.2d 28 (2d Cir. 1940). Indeed, to qualify as the first and original inventor, a third party must have enriched the art. Accordingly, a private and deliberately undisclosed use does not anticipate a later invention of the same subject matter because the public never receives the benefit of the initial invention. This rule corresponds well with the rule that a third party's deliberately secret use cannot erect a statutory bar under § 102(b). Again similar to § 102(b)'s scheme, a third party's public, noninforming uses do not follow the same rule. These noninforming uses preclude the patentability of the subject matter.

Subject matter is "known" within the meaning of § 102(a) if reasonably accessible to the interested public. For example, in *National Tractor Pullers Association v. Watkins*, 205 USPQ 892 (N.D. Ill. 1980), the alleged infringer asserted that the patent-in-suit, a resistance sled for tractor pulling contests, was invalid under § 102(a). The infringer produced evidence that a putative earlier inventor had sketched the invention on the underside of a kitchen tablecloth. Because that alleged earlier inventor had neither reproduced the drawings before their destruction nor commercialized the depicted device, the court correctly determined that this evidence was not anticipatory prior art because the interested public did not have reasonable access to it. This rule also sounds familiar because it correlates with the public accessibility requirement for printed publications, such as through indexing and cataloguing. *See e.g.*, *In re Klopfenstein*, 380 F.3d 1345 (Fed. Cir. 2004).

B. Section 102(a) Before the Patent and Trademark Office

Because the important date under § 102(a) is the inventor's date of invention, the Patent and Trademark Office permits patent applicants to show a date of invention before the prior art's disclosure date. But because a rejection under § 102(a) alone is rare, an applicant usually does not specify a date of invention until it becomes necessary to "swear behind" or antedate a reference. In other words, the date of filing serves as the presumptive invention date, until an inventor needs to show an earlier date of invention with a Rule 131 affidavit. Notably, once a patent applicant or patentee antedates a reference, the inquiry ends. That is, the PTO does not seek out an earlier date of invention for the prior art reference, which makes sense because those inventive activities are not publicly accessible. The administrative rule, 37 C.F.R. § 1.131, provides:

(a) When any claim of an application or a patent under reexamination is rejected, the inventor of the subject matter of the rejected claim ... may submit an appropriate oath or declaration to establish invention of the subject matter of the rejected claim prior to the effective date of the reference or activity on which the rejection is based. The effective date of a U.S. patent, U.S. patent application publication, or international application publication under PCT Article 21(2) is the earlier of its publication date or date that it is effective as a reference under 35 U.S.C. § 102(e).

Prior invention may not be established under this section in any country other than the United States, a NAFTA country, or a WTO member country.... Prior invention may not be established under this section if either:

(1) The rejection is based upon a U.S. patent or U.S. patent application publication of a pending or patented application to another or others which claims the same patentable invention as defined in Sec. 1.601(n); or

(2) The rejection is based upon a statutory bar.

(b) The showing of facts shall be such, in character and weight, as to establish reduction to practice prior to the effective date of the reference, or conception of the invention prior to the effective date of the reference coupled with due diligence from prior to said date to a subsequent reduction to practice or to the filing of the application. Original exhibits of drawings or records, or photocopies thereof, must accompany ... the affidavit....

Rule 131 allows inventors to establish a date of invention using inventive activities in certain foreign countries as well as the United States. Furthermore, the Rule specifies two categories where an affidavit cannot antedate a reference: interferences to determine priority over the same subject matter and statutory bars. Under the second category, if a printed publication precedes the filing date of a patent by more than a year, that printed publication serves as a bar under § 102(b) regardless of the applicant's or patentee's ability to show an earlier date of invention.

A Rule 131 affidavit must possess sufficient content to antedate an anticipatory reference. For example, in *In re Stryker*, 435 F.2d 1340 (CCPA 1971), the court considered whether an uncorroborated affidavit had to substantiate prior invention of the entire claimed subject matter or just the subject matter disclosed in the prior art reference. The court decided the latter: the affidavit did not need to substantiate prior invention of claimed features not found in the prior art. Instead, an antedating affidavit need only show prior invention of the features disclosed in the prior art. Otherwise, broad claims without a feature in both the reference and affidavit would escape anticipation, while narrower claims with features not present in either the reference or the affidavit would be invalid. The *Stryker* rule prevents this anomaly.

III.   PRIORITY UNDER SECTION 102(g)

A.   Section 102(g)'s Purpose

Perhaps the most complicated prior art section, § 102(g), recites:

(1) during the course of an interference conducted under section 135 or section 291, another inventor involved therein establishes, to the extent permitted in section 104, that before such person's invention thereof the invention was made by such other inventor and not abandoned, suppressed, or concealed, or

(2) before such person's invention thereof, the invention was made in this country by another

inventor who had not abandoned, suppressed, or concealed it. In determining priority of invention under this subsection, there shall be considered not only the respective dates of conception and reduction to practice of the invention, but also the reasonable diligence of one who was first to conceive and last to reduce to practice, from a time prior to conception by the other.

The first paragraph provides a mechanism for resolving interferences. The second paragraph serves a purpose distinct from, yet related to, interferences—permitting an alleged infringer to invalidate an issued patent based on either his own or a third party's prior invention (but only if "in this country"). In the first paragraph, a party seeks more than a mere denial of another's entitlement to a patent on the claimed subject matter; it seeks to secure a patent for itself.

The first paragraph thus determines priority of invention. As innovators across the world compete to develop new and valuable technologies, they will often arrive at similar or even identical inventions at approximately the same time. Where two inventive entities claim the same invention, the United States patent system has a winner-take-all approach: the first inventor obtains the exclusive right to the subject matter and the second inventor gets nothing, not even a right to continue to practice his independent development.

B. Statutory Framework

Although both paragraphs recite slightly different language, the step-wise procedure of resolving priority is the same. In § 102(g)(2), the statute sets forth the general rule of priority: "A person shall be entitled to a patent unless ... before such person's invention thereof, the invention was made in this country by another inventor." But there is an important and complicating exception: if the first inventor "abandoned, suppressed, or concealed" the subject matter, the second inventor has priority. In the case of an interference under this scenario, the second inventor would receive a patent covering the subject matter. In the case of a challenge to validity, the first inventor's patent is invalid even though the second inventor is not awarded a patent.

Furthermore, the last sentence of § 102(g) informs that a date of invention requires an examination of "not only the respective dates of conception and reduction to practice of the invention, but also the reasonable diligence of one who was first to conceive and last to reduce to practice, from a time prior to conception by the other." Thus the priority rule awards a patent to the first to reduce to practice unless the second person to reduce the invention to practice was the first to conceive of the invention and diligently worked to reduce the subject matter to practice. That basic rule, however, is subject to the abandonment, suppression, or concealment requirement.

1. Interferences

As noted, § 102(g) serves not only as a category of prior art but also as the source for interferences.

An interference is a very complex administrative proceeding, and interference practitioners can easily devote their entire career to learning the intricacies of these priority contests. An interference may occur between two pending applications or between a pending application and an issued, unexpired patent. The Patent and Trademark Office will declare an interference when "an application is made for a patent which ... would interfere with any pending application, or with any unexpired patent." 35 U.S.C. § 135. An interference may arise between two conflicting applications without any prompting by (or even knowledge of) either applicant. Alternatively, a patent applicant may provoke an interference upon discovery of a newly issued patent or published pending application that claims the same invention. In fact, an interference may even be declared between a reissue application and an issued patent.

Even a basic understanding of interference procedures requires knowledge of a certain vocabulary. To begin with, the two parties have uniform names: "A senior party is the party with the earliest effective filing date.... A junior party is any other party." 37 C.F.R. § 1.601(m). These senior and junior designations are not just names–they establish procedural and evidentiary burdens. For this reason, the senior party enjoys a greater probability of winning an interference than a junior party. With respect to other nomenclature, a "count" corresponds to the claimed invention over which both parties seek exclusive rights. The count defines the parameters of the dispute.

Importantly, the Patent and Trademark Office will only declare an interference in some circumstances, namely "when at least one claim of a party that is designated to correspond to a count and at least one claim of an opponent that is designated to correspond to the count define the same patentable invention." 37 C.F.R. § 1.601(j). Furthermore, "[i]nvention 'A' is the same patentable invention as an invention 'B' when invention 'A' is the same as (35 U.S.C. 102) or is obvious (35 U.S.C. 103) in view of invention 'B' assuming invention 'B' is prior art with respect to invention 'A.'" 37 C.F.R. § 1.601(n). This rule sets forth a two-way test that judges the patentability of each invention vis-à-vis the other. *Eli Lilly & Co. v. Bd. of Regents of the Univ. of Wash.*, 334 F.3d 1264 (Fed. Cir. 2003). Thus an interference requires claimed subject matter in one patent or application that either anticipates or renders the other obvious.

On rare occasions, the Patent and Trademark Office will issue two patents claiming the same subject matter. In such a case, § 291 permits an owner of an interfering patent to seek exclusive entitlement in a court proceeding. In other words, the district court conducts the interference in a proceeding satisfying the same standards as set forth in § 135. *Medichem, S.A. v. Rolabo, S.L.*, 353 F.3d 928 (Fed. Cir. 2003). More frequently than invoking § 291, however, an accused infringer will invoke § 102(g)(2) to invalidate the asserted patent when it has independently developed the subject matter it is accused of infringing. *See, e.g., Apotex USA, Inc. v. Merck & Co.*, 254 F.3d 1031 (Fed. Cir. 2001).

2. Conception

The touchstone of invention is conception, that is, the completion of the mental portion of the process of inventing. *Burroughs Wellcome Co. v. Barr Labs., Inc.*, 40 F.3d 1223 (Fed. Cir. 1994). An inventor conceives of an invention upon formation of "a definite and permanent idea of the complete and operative invention." *Hybritech Inc. v. Monoclonal Antibodies, Inc.*, 802 F.2d 1367, 1376 (Fed. Cir. 1986) (quoting 1 Robinson on Patents 532 (1890)). An idea is complete when a person having ordinary skill in the art would be able to reduce the invention to practice, including every claimed feature, without excessive research or experimentation. A general goal or research plan is not enough; the inventor must have a specific idea, or particular solution firmly in mind, even if knowledge that the invention will actually work is still lacking. Reduction to practice requires the inventor to make the invention work; conception occurs before the operative invention has actually worked.

Chemical compounds have an even more stringent conception rule. For example, in *Oka v. Youssefyeh*, 849 F.2d 581 (Fed. Cir. 1988), the court encountered a priority dispute over a count reciting a particular genus of chemical compounds, specifically 2–indanyl and 5–indanyl classes. The court divided conception for chemical compounds into two parts: (i) the idea of a structure or formula and (ii) the possession of an operative method of synthesizing that structure. Where the second step is within the knowledge of one of ordinary skill in the art, the standard rule for conception governs, namely the formation of a complete idea constitutes conception. In *Oka*, however, the junior party, Youssefyeh, attempted to show an earlier conception with two distinct sets of corroborated activities. First, Youssefyeh attempted to show that he had the idea of the 2–indanyl compounds along with the belief that those compounds could be synthesized according to conventional techniques. The court discounted that belief because the evidence showed that a person of ordinary skill in the art took over six months to obtain a method to formulate those compounds. Because Youssefyeh apparently never acquired an operative method, he could not show conception of the 2–indanyl compounds. Second, Youssefyeh attempted to show conception of the 5–indanyl compounds with an operative method of making such a compound, even though he did not also have the idea of the chemical structure until later. The court explained that conception occurred only when Youssefyeh had both the idea of the chemical structure and an operative method of synthesis.

Furthermore, because conception can be entirely mental, the inventor's challenge is often to produce contemporaneous evidence that corroborates the conception. The corroboration requirement compensates for the often ethereal nature of conception by requiring particular proof beyond the inventor's mere recollection. *Singh v. Brake*, 317 F.3d 1334 (Fed. Cir. 2003). A rule of reason governs this corroborating evidence. *See, e.g., Linear Tech. Corp. v. Impala Linear Corp.*, 379 F.3d 1311 (Fed. Cir. 2004).

3. Reduction to Practice

An inventor may reduce an invention to practice in two ways: constructively, by filing a patent application, or actually, by building and testing a physical embodiment of the invention. If the inventor relies on a constructive reduction to practice, the filed application must fully disclose the invention. As noted in *Travis v. Baker*, an application "must be for the same invention as that defined in the count in an interference, and it must contain a disclosure of the invention sufficiently adequate to enable one skilled in the art to practice the invention defined by the count, with all the limitations contained in the count, without the exercise of the inventive faculties." 137 F.2d 109, 111 (CCPA 1943).

An actual reduction to practice must show that the invention works for its intended purpose in the actual environment of its use. Once again, a rule of reason governs the sufficiency of the proof. The case of *Scott v. Finney*, 34 F.3d 1058 (Fed. Cir. 1994), illustrates these principles at work. The invention was a penile prosthesis. The inventor sought to show an actual reduction to practice, but had not tested the prosthesis in intercourse. Instead the inventor presented a videotape of the prosthesis inducing an erection during surgery to install the device. The court held that the junior party had sufficiently tested the relatively simple medical device. The court explained:

In cases requiring testing, this court's predecessor addressed many times the nature of testing necessary to show reduction to practice. Several important principles emerge from these cases. For instance, the testing requirement depends on the facts of each case, with the court guided by a common sense approach in weighing the sufficiency of the testing. Reduction to practice does not require that the invention, when tested, be in a commercially satisfactory stage of development. Testing need not show utility beyond a possibility of failure, but only utility beyond a probability of failure. When reviewing the sufficiency of evidence of reduction to practice, this court applies a reasonableness standard.

Complex inventions and problems in some cases require laboratory tests that accurately duplicate actual working conditions in practical uses. . . .

Less complex inventions and problems do no demand such stringent testing.

Scott, 34 F.3d at 1061–62 (quotations and citations omitted).

In some circumstances, conception and reduction to practice occur simultaneously. For example, an inventor does not conceive of a gene until identification of the gene's structure (and not just the principal biological property). Thus, conception and reduction to practice occur simultaneously upon discovery of the gene's sequence. *Amgen, Inc. v. Chugai Pharm. Co.*, 927 F.2d 1200 (Fed. Cir. 1991).

Similar to conception, a reduction to practice requires corroboration with contemporaneous evidence. Again, this rule prevents fraud, and in some circumstances can be quite stringent. In one case, a witness testified that he had read and understood a notebook entry on a specific date. The court rejected this proof of an earlier reduction to practice:

> Those affiants' statements that by a certain date they had "read and understood" specified pages of [the junior party's] laboratory notebooks did not corroborate a reduction to practice. They established only that those pages existed on a certain date; they did not independently corroborate the statements made on those pages.

Hahn v. Wong, 892 F.2d 1028, 1033 (Fed. Cir. 1989). In another case, the court upheld an inventor's offer of his lab notebook showing his practice of the claimed invention. As corroboration, the inventor proffered testimony of a co-worker from whom the inventor acquired supplies for the invention, testimony of another co-worker that he had seen the product produced by the claimed method, and general evidence that the company followed a program to record inventive activity. *Lacotte v. Thomas*, 758 F.2d 611 (Fed. Cir. 1985).

Also similar to conception, the court measures the sufficiency of evidence under a rule of reason:

Under the rule of reason, this court cannot ignore the realities of technical operations in modern day research laboratories. Recognizing these realities, a junior technician performing perfunctory tasks under the supervision of a senior scientist is not generally necessary to verify the reliability of evidence about scientific methods or data. In the absence of indicia calling into question the trustworthiness of the senior scientist's testimony, the rule of reason permits the Board [of Patent Appeals and Interferences] to rely on the trained supervisor's testimony to ascertain scientific methods or results.

Holmwood v. Sugavanam, 948 F.2d 1236, 1239 (Fed. Cir. 1991) (citation omitted). Various factors guide the rule of reason analysis. *See Price v. Symsek*, 988 F.2d 1187 (Fed. Cir. 1993).

4. Diligence

As noted earlier, an inventor who diligently pursues a reduction to practice after an early conception may win priority over the first reducer to practice. While diligence naturally depends on the factual circumstances, it requires persistent, dogged work from conception to reduction to practice. The classic case in this area is *Gould v. Schawlow*, 363 F.2d 908 (CCPA 1966). From that case, a clear rule emerged: "The party chargeable with diligence must account for the entire period during which diligence is required." *Id.* at 919. Gordon Gould, now in the Inventor's Hall of Fame, spent about a thousand hours over a 14–month period pursuing a reduction to practice of his conception of a laser, but he was not diligent enough. Specifically, Gould could not show work in a few gaps of several weeks.

A general averment of the number of days spent reducing the invention to practice does not show diligence without a concomitant showing the specific work accomplished on each day. In other words, the junior party must provide very specific evidence of diligence. Moreover the corroboration requirement also applies to diligence and makes overcoming the senior party's bid very difficult.

Diligence is *only* relevant where one party claims an earlier date of conception and a later date of reduction to practice. That is, only one party's diligence ever affects the outcome of a priority contest: the first to conceive but second to reduce to practice. The inventor who is both first to conceive and first to reduce an invention to practice wins the priority contest outright without any showing of diligence. Competing inventors do not engage in any sort of diligence race. The first inventor to reduce to practice never needs to show diligence.

The required period of diligence for the inventor who was first to conceive and last to reduce to practice begins "prior to the conception by the other" and extends to that inventor's own reduction to practice (constructive or actual). Diligence outside of those bounds is irrelevant, as long as the first conceiver and second reducer to practice commences a course of diligence before the date of conception by the second conceiver (and first reducer to practice).

5. Abandoned, Suppressed, or Concealed

A first inventor does not always win a priority contest. Indeed, a first inventor may lose by abandoning, suppressing, or concealing the invention. Section 102(g) thus provides an impetus to promptly file a patent application describing the subject matter (or otherwise publicly disclose it). Although these all relate to the general idea that an inventor must somehow enrich the public knowledge soon after finalizing the invention, they are slightly different concepts. When establishing abandonment, suppression, or concealment, the second inventor does not need to prove the category within which the first inventor's activities belong.

An inventor may abandon, suppress, or conceal the invention either actively or passively. That is, an inventor may actively conceal the invention as a trade secret. Alternatively the inventor may abandon or suppress the invention by unreasonably delaying its public disclosure. *E.g.*, *Fujikawa v. Wattanasin*, 93 F.3d 1559 (Fed. Cir. 1996); *Shindelar v. Holdeman*, 628 F.2d 1337 (CCPA 1980). Abandonment, suppression, or concealment most often appear in cases involving "spurring," that is, where the first inventor is spurred into filing a patent application by learning of second inventor's competing application or commercial activity. To avoid forfeiture, the first inventor must publicly disclose the invention within a reasonable amount of time after reducing it to practice by filing a patent application, describing it in a publicly available publication, or commercializing it in an informing way that enables the public to learn of the invention. *Dow Chem. Co. v. Astro–Valcour, Inc.*, 267 F.3d 1334 (Fed. Cir. 2001). The method of public disclosure impacts the types of activities that negate an inference of forfeiture. Although occasionally (and erroneously) called "diligence," the level of activity negating an inference of abandonment, suppression, or concealment is far less onerous than the diligence requirement.

An inventor who abandons, suppresses, or conceals the invention may still prevail in a priority fight. To win in that situation, the first inventor must "demonstrate that he renewed activity on the invention and that he proceeded diligently to filing his patent application, starting before the earliest date to which [the second inventor] is entitled." *Paulik v. Rizkalla*, 760 F.2d 1270, 1273 (Fed. Cir. 1985) (*en banc*). If that were not the rule, inventors would never return to projects that had been ignored for an extended period of time. Accordingly, an inventor may partially minimize the consequences of abandoning, suppressing, or concealing an invention if no one began work on the same invention prior to the inventor's return to the inventive project.

6.   The second paragraph of § 102(g)

To a large extent, the legal standards under § 102(g) are the same under both paragraphs. One difference is that § 102(g)(2) applies only if the prior invention was in this country. In some respects, furthermore, the subsection is similar to § 102(a), except that § 102(g)(2) applies to an earlier invention that is secret (so long as it was not abandoned, suppressed, or concealed).

Because the second paragraph permits invalidation of a presumptively valid patent, the procedure entails a different burden of proof. In *Apotex USA, Inc. v. Merck & Co.*, 254 F.3d 1031, 1037–38 (Fed. Cir. 2001), the court explained:

Because the patentee (analogous to the second-to-invent in the interference context) has the benefit of the presumption of validity, that party should only be held to bear a burden of producing evidence indicating that the prior inventor may have suppressed or concealed the invention once the challenger (analogous to the first-to-invent in the interference context) has established prior invention by clear and convincing evidence. That burden bears a rough similarity to placing the burden of proving suppression or concealment on the second-to-invent under interference law, but at the same time is appropriately limited to one of production, not persuasion, giving due regard to the presumption of validity.

We therefore interpret § 102(g) as requiring that once a challenger of a patent has proven by clear and convincing evidence that "the invention was made in this country by another inventor," 35 U.S.C. § 102(g), the burden of production shifts to the patentee to produce evidence sufficient to create a genuine issue of material fact as to whether the prior inventor has suppressed or concealed the invention. However, in accordance with the statutory presumption in 35 U.S.C. § 282, the ultimate burden of persuasion remains with the party challenging the validity of the patent. Once the patentee has satisfied its burden of production, the party alleging invalidity under § 102(g) must rebut any alleged suppression or concealment with clear and convincing evidence to the contrary.

7. Examples

The following examples provide a helpful guide—or a crib sheet—to who would win a priority dispute under § 102(g). In each of the examples, assume the events occur in chronological order.

A files; B files.	A prevails, because its reduction to practice predates B's. Note that both reductions to practice are constructive.
B reduces to practice; A files; B files.	B prevails, because its reduction to practice predates A's reduction to practice. Note that B's earliest reduction to practice is actual, while A's reduction to practice is constructive.
A reduces to practice; B reduces to practice; A files; B files.	A prevails, because its reduction to practice predates B's.
B conceives and proceeds	B prevails, because although it

with requisite diligence; A reduces to practice; A files; B files.	was the second to reduce to practice, it conceived first and diligently worked until reduction to practice.
A conceives and proceeds with requisite diligence; B conceives and proceeds with requisite diligence; A reduces to practice; A files; B files.	A prevails, because both its conception (with diligence) and its reduction to practice predates B's.
B reduces to practice; A reduces to practice; B abandons, suppresses, or conceals; A files; B files.	A prevails, because although B was the first to reduce to practice, B subsequently abandoned, suppressed, or concealed and did not resume activities prior to A's inventive activity.
B conceives and proceeds with requisite diligence; A reduces to practice; A files; B publicly discloses the invention; A obtains a patent.	A's patent is invalid, because B conceived first and diligently worked until publicly disclosing the invention.

IV. PRIOR INVENTION UNDER SECTION 102(e)

Although related to a priority fight under § 102(g), § 102(e) prevents the patenting of subject matter described in an earlier application, so long as that earlier application either matures into a patent or is published prior to grant. Thus, while § 102(g) focuses on the claimed invention, § 102(e) focuses on the disclosure of a patent or patent application. The section proscribes the patentability where

(e) The invention was described in—

(1) an application for patent, published under section 122(b), by another filed in the United States before the invention by the applicant for patent, except that an international application filed under the treaty defined in section 351(a) shall have the effect under this subsection of a national application published under section 122(b) only if the international application designating the United States was published under Article 21(2)(a) of such treaty in the English language; or

(2) a patent granted on an application for patent by another filed in the United States before the invention by the applicant for patent, except that a patent shall not be deemed filed in the United States for the purposes of this subsection based on the filing of an international application filed under the treaty defined in section 351(a)[.]

As first established by the Supreme Court in *Alexander Milburn Co. v. Davis–Bournonville Co.*, 270 U.S. 390 (1926), this paragraph fixes the date of an issued patent or published application as that patent's filing date, even though the contents of that patent or published application remain secret until issuance or publication. While the secret prior art discussed in this section may negate novelty, it may negate nonobviousness as well. That is, the novelty requirement defined by § 102(e) also established prior art that can be combined or modified in an obviousness analysis. *Hazeltine Research, Inc. v. Brenner*, 382 U.S. 252 (1965).

V. DERIVATION UNDER SECTION 102(f)

Because a patent should issue to only the correct inventor, § 102(f) negates the patentability of subject matter if the applicant or patentee "did not himself invent the subject matter sought to be patented." Thus, one cannot file a patent application claiming subject matter that another invented. For instance, a corporation cannot establish a policy whereby the president is always named the sole inventor regardless of the actual inventor(s). The Supreme Court explained this commonsense rule in *Agawam Woolen Co. v. Jordan*, 74 U.S. (7 Wall.) 583, 602–03 (1868):

> No one is entitled to a patent for that which he did not invent unless he can show a legal title to the same from the inventor or by operation of law[.] . . .

> Suggestions from another, made during the progress of such experiments, in order that they may be sufficient to defeat a patent subsequently issued, must have embraced the plan of improvement, and must have furnished such information to the person to whom the communication was made that it would have enabled an ordinary mechanic, without the exercise of any ingenuity and special skill on his part, to construct and put the improvement in successful operation.

The Court indicated that the prior inventor must have disclosed the subject matter to the person seeking to patent the subject matter. Furthermore, it is not enough that the disclosure rendered the subject matter obvious; rather, the strict anticipation test governs this rule, just like the other subparagraphs in § 102. *Gambro Lundia AB v. Baxter Healthcare Corp.*, 110 F.3d 1573 (Fed. Cir. 1997).

Like prior disclosure in a patent or published patent application under § 102(e), the anti-derivation requirement of § 102(f) may also operate in an interference under § 102(g). In fact, parties in a priority fight will occasionally assert that the opposing parties derived the subject matter of the count from them. In such a circumstance, "the person attacking the patent must establish prior conception of the claimed subject matter and communication of the conception to the adverse claimant." *Price v. Symsek*, 988 F.2d 1187, 1190 (Fed. Cir. 1993). This standard applies equally to all inquiries under § 102(f), even where § 102(g) is not at issue.

CHAPTER 8

NONOBVIOUSNESS

I. INTRODUCTION

In addition to being novel, an invention must be nonobvious, that is, a sufficient advance beyond the collective knowledge in the art to warrant an exclusive right. Novelty mandates that the invention cannot already be expressly or inherently disclosed to the public. An invention, however, may be strictly new in the sense that it did not exist in its entirety before the invention, but still be little more than an obvious variation on prior technology. Exclusive rights are not necessary nor offered to encourage the creation of obvious variations. Obviousness, therefore, compares the invention to the prior art to determine whether a single or, most often, multiple references would have led a person of ordinary skill in the art to formulate the claimed invention at the time of invention.

Some combinations of old prior art are very inventive and worthy of an exclusive right. In fact, inventions are very often combinations of elements already in the prior art. These combinations are not necessarily obvious. Rather the obviousness inquiry requires a factual assessment of the prior art compared to the invention as a whole. Section 103(a) sets forth the statutory test:

A patent may not be obtained though the invention is not identically disclosed or described as set forth in section 102 of this title, if the differences between the subject matter sought to be patented and the prior art are such that the subject matter as a whole would have been obvious at the time the invention was made to a person having ordinary skill in the art to which said subject matter pertains. Patentability shall not be negatived by the manner in which the invention was made.

Though not a model of clear and efficient language, each phrase of this section contains a vital part of the obviousness test.

To begin with, the statute refers to inventions that are "not identically disclosed or described as set forth in section 102." This phrase clarifies that obviousness is a requirement beyond novelty. Accordingly, an innovation may be novel yet still unpatentable because it is obvious. The statute next refers to "the differences between the subject matter sought to be patented and the prior art." This passage requires a factual comparison between the claimed invention, that is, "the subject matter sought to be patented," and the prior art, that is, knowledge predating the date of invention. As discussed earlier, a printed publication, patent, or any other form of information specified in section 102 defines the prior art categories. Although narrowly failing to anticipate a claimed invention, these prior art references nonetheless count as part of the ongoing patentability equation as the critical components of an obviousness analysis.

After identification of the prior art, the obviousness inquiry weighs, as a factual matter, the "differences between the subject matter sought to be patented and the prior art." Assessing the significance of these differences requires great judgment. With some inventions, a very slight difference—a slight shift in the angle of entry or in molecular structure—can greatly distinguish the invention from the prior art and greatly advance the scientific field. *See Eibel Process Co. v. Minn. & Ontario Paper Co.*, 261 U.S. 45 (1923). With other inventions, large changes—such as the key to triggering a gene to express itself—still do not distinguish the invention from the prior art because the significant advance was expected by an artisan of ordinary skill. *See In re O'Farrell*, 853 F.2d 894 (Fed. Cir. 1988). Thus, application of the obviousness test, though easily explained in a paragraph or two, may only be applied confidently after years of scientific and legal experience.

The statute specifically requires application of the obviousness test to the claimed invention "as a whole." This cryptic instruction is critical; it ensures that, for new combinations of old elements, an invention cannot be broken down into its constituent parts when comparing it to the scope and content of the prior art. For example, an invention claiming the combination of A, B, and C is not necessarily rendered obvious by finding references showing that A, B, and C were individually known. Without this simple statutory phrase, the value in combining the elements—often a central creative feature—would be inappropriately foreclosed. Indeed, many innovations otherwise deserving of an exclusive right would be rendered obvious if not evaluated as a whole.

Very often inventive genius lies in recognizing that a combination of old elements will advance the art. For instance, the best antacid in its class, the billion-dollar pharmaceutical named famotidine and sold under the trademark Pepcid®, was the combination of three molecular elements known in the prior art. *Yamanouchi Pharm. Co. v. Danbury Pharmacal, Inc.*, 231 F.3d 1339 (Fed. Cir. 2000). Although each element of this marvelous invention was already in the prior art, it took researchers many years, great expense, and counterintuitive inventiveness to discover this unique new combination. Without the "as a whole" requirement, the Patent Office or courts might be tempted to simply parse the invention into its three molecular components, then using the invention as a "blueprint for obviousness," locate each component in the prior art, and discount the advance as obvious.

The statute next provides the succinct legal test for patentability in this section, reciting that the inquiry turns on whether the claimed invention "would have been obvious." This legal test is deceptively difficult and proves simple to recite yet elusive to apply. Other condensed words and phrases other than "obviousness" that describe this legal test include, "inventiveness," "inventive intellectual product," and internationally "inventive step." The obviousness doctrine prohibits patent protection for trivial, routine, easy, or straightforward advances within the ordinary state of the art. While difficult to summarize, obviousness provides an objective standard that ensures the quantum of advancement is more than a mere modicum. It thus creates an unpatentable zone around the state of the art, proscribing persons in the art from obtaining exclusive rights to routine improvements and straightforward advances.

Finally, the statute evaluates obviousness "at the time the invention was made." Like the "as a whole" requirement, this aspect of the test is both difficult and essential. This temporal injunction prevents hindsight—a particularly insidious phenomenon that uses the inventor's own work and disclosure as a blueprint or roadmap against its own validity. As noted earlier, inventions very often combine existing elements in new and productive ways. After the invention, this combination may appear self-evident because the constituent elements were already known. This type of analysis, however, evinces hindsight, or using the new combination to identify its preexisting components. To prevent hindsight from threatening the patentability of almost every invention, the legal test deliberately propels the evaluator back to the time before the invention. The Patent Office examiner or court must instead forget the claimed invention when evaluating and comparing the scope and content of the prior art with the claimed invention. Casting oneself back to before the invention—a self-induced amnesia—is hardly easy. The invention often colors our perception of the art field or even the vocabulary of the new area.

Lastly, the statute states that "a person having ordinary skill in the art to which said subject matter pertains" serves as the objective lens through which obviousness can be determined, much like the reasonably prudent person in tort law. This prevents the obviousness inquiry from being clouded with the decision maker's own knowledge, skill, and intellect. Notably, the ordinarily skilled artisan is neither the inventor, who may have extraordinary skill in the art, nor a novice, who may have only minimal technical knowledge. Obviousness is thus an objective test to assess the worthiness of the technical advance to receive a patent. The inquiry depends on factual differences between the claimed invention and prior art at the time of the invention as understood by one of ordinary skill in the art.

Fields populated with the highly skilled practitioners—such as the satellite communications industry—thus require a more stringent standard for patentability. *See In re Rouffet*, 149 F.3d 1350, 1356–57 (Fed. Cir. 1998) (noting the "lofty skill level for ordinary artisans" in that field). While courts generally speak of the need for determining the skill in the art, even the plentiful case law of the Federal Circuit does not routinely produce cases that turn solely on the level of skill in the art.

Nonetheless, at least in theory, nearly everything would be patentable in a field where everyone is a dullard, while almost nothing would be patentable in a field where the ordinary level of skill requires a Nobel prize. In fact, Albert Einstein worked in the Swiss patent office. If he had performed examinations, it would be easy to imagine him tossing a week's worth of applications over his shoulder as obvious in a few minutes and then returning to writing his theory of relativity.

II. HISTORY OF PATENT LAW'S "CROWN JEWEL"

The lengthy historical development of the "novelty-plus" test discloses the difficulty in framing a measure of inventiveness sufficient to warrant an exclusive right. During the first 60 years, patentability rested principally on novelty and utility. In fact, the 1952 Patent Act established the first statutory requirement for patentability beyond novelty and utility. Prior to 1952, courts developed "negative rules" for determining patentability, which prevented patent protection for mere changes in material, proportion, or form over existing technology or mere combinations of known mechanisms.

The first recognition of a need for a measure of inventiveness—as well as its doctrinal moorings—came in *Hotchkiss v. Greenwood*, 52 U.S. (11 How.) 248 (1851). Dealing with a purported invention that merely fashioned a common door knob out of a material (ceramics) that had recently become more amenable to new applications, the Court stated that only "inventions" were patentable. The Court then elaborated that new technology only constituted an invention when it transcends the everyday or routine efforts of a skilled mechanic. The ceramic doorknob did not qualify.

Although foreshadowing the objective person of ordinary skill in the art, the early *Hotchkiss* decision focused on the ingenuity or "inventiveness" of the subject matter without a neutral standard to distinguish the unpatentable improvements of a skilled mechanic from the patentable advances of an inventor. With the focus on the invention, this test invited courts to use hindsight. If the inventive subject matter impressed the court, it received approval as being the "product of an inventor." If the subject matter did not evoke a "gee whiz" reaction, it was merely a mechanic's handiwork. By its very nature, this test invited insidious hindsight. Few advances qualified for a patent.

After percolating for roughly a century, the *Hotchkiss* test for patentability evolved to embrace slightly different terminology: did the subject matter exhibit "a flash of creative genius?" *Cuno Eng'g Corp. v. Automatic Devices Corp.*, 314 U.S. 84, 91 (1941). This verbal construct was just the hindsight reaction analysis in slightly more demanding terminology. This stringent patentability standard caused Justice Jackson to comment: "[T]he only patent that is valid is one which this Court has not been able to get its hands on." *Jungersen v. Ostby & Barton Co.*, 335 U.S. 560, 572 (1949) (Jackson, J., dissenting).

The hindsight-reaction test reached its high-water mark in *Great A. & P. Tea Co. v. Supermarket Equipment Corp.*, 340 U.S. 147 (1950). The invention was a supermarket counter that combined several features to improve the efficiency and speed of the check-out counter. Beyond a "flash of genius," the Supreme Court required some synergistic effect in the invention. In other words, the invention had to surprise or amaze beyond the sum of its parts. Otherwise the new technology was merely the combination of known elements. The Supreme Court did not seem to acknowledge that nearly every invention would be a combination or reconstruction of available and known elements. If characterized as a "mere combination," any inventive subject matter in this era lacked sufficient "genius" or "synergy."

In desperation, the Patent Office and the patent bar turned to Congress. The result was the 1952 Patent Act. The 1952 Act sets forth the objective test for obviousness discussed earlier. Patentability hinged on factual evidence about the likelihood that a person of ordinary skill in the art would have found the subject matter obvious at the time of the invention.

The Supreme Court did not interpret that Act until nearly a decade and a half later. *Graham v. John Deere Co.*, 383 U.S. 1 (1966); *Calmar, Inc. v. Cook Chem. Co.*, 383 U.S. 1 (1966); *United States v. Adams*, 383 U.S. 39 (1966). Then, after upholding the objective factual analysis of the new § 103, the Supreme Court slipped again into its hindsight reaction methodology in *Anderson's-Black Rock, Inc.*

v. Pavement Salvage Co., 396 U.S. 57 (1969) and *Sakraida v. Ag Pro, Inc.*, 425 U.S. 273 (1976). These cases reinvigorated the synergism test employed prior to the 1952 Act, bringing along with it the use of hindsight reasoning to find patents invalid as a matter of course.[4]

With the various circuits unable to discern the uniform test for inventiveness, Congress again stepped in. This time the legislature created the United States Court of Appeals for the Federal Circuit. The Federal Circuit quickly opted to follow the Supreme Court's more responsible *Graham* test. *See, e.g., Chore-Time Equip., Inc. v. Cumberland Corp.*, 713 F.2d 774 (Fed. Cir. 1983). Thus, beginning in 1982, the objective standard for obviousness prevailed nationwide.

In its obviousness jurisprudence, the Federal Circuit placed a particular emphasis on the "teaching, suggestion, motivation" (TSM) test to prevent hindsight, *In re Rouffet*, 149 F.3d 1350 (Fed. Cir. 1998), and secondary considerations as part of the obviousness test, *Hybritech, Inc. v. Monoclonal Antibodies, Inc.*, 802 F.2d 1367 (Fed. Cir. 1986) (secondary considerations are "not just icing on the cake"). Over time, some Federal Circuit opinions applied the motivation to combine test rigidly to require reference to a specific prior art teaching that suggested the combination without taking into account the creativity and common sense of a person having

4. In *KSR Int'l Co. v. Teleflex, Inc.*, the Supreme Court recently attempted to reconcile *Anderson's-Black Rock* and *Sakraida* with the traditional *Graham* test for obviousness. 550 U.S. ___, 82 USPQ2d 1385.

ordinary skill in the art. *See, e.g., In re Lee*, 277 F.3d 1338 (Fed. Cir. 2002). One of these instances, *KSR Int'l Co. v. Teleflex, Inc.*, 550 U.S. ___, 82 USPQ2d 1385 (2007), brought the issue of obviousness back to the Supreme Court. In *KSR*, the Supreme Court reversed the Federal Circuit. In its lengthy unanimous opinion, the Court reaffirmed the basic principles enunciated by *Graham* and urged an "expansive and flexible approach" to obviousness in general. 82 USPQ2d at 1395.

III. PRIOR ART

The obviousness test rests on the foundation of an accurate and complete picture of the prior art. Section 102 usually—but not exclusively—defines the categories that supply that art. Statements and admissions by the patentee or applicant, for instance, provide another less common, even if potent, source of knowledge. The broad categories of "printed publications" or "patents," however, do not narrow the range of prior art to the knowledge most pertinent to the claimed invention. Thus, beyond the simple qualification of falling within a § 102 category, a prior art candidate for the obviousness calculus must also be "analogous" to the claimed subject matter. A prior art candidate is "analogous" if sufficiently related to the claimed invention to fairly count as part of the obviousness equation.

A. Section 102

With only two exceptions (the analogous art requirement and the joint venture exclusion), the rule defining prior art is simple: art that applies to the novelty determination also applies for obviousness. Thus, the same references relevant for novelty often apply as well in an obviousness inquiry. For example, a patent or printed publication qualifying under either § 102(a) or (b) commonly serves as a reference for obviousness. Patent law includes a limited exception, however, where a reference described by § 102(a) does not constitute prior art under § 103 if the applicant had earlier possessed an obvious variation of the reference. *In re Stryker*, 435 F.2d 1340 (CCPA 1971). Similarly, a patent filed but not issued before the filing of another patent may serve as so-called "secret" prior art under § 102(e) and § 102(g). *Hazeltine Research, Inc. v. Brenner*, 382 U.S. 252 (1965); *In re Bass*, 474 F.2d 1276 (CCPA 1973). Thus, a prior invention—even if unpatented and not disclosed until after the priority date of a patent—may serve as an obviousness reference under § 102(g)(2). Left unchecked, this would even mean that related work by inventors employed by the same company could render subsequent work obvious. Because of this clear inequity, subsection (c) of § 103—discussed below—prevents some provisions of section 102 from creating prior art in limited circumstances. Moreover, prior art for obviousness is not necessarily public; under § 102(f), a person may not obtain a patent on subject matter obtained, that is, derived, from someone else. Section 102(f) notably applies not only to public disclosures but also to private communications. *See Oddz-*

On Prods., Inc. v. Just Toys, Inc., 122 F.3d 1396 (Fed. Cir. 1997).

1. Analogous Art

As noted above, the general § 102 categories do not focus on prior art genuinely relevant to the obviousness equation. The prior art technology must also issue from an "analogous art"—a technical area judged sufficiently germane to the claimed invention's field. Thus, an applicant or inventor is really only presumed to have access to all technical knowledge within a field reasonably related to the inventive subject matter. In sum, prior art is analogous (and thus available for obviousness) if it is either in the same field of endeavor as the inventive subject matter (regardless of the problem addressed by the invention) or reasonably pertinent to the particular problem addressed by the invention. *In re Clay*, 966 F.2d 656 (Fed. Cir. 1992).

The *Clay* case illustrates analogousness in practice. The claimed invention recovered residual oil in storage tanks when the outlet port was located above the bottom of the tank. The invention filled the tanks with gel to bring the oil up to the drainage pipe level. The prior art extracted more oil from *natural* rock formations by filling formation anomalies with a gel to improve oil flow and production. The Federal Circuit defined the problem addressed by the invention narrowly. If the Federal Circuit had defined the problem as filling dead spaces to improve petroleum extraction, then the similarities between the prior art and the invention might have resulted in obviousness. The Federal Circuit, however, confined the problem to extracting oil from man-made tanks. Thus, despite similarities between the claims and the prior art, the rock formation prior art was not pertinent to the inventive problem and not available for the obviousness analysis.

The analogous art test is really a court-created fairness doctrine. The law will not hold an inventor accountable for prior art far removed from the inventive subject matter either by field or by pertinence. Under the simple terminology that governs prior art theory, "libraries before laboratories" is still the governing principle, the analogous art test ensures that only relevant sections of the library apply for obviousness.

In reality, this requirement for "analogous art" rarely limits the scope of prior art. In fact, this threshold requirement for prior art is probably best understood as a corollary of the § 103 principle that only knowledge accessible by one of ordinary skill in the inventive field of art renders subject matter obvious.

2. Joint Research Exception

As briefly described above, § 103(c) states:

Subject matter developed by another person, which qualifies as prior art only under one or more of subsections (e), (f), and (g) of section 102 of this title, shall not preclude patentability under this section where the subject matter and the claimed invention were, at the time the invention

was made, owned by the same person or subject
to an obligation of assignment to the same person.

Accordingly, § 103(c) exempts § 102(e), (f), and (g)
art from an obviousness inquiry where the inventions were subject to a common assignment. In
practice, the assignment condition usually means
that the inventions and the prior art were the
product of the same research team or facility. Subsection (c) contains narrow limits: If, for instance, a
reference is otherwise available as prior art, such as
under § 102(a) or (b), it remains available for obviousness.

This subsection addresses a specific problem involving research teams. Any corporate or university
research team likely features several different scientists working together. A team might make several
inventions over a period of years. The applications
for the various team inventions, however, may list
in each case a different combination of inventors.
Thus, although the entire team contributed to the
advances, the team's first inventions will serve as
prior art against the team's later inventions because each invention technically lists a different
"inventor." Without § 103(c), the rules of prior art
would discourage collaborative research. *See In re
Bass*, 474 F.2d 1276 (CCPA 1973). Under this section, the team—in essence, the inventor—does not
create prior art against itself.

B. Prior Art by Admission

A second, less common, category for prior art
occurs when the patent applicant (or patentee)

identifies the work of another as prior art, regardless of whether it actually is prior art. This nonstatutory category—admissions—also contains a limited exception analogous to § 103(c). Under that exception, work by the same inventive entity—a narrower category than the common obligation of assignment category in § 103(c)—does not qualify as prior art unless falling within one of the categories enumerated in § 102. *Riverwood Int'l Corp. v. R.A. Jones & Co.*, 324 F.3d 1346 (Fed. Cir. 2003). If, for example, the specification (including the drawings) identifies some technology as prior art, that prior art applies for an obviousness determination. Similarly, a claim drafted in *Jepson* format—a format that recites the invention as an improvement on the subject matter identified in the preamble—admits that the subject matter in the preamble is prior art.

IV. THE SUPREME COURT TRILOGY

While the 1952 Act codified the ultimate patentability test now called nonobviousness, the proper understanding of § 103 remained unclear until Supreme Court examined it in a trilogy of cases in 1966: *Graham v. John Deere*, *Cook Chemical*, and *Adams*. These long-awaited cases—it took an eternity of 13 years before the Court addressed the new statute—are the most important to understanding obviousness. In fact, they might just be the most important patent cases of the modern era. Indeed the Federal Circuit deserves praise for elevating the trilogy to that lofty status. Recently the Supreme Court itself acknowledged that prominence for these cases: "*Graham* . . . set out a framework for applying the statutory language of § 103." *KSR*, 82 USPQ2d at 1391.

In *Graham v. John Deere Co.*, 383 U.S. 1 (1966), the Supreme Court explained that obviousness is a legal conclusion buttressed by four factual inquiries. The Court specified these factual underpinnings:

(1) the scope and content of the prior art;

(2) differences between the prior art and the claims at issue;

(3) the level of ordinary skill in the pertinent art; and

(4) secondary considerations of obviousness or nonobviousness, such as commercial success, long felt but unsolved needs, and failure of others.

Although giving prominence to the first three as the background for determining obviousness, the Court also explained that the secondary considerations are relevant indicators of nonobviousness. The Court recognized, furthermore, the inherent difficulties in determining obviousness:

What is obvious is not a question upon which there is likely to be uniformity of thought in every factual context. The difficulties, however, are comparable to those encountered daily by the courts in such frames of reference as negligence and scienter, and should be amenable to a case-by-case development.

Graham, 383 U.S. at 18.

The *Graham* case began when Graham sued the Deere Corporation for infringement of the '798 patent on a plow with a spring clamp. The defendant questioned the validity of the patent in light of an earlier patent, the '811 patent, to the same inventor, Graham. The prior art patent was the same plow with one variation—a hinge plate was moved from one side of the shank to the other. This seemingly slight change, however, meant that the shank would not break when it hit a stone—a significant improvement in the performance of the plow. Indeed Graham had successfully weathered validity challenges, including a prior appeal to a regional circuit, and had asserted his patent against other infringers before this case. Nonetheless the Supreme Court upheld a determination that the '798 was invalid.

In reaching its conclusion that the patent would have been obvious, the Court applied, for the first time in Supreme Court jurisprudence, the objective test of § 103 with its factual underpinnings. After examining the differences carefully, the Court rather abruptly skips some other factual underpinnings and reaches a conclusion of obviousness: "Certainly a person having ordinary skill in the prior art, given the fact that the flex in the shank could be utilized more effectively if allowed to run the entire length of the shank, would immediately see that the thing to do was what Graham did, i.e., invert the shank and the hinge plate." 383 U.S. at 25. Although quick to resolve some factual issues on appeal (such as the level of ordinary skill and that artisan's

chance of recognizing the problem and "immediately" seeing the solution) and perhaps too hesitant to
examine the secondary considerations, the Court
still set a landmark standard for neutral application
of the obviousness test.

In *Calmar v. Cook Chemical*, the Court similarly
invalidated the Scoggin '943 patent on a leak-proof
cap for a pump-sprayer insecticide dispenser. The
prior art that the Supreme Court found most important to the obviousness inquiry, the Livingstone '480 patent, had not even been considered by
the PTO examiner that granted Scoggin's patent.
After noting that the '943 patent involved only
"small and nontechnical mechanical differences,"
the Court observed that those "differences were
rendered apparent" by the Livingstone prior art
patent. 383 U.S. at 36. The Court, however, emphasized that obviousness depended on "prior art as it
stood at the time of the invention," *id.*, thus es-
chewing the history of hindsight that bedeviled pri-
or validity determinations at the Court.

After *Cook Chemical*, the Court wisely considered
a third case that upheld an important patent under
the new standard. The United States used the battery technology featured in this case during World
War II and Adams, the inventor, sued for infringement. In *United States v. Adams*, the patent
claimed a battery whose electrolyte, or battery fluid,
was water. Adams did not, however, claim this
important distinguishing feature of his invention.
Reading those claims in light of the specification,
the Court nonetheless determined "the stated ob-

ject" of the invention included a "water-activated cell." 383 U.S. at 49. In fact, this feature plays the central role in one of the great stories of patent litigation lore: Adams's attorney arose before the Supreme Court, took a drink from his glass of water, and then dropped a tiny Adams battery into the glass. The inventive battery immediately lit a tiny light that continued to burn throughout the argument. Some accounts suggest that the attorney knew he had won the case when the Justices kept their eyes on the tiny burning light throughout the remainder of the argument.

The Supreme Court's *Adams* opinion invokes several secondary considerations in favor of nonobviousness. In particular, the Court observed that the record disclosed the skepticism of experts before the invention, the endorsement of experts after disclosure, and unexpected results. In a case that featured a great deal of prior art very close to the invention, these secondary considerations evidently played an important, perhaps even dispositive, role.

The recent *KSR* pronouncement adds significance to *Graham* and the rest of the trilogy. A review of the Federal Circuit's obviousness jurisprudence brings *KSR* into better focus.

V. THE FEDERAL CIRCUIT

While *Graham* set forth the basic test for obviousness, the Federal Circuit refined that test in its later evolution of the doctrine. In particular, the Federal Circuit focused the test on evidence suggesting or motivating the combination or modification of prior art to render an invention obvious. While increasing vigilance against hindsight reasoning, the Federal Circuit also placed an emphasis on objective criteria that indicate nonobviousness.

A. Motivation or Suggestion to Combine

Under § 103, the comparison of the prior art with the claimed invention must be done "as a whole." Thus, the analysis cannot be done piecemeal by parceling the claimed invention into its constituent parts and finding an analog for each separate feature of the new combination. In *KSR*, the Supreme Court reiterated the importance of this "as a whole" methodology: "[A] patent composed of several elements is not proved obvious merely by demonstrating that each of its elements was, independently, known in the prior art." 82 USPQ2d at 1396 This essential "as a whole" provision suggests a methodology that shows the factors would have motivated one of ordinary skill in the art at the time of the invention to make the new combination as a routine or obvious next step in the relevant art. This method distills down to an essential finding supported by concrete evidence that an ordinarily skilled artisan confronted with the same problems as the inventor would have selected the elements from the most relevant prior art and combined them to create the claimed invention.

In practical terms, this test seeks concrete evidence of a motivation or suggestion to modify or combine prior art elements without using the inventor's disclosure as a blueprint. This last point has special significance. If that evidence is to remain untainted by hindsight, it must date back to a time before the invention.

Although a finding of motivation was often coterminous with or synonymous with the legal conclusion of obviousness, the Federal Circuit treated the inquiry for a motivation or suggestion to combine or modify the prior art as a question of fact. Evidence of a teaching, suggestion, or motivation to combine references appears in three different forms: the nature of the problem may itself suggest a combination, *Ruiz v. A.B. Chance Co.*, 357 F.3d 1270 (Fed. Cir. 2004); the teachings of the pertinent references may suggest a combination, *In re Rouffet,* 149 F.3d 1350 (Fed. Cir. 1998); or the customary knowledge of those ordinarily skilled in the art may suggest a combination. *Nat'l Steel Car v. Can. Pac. Ry., Ltd.*, 357 F.3d 1319 (Fed. Cir. 2004). The Federal Circuit cautioned, however, against unsupported use of the customary knowledge category. In reversing the Patent and Trademark Office's conclusion of obviousness, the court explained:

> [The Board] relied upon the high level of skill in the art to provide the necessary motivation. The Board did not, however, explain what specific understanding or technological principle within the knowledge of one of ordinary skill in the art would have suggested the combination. Instead, the Board merely invoked the high level of skill in the field of art. If such a rote invocation could suffice to supply a motivation to combine, the

more sophisticated scientific fields would rarely, if ever, experience a patentable technical advance. *Rouffet*, 149 F.3d at 1357–58. Thus to ensure relevant, accurate, and reliable TSM evidence, the Federal Circuit in some cases discounted the customary knowledge category and instead required some actual reference from before the invention to support the suggestion. *In re Lee*, 277 F.3d at 1343–4. Indeed the Federal Circuit in its *KSR* opinion had adopted this strict type of reasoning.

B. *KSR*

KSR featured rather simple technology—an adjustable throttle pedal for an automobile. Teleflex owned the Engelgau patent (U.S. Pat. No. 6,237,-565) which combined an adjustable pedal with an electronic sensor to measure the pedal depression. Adjustable pedals, of course, make the throttle more accessible to drivers of different heights. Electronic sensors on those pedals measure movement without cumbersome mechanical cables. Both of these features were in the prior art. An Asano patent described an adjustable pedal like that in Engelgau; a Rixon patent (as modified by a Smith reference) described the particular electronic calibration features of the Engelgau patent. Asano incidentally was not before the PTO when it granted the Engelgau patent.

When Teleflex sued KSR for infringement, the District Court invalidated the '565 patent on summary judgment. The Federal Circuit reversed because the trial court had not made specific findings to show a teaching, suggestion, or motivation to combine. The Supreme Court, in turn, reversed the Federal Circuit: "A person having ordinary skill in the art could have combined Asano with a pedal position sensor in a fashion encompassed by claim 4, and would have seen the benefits of doing so." *KSR*, 82 USPQ2d at 1398.

On one level, KSR may have only corrected a rather fundamental and simple error by the Federal Circuit. The error appears right before footnote 3 in the Federal Circuit's opinion[5]:

In this case, the Asano patent does not address the same problem as the '565 patent. The objective of the '565 patent was to design a smaller, less complex, and less expensive electronic pedal assembly. The Asano patent, on the other hand, was directed at solving the "constant ratio problem."

Teleflex, Inc. v. KSR Int'l, Co., 119 Fed. Appx. 282, 288 (Fed. Cir. 2005). This passage shows that the Federal Circuit overlooked the fundamental proposition that obvious variants of prior art references are themselves part of the public domain. A British case makes this point forcibly:

Anything which is obvious over what is available to the public cannot subsequently be the subject of valid patent protection even if, in practice, few would have bothered looking through the prior

5. The error appeared in a nonprecedential opinion that would not have been reviewed, or even seen, by any judges on the Federal Circuit except the three on the panel.

art or would have found the particular items relied on. Patents are not granted for the discovery and wider dissemination of public material and what is obvious over it, but only for making new inventions.

Lilly Icos LLC v. Pfizer Ltd., [2000] EWHC Patents 49 at ¶ 62. In the context of *KSR*, the Asano teachings and its obvious variants were in the prior art, even if that patent did address a different problem (the constant ratio problem). Therefore the Federal Circuit erred by dismissing Asano. The Supreme Court identified that error in its opinion:

> The second error of the Court of Appeals lay in its assumption that a person of ordinary skill attempting to solve a problem will be led only to those elements of prior art designed to solve the same problem. The primary purpose of Asano was solving the constant ratio problem; so, the court concluded, an inventor considering how to put a sensor on an adjustable pedal would have no reason to consider putting it on the Asano pedal. Common sense teaches, however, that familiar items may have obvious uses beyond their primary purposes, and in many cases a person of ordinary skill will be able to fit the teachings of multiple patents together like pieces of a puzzle.

KSR, 82 USPQ2d at 1397 (citations omitted).

The Supreme Court also condemned the Federal Circuit's "rigid and mandatory" TSM test as a primary source of error: "The obviousness analysis cannot be confined by a formalistic conception of the words teaching, suggestion, and motivation, or by overemphasis on the importance of published articles and the explicit content of issued patents." *KSR*, 82 USPQ2d at 1396. Instead the Supreme Court repeatedly advised that "common sense" would broaden the use of customary knowledge in the obviousness equation. Indeed, the Court observed, "[a] person of ordinary skill is also a person of ordinary creativity, not an automaton." *Id.* at 1397. Thus, at a minimum, the Supreme Court's decision overruled instances of "rigid" application of the TSM test and broadened use of customary knowledge as an ingredient for obviousness.

At one point in its analysis, the Court observed that the Federal Circuit had also "elaborated a broader conception of the TSM test than was applied" in the case it reversed. *See KSR*, 82 USPQ2d at 1397. Specifically the Court referred to *DyStar Textilfarben GmbH & Co. v. C.H. Patrick Co.*, wherein the Federal Circuit had opined: "Our suggestion test is in actuality quite flexible and not only permits, but *requires*, consideration of common knowledge and common sense." 464 F.3d 1356, 1367 (Fed. Cir. 2006) (emphasis original). The Court did not expressly endorse this formulation of the TSM test, but hinted that it would be "more consistent" with the Supreme Court's requirements. *KSR*, 82 USPQ2d at 1397. In sum, the TSM test in its more flexible and expansive form is likely to survive the correction of the *KSR* mistake.

Moreover, with respect to obviousness in general, the Supreme Court rejected any "rigid rule." Indeed, as the Court counseled, "a court can take account of the inferences and creative steps that a person of ordinary skill in the art would employ." *Id.* at 1396.

C. Scrutiny of Hindsight

As a corollary to the factual requisite for a suggestion or motivation to combine or modify the prior art, the Federal Circuit required great caution to avoid hindsight reasoning. Hindsight can take many forms. Because an inventor is charged with the knowledge of all prior art, one method to imagine whether the claimed invention would have been obvious is to picture the inventor working in his shop with the prior art references hanging on the walls around him. *See In re Winslow*, 365 F.2d 1017 (CCPA 1966). While this depiction of a hypothetical event is vivid and compelling, it is a suspected form of dangerous hindsight—namely hindsight in selecting the prior art that might hang on the laboratory walls. For example, this image cannot convey that the most pertinent prior art would in fact be hidden and obscured by voluminous amounts of irrelevant art. To visualize the inventor with only the most relevant art invites insidious hindsight, having edited out the most applicable references from those which are inapplicable or even misleading. The Federal Circuit has abandoned this antiquated visual, relying on the facts and evidence in each case to discern a suggestion or motivation to combine or modify references.

KSR did not ignore the dangers of hindsight: "A factfinder should be aware, of course, of the distortion caused by hindsight bias and must be cautious of arguments reliant on *ex post* reasoning." 82 USPQ2d at 1397. This caution, however, cannot lead to "[r]igid preventative rules." *Id.* Thus, the legal prevention of hindsight, such as rejecting the *Winslow* formulation, also survives *KSR*.

D. Objective Criteria (Secondary Considerations)

Secondary considerations remain, of course, germane to the ultimate conclusion of obviousness. Although the legal test of obviousness does not differ between prosecution and litigation, the methodology used by the Patent and Trademark Office provides a useful example of how secondary considerations can affect an obviousness determination. Before reevaluating obviousness by including secondary considerations, a *prima facie* case of obviousness should exist based solely on the first three *Graham* factors. The Federal Circuit explained the dance between applicant and the Office:

> The *prima facie* case is a procedural tool of patent examination, allocating the burdens of going forward as between examiner and applicant. The term *"prima facie"* case refers only to the initial examination step. As discussed in *In re Piasecki*, [745 F.2d 1468, 1472 (Fed. Cir. 1984),] the examiner bears the initial burden, on review of the prior art or on any other ground, of presenting a *prima facie* case of unpatentability. If that burden is met, the burden of coming forward with evidence or argument shifts to the applicant.

After evidence or argument is submitted by the applicant in response, patentability is determined on the totality of the record by a preponderance of evidence with due consideration to the persuasiveness of argument.

If examination at the initial stage does not produce a *prima facie* case of unpatentability, then without more the applicant is entitled to grant of the patent.

In reviewing the examiner's decision on appeal, the Board [of Patent Appeals and Interferences] must necessarily weigh all of the evidence and argument. An observation by the Board that the examiner made a *prima facie* case is not improper, as long as the ultimate determination of patentability is made on the entire record.

In re Oetiker, 977 F.2d 1443, 1445 (Fed. Cir. 1992) (citations omitted). Thus, obviousness before the Patent Office divides into two phases—one with and one without secondary considerations. Importantly, in the latter phase (post *prima facie* case) with secondary considerations, the inquiry mandates that all evidence, including the differences between the scope and content of the prior art, be reevaluated before concluding that the claimed invention is in fact obvious.

These secondary considerations are secondary in name only; the Federal Circuit often views them as essential to the obviousness inquiry. *Hybritech Inc. v. Monoclonal Antibodies, Inc.*, 802 F.2d 1367 (Fed. Cir. 1986). As such, the more apt nomenclature is to call them "objective indicia." Indeed, empirical evidence, such as the reaction of the marketplace and competitors, provides much firmer ground than a purely hypothetical exercise in the courtroom.

Objective indicia, however, must bear some relationship to the claimed invention, that is, there must be a nexus between the claimed invention and the proffered objective evidence. In the case of commercial success, for example, the applicant or patentee must show that the success is the result of innovative claims, not merely the result of effective marketing strategies or general popularity of like products in the prior art.

Although the Supreme Court identified a few examples of objective indicia, creative litigants over the years have added a few more. As would be expected, all objective indicia are not equal, with some showing nonobviousness to a greater extent than others. The following is a nonexhaustive list in order of the strongest to the weakest evidence showing nonobviousness: skepticism, long-felt need, prior failure, unexpected results, licenses, copying, and commercial success. Note that the most potent, relevant indicia occur less frequently and share a greater connection to the claimed invention than the least potent.

First, skepticism of other experts in the art expressed before the inventor's work bolsters the case for nonobviousness. *Burlington Indus., Inc. v. Quigg*, 822 F.2d 1581 (Fed. Cir. 1987). Because this evidence arises before the invention, it has particular persuasive value, but it is extremely rare that experts will "rule out" or criticize a line of research or inventive concept that later revolutionizes their field.

Second, a long-felt need for a solution to a particular problem also supports nonobviousness. *Tex. Instruments, Inc. v. U.S. Int'l Trade Comm'n*, 988 F.2d 1165 (Fed. Cir. 1993). Oftentimes, however, the expressions of long-felt need do not correlate exactly with the problem solved by the invention. Moreover an invention can sometimes create its own market, meaning that the invention identified a problem which others had not recognized at all. In any event, the nexus requirement, of course, assures that the long-felt need correlates with the problem solved by the invention.

Third, prior failures by other inventors certainly supplement the case for nonobviousness. *Heidelberger Druckmaschinen AG v. Hantscho Commercial Prods. Inc.*, 21 F.3d 1068 (Fed. Cir. 1994). But prior failures are not helpful if the person who failed had either a limited knowledge of the relevant prior art (that is, an incomplete understanding of the scope and content of the prior art) or little motivation or desire to succeed due to satisfaction with the extant technology. *In re Sneed*, 710 F.2d 1544 (Fed. Cir. 1983). Furthermore, evidence of other failures rarely relates to exactly the same problem addressed by the invention. Again the nexus requirement tries to assure this correlation.

Fourth, unexpected results—in one form similar to the now-defunct synergism test for nonobviousness—can include evidence of surprise and commendation by those skilled in the art upon learning of the invention. *Specialty Composites v. Cabot Corp.*, 845 F.2d 981 (Fed. Cir. 1988). In another form, unexpected results can be documentary evidence that exceeds the expectations of skilled artisans. This evidence can suffer from hindsight, because it necessarily appears after the invention, which perhaps changed expectations. Furthermore, expectations are inherently subjective, and litigation can influence the nature and intensity of those expectations.

Fifth, evidence of extensive licensing supports nonobviousness, because it shows that the industry respects the invention. At the same time, however, a long period of no infringement may show that the licenses are truly motivated by a desire to avoid the costs of litigation, rather than by respect for the nonobviousness of the invention. *Pentec, Inc. v. Graphic Controls Corp.*, 776 F.2d 309 (Fed. Cir. 1985). In a healthy market, moreover, many licenses are part of a larger cross-licensing arrangement that undermines the nexus between a particular license in a large package and the claimed features it licenses.

Sixth, copying—particularly when done by the accused infringer without concomitantly copying other subject matter—also can show that the invention is nonobvious. *Advanced Display Sys., Inc. v. Kent State Univ.*, 212 F.3d 1272 (Fed. Cir. 2000). But copying is not persuasive in all contexts. For

example, copying is not reliable evidence of nonobviousness where the accused product is not identical
to the claimed invention and the accused infringer
vigorously denies infringement. While copying is a
high form of flattery, it may have been done solely
because the copyist reasonably believes that the
patent is not valid or enforceable.

And seventh, commercial success may, in some
cases, show nonobviousness. *Hybritech Inc. v. Monoclonal Antibodies, Inc.*, 802 F.2d 1367 (Fed. Cir.
1986). In fact, commercial success includes the sales
of infringers as well as those of the patentee and its
licensees. *Syntex (U.S.A.) Inc. v. Paragon Optical
Inc.*, 7 USPQ2d 1001 (D. Ariz. 1987). But the commercial success could be due to any number of
market factors, including superior business acumen
or marketing. Accordingly, the nexus requirement
serves as an effective check on the evidence of
commercial success. Even though it is often viewed
with some skepticism and has problems with causation, commercial success is often presented to show
nonobviousness, because data regarding sales are
easy to acquire.

While those are the categories most commonly
invoked to show nonobviousness, an accused infringer may introduce an objective criterion of its
own to support a case of obviousness. Indeed, evidence of contemporaneous independent—that is,
not based on derivation—invention shows that other could (and did) invent the same subject matter. It
provides real evidence showing persons of ordinary

skill in the art would have found the claimed subject matter obvious at the time of invention.

KSR does not disturb the role of secondary considerations at all. In the context of that case, the Court noted: "[W]e conclude Teleflex has shown no secondary factors to dislodge the determination that claim 4 is obvious." 82 USPQ2d at 1399.

E. Obviousness "Traps"

Because obviousness is an exceptionally slippery doctrine that proves elusive to master, there are a few admonitions that, if heeded, aid one's understanding of the requirement.

1. Standard of Proof

Importantly, the standard of proof differs between an issued patent and a pending patent application. Prior to issuance, the factual predicates need only be established by a preponderance of evidence. But once a patent issues, that patent enjoys a presumption of validity under 35 U.S.C. § 282. Accordingly, the patent's invalidity must be proven by clear and convincing evidence. This heightened standard of proof stems from a respect for the administrative and scientific expertise of the Patent and Trademark Office. *Am. Hoist & Derrick Co. v. Sowa & Sons, Inc.*, 725 F.2d 1350 (Fed. Cir. 1984). This rationale does not apply to questions that were not considered by the Patent and Trademark Office. Moreover *KSR* will have some bearing on the presumption. Although the Supreme Court did not directly address the presumption of validity, it made a comment that calls into question its universal application: "We nevertheless think it appropriate to note that the rationale underlying the presumption—that the PTO, in its expertise, has approved the claim—seems much diminished here." *KSR*, 82 USPQ2d at 1399.

2. Manner of Invention Irrelevant

The first sentence of § 103(a) indicates that "patentability shall not be negatived by the manner in which the invention was made." This language overruled the "flash of genius" test. One of the weaknesses of this old Supreme Court regime was that it discounted a methodical, yet plodding, path of exhaustive research and development. The "shall not be negatived" phrase placed the plodding research effort on a level footing with inventions inspired by a "flash of genius." Thus, the statute offers its awards to accidental or lucky inventors, even though such incentives had nothing to do with the development of the invention. Thus, the inventor's motivation or path to derive the claimed invention is simply irrelevant to the judgment of a person of ordinary skill in the art at the time of the invention.

A corollary to this statutory prohibition suggests no special rule for combination inventions. New combinations neither enjoy an advantage nor suffer heightened obstacles to obviousness. Rather, obviousness of combinations depends, to a large extent, on the presence or absence of a teaching, motivation, or suggestion to combine bits and pieces of the prior art (as flexibly applied) to create the claimed invention. Moreover, this portion of the statute guards against finding all "easy" inventions obvious; sometimes the "easy" solution is the hardest to achieve.

3. Obvious to Try

An inquiry that does not find an invention obvious will often state that the evidence only shows that the invention was "obvious to try." This terminology suggests that the obviousness analysis is incomplete, or short of the necessary factual finding of a motivation or suggestion to combine or modify the teachings of prior art references. The "obvious to try" label emphasizes that it is not correct "to pick and choose among individual parts of assorted prior art references 'as a mosaic to recreate a facsimile of the claimed invention.'" *Akzo N.V. v. U.S. Int'l Trade Comm'n*, 808 F.2d 1471, 1481 (Fed. Cir. 1986) (quoting *W.L. Gore & Assoc., Inc. v. Garlock*, 721 F.2d 1540, 1550 (Fed. Cir. 1983)). Thus, an "obvious to try" test may point to hindsight. Prior to *KSR,* the Federal Circuit clearly rejected an "obvious to try" approach to obviousness:

> The admonition that "obvious to try" is not the standard under § 103 has been directed mainly at two kinds of error. In some cases, what would have been "obvious to try" would have been to carry all parameters or try each of numerous possible choices until one possibly arrived at a successful result, where the prior art gave either no indication of which parameters were critical or

no direction as to which of many possible choices is likely to be successful. In others, what was "obvious to try" was to explore a new technology or general approach that seemed to be a promising field of experimentation, where the prior art gave only general guidance as to the particular form of the claimed invention or how to achieve it.

In re O'Farrell, 853 F.2d 894, 903 (Fed. Cir. 1988) (citations omitted).

KSR also made a passing reference to the "obvious to try" concept: "That it might have been obvious to try the combination of Asano and a sensor was likewise irrelevant...." *KSR*, 82 USPQ2d at 1394. Actually any discussion of "obvious to try" had no place in the *KSR* case. The movable pedal technology only provided two places to put the electronic sensor—on the car or on the movable unit. The prior art had always chosen the car. Therefore the invention's choice to locate the sensor on the car was obvious wholly irrespective of "obvious to try" principles.

Nevertheless, the Supreme Court explained that the Federal Circuit erred in concluding "that a patent claim cannot be proved obvious merely by showing that the combination of elements was 'obvious to try.'" *KSR*, 82 USPQ2d at 1397. The Supreme Court further explained:

When there is a design need or market pressure to solve a problem and there are a finite number of identified, predictable solutions, a person of ordinary skill has good reason to pursue the known options within his or her technical grasp. If this leads to the anticipated success, it is likely the product not of innovation but of ordinary skill and common sense. In that instance the fact that a combination was obvious to try might show that it was obvious under § 103.

Id.

An example illustrates the distinction between nonobviousness and "obvious to try." Suppose that a sporting magazine suggests that some alloy of aluminum and titanium will produce a light-weight baseball bat that will hit balls farther than any other metal bat. If the evidence shows only three possible alloys of aluminum and titanium, the prior art article will no doubt (absent objective indicia for instance) render all three possible alloys obvious. After all, the prior art clearly suggested that one of ordinary skill could make the combination easily. On the other hand, if the evidence shows five thousand possible alloys and only one of them sends a ball twenty feet beyond all the others, then the article has probably only made it obvious to try to make the invention. The article did not render the inventive combination obvious.

4. Patentability vs. Validity

The procedures to obtain a patent invariably involve the obviousness test, and obviousness is a central patentability doctrine at the Patent Office. During infringement litigation, a defendant may also put up a defense of patent invalidity. Obviousness is a central doctrine of patent validity in court proceedings. Patentability, however, differs in important respects from validity.

In patentability, the obviousness inquiry begins with the *prima facie* test for obviousness (the first three steps) and only proceeds to objective criteria if necessary. With validity challenges, obviousness does not usually subdivide in this manner although the defendant will often present a *prima facie* case of obviousness which the patent owner will rebut with evidence of objective criteria.

During patentability proceedings at the Patent Office, the examiner will give the claims of the invention the "broadest reasonable interpretation." *In re Morris*, 127 F.3d 1048, 1053–54 (Fed. Cir. 1997). During validity proceedings, a court will conduct proceedings to determine the precise bounds of the claims. In any event, differences between patentability and validity proceedings often explain different applications of the obviousness test. *In re Dillon*, 919 F.2d 688 (Fed. Cir. 1990) (*en banc*).

F. Chemistry and Biotechnology

Although the Federal Circuit has stated that "the requirement for unobviousness in the case of chemical inventions is the same as for other types of inventions," *In re Johnson*, 747 F.2d 1456, 1460 (Fed. Cir. 1984), obviousness in the context of chemical and biotechnological technologies presents a distinct set of issues. Patenting in the chemical and biotechnological areas focuses to a large extent on claiming "new entities," such as new molecules in chemistry and new chains of amino acids or genetic materials in biotechnology. For many years, the obviousness of chemical compound was judged primarily by the proximity of the structure or nomenclature of the claimed compound to the prior art. This emphasis on "structural obviousness" dominated the *prima facie* obviousness inquiry and discounted any objective indicia of nonobviousness, such as a showing of unexpected results.

1. Chemistry

While historically "structural obviousness" may have controlled patentability, the Federal Circuit's predecessor rightfully differentiated a compound's formula from the compound itself, including all of its properties. *In re Papesch*, 315 F.2d 381, 391 (CCPA 1963). Nevertheless, structural similarity in the prior art will nearly always erect a *prima facie* case of obviousness against a new chemical which the applicant may attempt to rebut with evidence of unexpected results. *In re Dillon*, 919 F.2d 688 (Fed. Cir. 1990) (*en banc*). The applicant may not rebut a *prima facie* case of obviousness based on structural similarities by identifying a property shared by the prior art, even if unknown. Obviousness in chemical compounds takes on heightened importance when viewed in the setting of the Hatch–Waxman Act, which regulates the interplay between generic drug companies and research-based drug companies.

2. Biotechnology

Even though chemistry and biotechnology share many aspects, they do not share the same emphasis on structure. Rather, many biotechnological inventions relate to genetic material composed of four building blocks (the nucleotide bases—adenine, guanine, cytosine, and thymine) that predictably pair up. Chemistry's emphasis on structure—remember there are an infinite number of molecules made from over a hundred elements—may have limited applicability to biotechnology. Even so, the body of law regarding obviousness in chemical cases has been imported to biotechnology. And the Federal Circuit has accordingly held that a nucleic acid sequence is only obvious if the prior art suggests the claimed compound, even if well-known techniques coupled with the knowledge of the encoded protein's amino acid sequence might have provided motivation to prepare that nucleic acid. *In re Deuel*, 51 F.3d 1552 (Fed. Cir. 1995).

In *Deuel*, the invention claimed a DNA sequence that encoded for a human growth hormone protein. In simple terms, the protein was a sequence of 168 amino acids. In rejecting this claim under § 103, the PTO cited the teachings of Bohlen and Maniatis. Bohlen disclosed the 19 amino acid N-terminal sequence of the protein. Maniatis, as any biotechnologist will attest, is the "Bible" of biotechnology with libraries and cloning procedures to derive entire proteins from smaller segments of the coded genomic material.

The Federal Circuit reversed the PTO and upheld the claims. In reaching this judgment, the Federal Circuit treated these proteins and DNA sequences like chemical compounds and determined obviousness based on structure. Because Bohlen's 19 amino acids differed structurally from the entire 168 amino acids of the HGH protein, the Federal Circuit rejected the PTO's obviousness determination on that basis alone. The Federal Circuit refused to inquire whether one of skill in the art could easily obtain the entire protein from the Bohlen reference by following the well-known Maniatis procedures. Rather, the court opined that "the existence of a general method of isolating cDNA or DNA molecules is essentially irrelevant to the question." *Deuel*, 51 F.3d at 1559. How can the chief tool and central understanding of ordinary biotechnicians be irrelevant to an inquiry that asks for their judgment? Can the "Bible" really be irrelevant to their "religion?" Most biotechnicians would support the PTO's judgment that it was easy to derive the entire protein with even fewer then 19 amino acids as the starting point. Indeed, none of the world's patent systems have followed the reasoning of *Deuel*. Instead, they ask whether the method of finding the gene was obvious or to use the terminology of a prior Federal Circuit opinion, whether application of the method would yield a "reasonable expectation of success" in finding the gene. *In re O'Farrell*, 853 F.2d 894, 904 (Fed. Cir. 1988).

The implications of this Federal Circuit decision have been far-reaching. If Maniatis and other procedures were "irrelevant," obviousness disappeared as a discipline for claims on genetic coding inventions. An initial discovery of genetic code could not render obvious the proteins or further sequences easily obtained from that genomic information. Thus, each little piece of DNA became a separate invention. *Deuel* set off a "gold rush" to obtain snippets of genetic information, called ESTs (expressed sequence tags). In the "gold rush," several inventors might obtain overlapping portions of an important protein sequence. In other words, several patents might claim a part of the same protein, thus complicating the legal rights to the real useful component, the protein. *See, e.g.*, Dan L. Burk, *Biotechnology in the Federal Circuit: A Clockwork Lemon*, 46 ARIZ. L. REV. 441, 449 (2004) (noting the tragedy of the "anticommons" caused by too many property rights); Arti K. Rai & Rebecca Eisenberg, *Bayh-Dole Reform & the Progress of Biomedicine*, 66 LAW & CONTEMP. PROBS. 289, 297 (2003) (noting the same concern for an "anticommons" or "patent thicket").

As discussed above, most foreign systems assess the patentability of gene claims without undue rote comparison of nucleic acid structure. The structure comparison invariably insures that nucleic acid claims are nonobvious. As an institution, the USPTO might responsibly make every effort to achieve a workable formulation of the law (such as insisting that its examiners use the more accurate *O'Farrell* test rather than the faulty *Deuel* test). Perhaps one benefit of *KSR* will be to provide a framework to reconsider the misguided *Deuel* doctrine.

As noted in the utility and disclosure chapters, the PTO and courts have struggled to find some discipline for the loss of obviousness as a substantive requirement for patentability in biotechnological inventions. Furthermore, § 103(b) provides a specific avenue for a special subset of biotechnological inventions relating to processes.

VI. OBVIOUSNESS (INVENTIVE STEP) IN FOREGIN PATENT SYSTEMS

As one might expect the verbal formulas used to determine obviousness (inventive step) varies somewhat from system to system. Yet all of them require an identification and understanding of the teachings of the prior art and a comparison of that prior art with the claimed advance. The well-known "problem and solution" approach to determining inventive step fails in cases where at least part of the invention lies in understanding the problem. In such cases, the solution is easy or obvious once the problem is understood. This approach exhibits another weakness as well, namely a predisposition to identify the problem as that associated with the closest prior art reference. This defect may divert attention away from other art that might render the claimed invention obvious. The U.S. obviousness test avoids these defects.

Nevertheless, as suggested earlier, obviousness and inventive step analyses invariably demand considerable legal and technical judgment. Any judgment call of this magnitude will produce reasonable disagreements. Thus any patent system relies heavily on the knowledge and wisdom of the inherently human (and therefore faulty) vessels charged with its administration. The legal formulas for the obviousness/inventive step test are important, but equally important are the institutional arrangements that affect the judgment calls. Thus, the efficiency and operation of patent offices around the world greatly affect the quality of patents and the success of the patent system in general.

CHAPTER 9

ADEQUATE DISCLOSURE

I. INTRODUCTION

In one sense, patents are contracts between the public and inventors. In exchange for an exclusive right, the inventor agrees to disclose new and non-obvious technology. Thus, for the public to get its part of the bargain, the inventor must fully disclose the invention. In other words, the inventor's primary obligation in the deal is adequate disclosure of the technology to ensure that, at the end of the patent term, others can make and use the invention, and that, at the time of the disclosure, others may study and improve upon the invention. The statutory language governing the disclosure requirement appears in § 112, first paragraph:

> The specification shall contain a written description of the invention, and of the manner and process of making and using it, in such full, clear, concise, and exact terms as to enable any person skilled in the art to which it pertains, or with which it is most nearly connected, to make and use the same, and shall set forth the best mode contemplated by the inventor of carrying out his invention.

The courts have interpreted this important (and cryptic) section to contain three requirements: enablement, written description, and best mode.

Enablement is the core doctrine that ensures adequate disclosure. This doctrine requires that the patent, when filed, includes sufficient technical information to enable a person of ordinary skill in the relevant art to make and use the claimed invention without undue experimentation. Enablement thus requires disclosure beyond a simple description or laconic explanation. Indeed the inventor must genuinely enrich the public's technical knowledge. Beyond disclosure of inventive details, enablement serves two other vital purposes. Enablement polices the boundary between abstract theoretical science and actual technical contributions. This patent law principle thus ensures a technical solution to a real problem, not just visionary theories and hypotheses. In addition, and of vital importance, enablement polices the scope of the claims and prevents an inventor from overreaching. This principle accordingly ensures that the scope and content of the inventor's claimed exclusive right is commensurate with the actual invention. Stated otherwise, the boundary of the exclusive right granted by the patent cannot be more expansive than the inventor's technical contribution.

Case law has generated a separate disclosure doctrine to complement enablement. This doctrine, the written description requirement, emerges from the same phrases in § 112. This doctrine has its origins in preventing a patent applicant from adding new subject matter to his specification—either in the claims or the description—once filed. The written description doctrine thus polices priority by ensuring that an inventor may not improperly amend a pending application to claim later technological advances. In § 132, the Patent Act expressly proscribes the addition of new matter to a pending application. The courts initially used § 112, first paragraph, as the mechanism to enforce § 132.

This traditional written description/new matter requirement, however, has since morphed into a separate substantive disclosure requirement for patentability. That is, at the risk of invalidity, a patent specification, which already includes the claim, must nonetheless describe the subject matter of the claim in other terms as well. Due to the relative nascency of this disclosure requirement, the precise standards for satisfying the doctrine have not yet emerged, but it seems to be merging with enablement, the long-standing and universal rule governing the scope of the claims.

The third requirement—best mode—is unique to U.S. patent law. According to the last clause of § 112, first paragraph, the inventor must ''set forth the best mode ... of carrying out his invention.'' This requirement mandates disclosure in the patent specification of any specific instrumentalities or techniques that the inventor recognized at the time of filing as the best way of carrying out the invention. That is, inventors cannot obtain an exclusive right without also disclosing to the public their trade secrets for practicing the invention. For example, if an inventor invents a new configuration for a bookshelf that bears the load of texts more efficiently and knows of a particularly beneficial material for the new bookshelf, he must disclose that material as part of the application.

II. ENABLEMENT

A. Purpose

Enablement, the other core validity doctrine alongside obviousness, ensures that the patent specification serves as an instruction manual teaching those of ordinary skill in the art to make and use the invention. Of course, the specification need not contain an overly exhaustive description. Rather, the description need only contain those details that, when combined with the baseline knowledge of a person of ordinary skill in the art, provide a comprehensive understanding of the invention's use and fabrication.

The primary function of enablement is to ensure that the public receives useful information, not just theoretical hopes. Accordingly, enablement demarks the boundary between science fiction or visionary hopes and real technological advance. Jules Verne postulated and hypothesized about submarines and space ships decades before these became real technology. Had he attempted to patent these unspecific, incomplete ideas, he would not have been able to enable them. Furthermore, the knowledge of a person of ordinary skill in the art would not have filled out a purely hypothetical disclosure. Enablement, therefore, provides an objective test demarking the boundary between a pioneering invention and visionary hypothesis.

Furthermore, enablement ensures that claim scope does not exceed the inventor's actual technological contribution to the art. *See, e.g., O'Reilly v. Morse*, 56 U.S. (15 How.) 62 (1854). An inventor thus cannot assert rights to an invention without sufficiently supporting the full scope of that assertion with enabling disclosure. Armed with the inventor's instruction in the patent's disclosure, other inventors can devise further improvements on the invention to advance technological progress in that area. In other words, by delineating the accurate boundary of the invention, enablement facilitates and encourages additional discoveries by creating incentives for subsequent improvements in the field. Enablement thus promotes further patentable improvements on patented inventions. *See, e.g., Consol. Elec. Light Co. v. McKeesport Light Co.*, 159 U.S. 465 (1895). A patent on a nonobvious improvement would, of course, require additional disclosure beyond the patent on the earlier invention.

B. Test

Enablement requires that the specification, when filed, contain disclosure sufficiently clear and complete to enable one of ordinary skill in the art to make and use the invention, as claimed, without undue experimentation. This test can be parsed into three critical portions. First, enablement is judged at the time of filing, preventing later developments from validating an inventor's prophetic guess about the progression in the art. Second, the disclosure must be clear and complete enough to enable the claimed invention, ensuring that the scope of the disclosure is commensurate with the scope of the claims. Third, a person of ordinary skill in the art must be able to make and use the invention without undue experimentation, permitting some (but not excessive) additional testing or research to make an operative embodiment of the invention.

1. At the Time of Filing

The first portion of the enablement test ensures that inventors have a complete idea before filing a patent application. Once again, Gordon Gould, the laser scientist, provides the classic example. In *Gould v. Hellwarth*, 472 F.2d 1383 (CCPA 1973), the court adjudicated an interference over a count concerning a "Q-switched" laser. By filing in April of 1959, Gould became the senior party. The junior party, Hellwarth, filed in August of 1961. Gould should have won the interference except for one problem: no one anywhere in the world built an operative laser until 1960. Accordingly, the court ruled that Gould could not have enabled a person of ordinary skill in the art to make an operable laser when neither he, nor anyone else, did it until later.

The court's opinion also noted that several renowned scientists testified years later at the trial that Gould's disclosure enabled a sodium mercury laser. Yet, as of 1968, no one had built an operative sodium mercury laser. How could they testify contrary to scientific history? Their testimony reveals another aspect of enablement: the as-filed disclosure cannot simply prophesy accurately about the development of new technology, rather it must enable operative technology at the time of filing. Gould evidently, as these noted scientists confirmed, predicted the fabrication and operation of a sodium mercury laser many years before it occurred. In the years after his basic disclosure, engineers learned the details necessary to make an operable laser, including (later) a sodium mercury laser. Prediction, even accurate prediction, however, is not enablement. Gould in fact did not adequately detail the making of a complete laser or he would have done it himself. Even though later developments confirmed his inadequate disclosure was "on the right track," it was still inadequate to enable. Enablement proceeds according to the state of the art at the time of filing. This classic Gould case illustrates that this rule precludes a patent on visionary, even if accurate, theoretical science that cannot produce operable technology.

As an aside, the court probably erred in awarding priority to Hellwarth over Gould. The court's fundamental error was in its reading of Gould's claims. The court read Gould's claims to cover lasers in general. In reality, Gould did not claim lasers in general, but an improvement, Q switching, on operable lasers. An inventor of an improvement may await the development of the basic technology before incurring the obligation to reduce the improvement to practice by showing it works for its intended purpose in the basic technology. *See, e.g., Columbia Broadcasting Sys. v. Sylvania Elec. Prods., Inc.*, 415 F.2d 719 (1st Cir. 1969) (noting that certain well-known techniques did not have to be disclosed in a patent relating to advances in color television). In this case, Gould should have received a chance to reduce his narrow invention to practice (and enable it) upon invention of the operable laser. Of course, Gould may well not have wished to claim this narrow victory when he instead wanted his disclosure to make him the father of all laser technology. In that context, the court was certainly correct to bar a broad claim to the laser in general for lack of enablement. In any event, enablement requires an operable technology, not a theory (even if later proved workable).

2. Scope of Disclosure

The second portion of the enablement test matches the scope of the disclosure to the scope of the claims. This requirement often depends on the state of knowledge in the scientific field of the invention. Thus, inventions in unpredictable fields require far more disclosure than inventions in more conventional fields. The necessary level of detail, however, never requires instruction on mass-producing the claimed invention. *Christianson v. Colt Indus. Operating Corp.*, 822 F.2d 1544, 1562 (Fed. Cir. 1987) (commenting that it is not "an objective of the patent system to supply, free of charge, production data and production drawings to competing manufacturers"). Rather, the disclosure must be as detailed and revelatory as necessary to enable the full breadth of the claims.

An early biotechnology case provides an illustration. In *In re Wright*, 999 F.2d 1557 (Fed. Cir. 1993), Dr. Stephen E. Wright claimed processes for producing vaccines against pathogenic RNA viruses, further claimed the vaccines themselves, and finally claimed methods of using those vaccines against RNA viruses. RNA viruses comprise a varied, genetically diverse group of submicroscopic infective agents that produce terrible maladies like HIV, some leukemias, and some sarcomas. Dr. Wright claimed, among other things, a process to produce vaccines against RNA viruses in general. In contrast, Dr. Wright's specification disclosed and detailed a single working example: the production of a vaccine that immunizes chickens against Prague Avian Sarcoma Virus, a particular type of RNA virus belonging to the Rous Associated Virus family. The USPTO granted Dr. Wright the claims to his chicken vaccine and the processes for making it. The USPTO declined to grant Dr. Wright a patent on general RNA viruses or methods of making them, so he appealed.

The Federal Circuit sustained the USPTO's rejections for lack of enablement. In classic understatement, the court noted that the physiological activity of RNA viruses was not sufficiently predictable even five years after Wright's priority date, let alone at the effective filing date. Accordingly, a person of ordinary skill in the art would not have reasonably believed that, as claimed by Wright, all living organisms could be immunized against infection by any RNA virus by following the generalized methods and processes disclosed in the application. In more direct terms, the court could have said: "You have not cured AIDS or leukemia! You do not deserve a patent on cures for all RNA viruses!" Wright's disclosure, at best, merely invited experimentation to develop vaccines for specific types of RNA viruses. In fact, Wright had invented little, if anything, beyond a chicken virus vaccine.

Apparently conceding the audacity of his broad claims in light of his incredibly thin disclosure, Wright offered to narrow his claims to vaccines for all avian RNA viruses. Wright was still vastly overreaching. He had not even cured other chicken viruses, let alone all potential viruses in all species of birds. Stated in more careful legal terms, the sophistication of the ordinary practitioner in this field would not permit extrapolation of the particular chicken RNA virus to all avian RNA viruses. The court, therefore, upheld the Patent Office's rejection of the overbroad claims. If, purely hypothetically, Wright had been able to posit a scientific principle that governed all avian viruses and showed that results against one would apply with equal force to another, then his single working example might have enabled a broader claim to cover all avian RNA viruses. Or, again completely hypothetically, if Dr. Wright had shown scientific principles that linked the chicken genome to turkeys and produced the same results for both, then he might have enabled a turkey vaccine beyond the chicken vaccine. Of course, in the treatment of viruses, that kind of understanding and technological achievement still lies in the distant future.

The second portion of the enablement test may be thought of as a comparison of the scope of enabling disclosure with the scope of the claims. When coupled with the reasonable knowledge and expectations of a person of ordinary skill in the art at the time of application, the description—taking into account the specific examples as well as generalized statements—cannot cover and explain less subject matter than the scope of the claims. That is, patentees may not overreach by asserting exclusive rights to subject matter beyond what they have actually invented and taught others to replicate.

Returning to biotechnology for a moment, as the science of genetic manipulation progressed, it became apparent that biotechnological inventions, such as the microorganisms at issue in *Diamond v. Chakrabarty*, 447 U.S. 303 (1980), could not be effectively enabled through a lifeless description in the patent or application. Instead, an inventor enables such an invention by providing a publicly accessible sample—a deposit—and identifying the source of that deposit. *See In re Lundak*, 773 F.2d 1216 (Fed. Cir. 1985). To minimize the transaction costs involved in depositing samples in each country, patent-savvy countries signed the Budapest Treaty on the International Recognition of Deposits of Microorganisms for the Purposes of Patent Protection. The Budapest Treaty established a uniform certification process for depositing microorganisms.

Under this international agreement, a patentee may refer to a single deposit in a single depository regardless of the country of application. But again, the scope of the claims cannot exceed the scope of enabled subject matter, even where the subject matter is enabled through a publicly accessible sample in a depository.

3.　Without Undue Experimentation

The third portion of the enablement test limits the amount of work or effort by a person of ordinary skill in the art that the patentee may reasonably rely upon to supplement the patent's disclosure. Because the enablement rule permits some, but not unduly excessive, experimentation, this part of the test is again influenced by the nature of the scientific field. In *Atlas Powder Co. v. E.I. du Pont De Nemours & Co.*, 750 F.2d 1569 (Fed. Cir. 1984), the Federal Circuit reviewed a determination that claims directed to emulsion blasting agents (explosives detonated by a high strength explosive primer) were not invalid for lack of enablement. The patent disclosed a large number of ingredients—salts, fuels, and emulsifiers—that combined to form thousands of potential emulsions. The patent, however, did not identify the operable, as opposed to the inoperable, combinations. Without specifying any working examples, this patent might seem to have a fatal flaw. To the contrary, the court determined that the patentee was not required to distinguish operable combinations for two reasons. First, a well-known principle of chemistry, "Bancroft's Rule," would have assisted a person of ordinary skill in the art in selecting operative combinations. Second, the claims may include inoperative embodiments so long as a person of ordinary skill in the art can identify the operable embodiments without undue experimentation. Indeed, the claims may also encompass embodiments that work but not well because patent law does not require disclosure of only the most effective subject matter (unless it is a best mode as appears later).

The patent had also described several prophetic examples—that is, experiments that the inventor has not actually performed. These descriptions did not render the patent invalid, because the inventor reasonably believed that those examples would, in fact, enable the claimed invention.

To be specific, Du Pont, the party attacking Atlas Powder's patent, tested the combinations in the claims. Out of 300 tests, forty percent failed outright and only two emulsions worked. Again, these results would seem to be fatal to a case for enablement. To the contrary, the court explained that bulk statistical aggregations do not necessarily reflect the difficulty of the experimentation to reach the claimed results. In this case, a person of ordinary skill, using Bancroft's well-known rule, would have quickly eliminated inoperable combinations and derived the optimal explosives. The patent required experimentation, but even the multiple experiments required in this case were not overly burdensome or undue.

Because the extent of experimentation depends on the facts of each dispute, courts have adopted an eight-factor test to discern the boundary between undue and customary experimentation in a particular field. These factors, commonly known as the *Wands* factors, include:

(1) the quantity of experimentation necessary,

(2) the amount of direction or guidance presented,

(3) the presence or absence of working examples,

(4) the nature of the invention,

(5) the state of the prior art,

(6) the relative skill of those in the art,

(7) the predictability or unpredictability of the art, and

(8) the breadth of the claims.

In re Wands, 858 F.2d 731, 737 (Fed. Cir. 1988). Although universally applicable, these factors have particular relevance with respect to biotechnological inventions. *See, e.g.*, *Enzo Biochem, Inc. v. Calgene, Inc.*, 188 F.3d 1362 (Fed. Cir. 1999).

C. Relationship to Utility

The § 112, paragraph 1, requirement that a patentee must enable others to make and use the claimed invention is similar to the utility requirement in § 101. As discussed in Chapter 4, utility serves as an insubstantial hurdle to patentability in most instances, except with respect to chemical and biotechnological inventions. But even in those technologies, the utility requirement merely requires that the patentee designate some application for the claimed subject matter. Enablement complements this requirement by ensuring some description in the specification to teach the skilled artisan that application. In fact, a patent lacking utility is necessarily not enabled: no person of ordinary skill in the art could ever practice the invention. *In re Swartz*, 232 F.3d 862 (Fed. Cir. 2000).

For example, in *In re Ziegler*, 992 F.2d 1197 (Fed. Cir. 1993), Ziegler, a patent applicant, attempted to claim the benefit of priority to a foreign application to avoid an anticipatory reference. The Court, however, determined that the foreign application did not enable the polypropylene as claimed in his domestic patent application, because Ziegler's foreign application lacked a disclosure of a specific utility. Ziegler's foreign application had merely disclosed that polypropylene could be pressed into a flexible film. Notably, Ziegler had not disclosed any practical use. (Polypropylene, of course, has numerous uses, most notably as semi-rigid packaging.)

III. WRITTEN DESCRIPTION

A. Purpose

Related to the enablement requirement, written description primarily serves a complementary purpose: to ensure that an inventor does not obtain claims on subject matter not initially disclosed in the application as filed and, thus, to which he is not entitled under the earlier priority date. If the inventor was the first to invent the new matter, then he may deserve claims to those improvements, but that assessment would require an accurate assessment of invention dates for the improvement. Others may have actually made the improvement first. In any event, the written description/new matter requirement prevents an applicant from perpetually "updating" his original disclosure to claim later developments. Thus, the written description requirement polices priority.

Assume an inventor creates a new superconductive metal alloy that speeds electronic communications. He files a patent application that describes and claims his new alloy for electric wires. While that application is pending, the inventor discovers several other derivative alloys that work even better as a communication medium. The inventor, however, can neither amend his claims in the initial application to recite the newer alloys nor amend his initial specification to describe the more recent advances. Instead, he must file a continuation-in-part that discloses and claims the newer developments. This new application will, of course, receive a later filing date. (Alternatively but at great risk as shown in Chapter 13, the inventor may choose to rely solely upon the doctrine of equivalents to preclude others from using an insubstantially different form of his invention.) While the inventor obtains the benefit of the filing date of his initial application for the initial alloy, he may only enjoy the benefit of the filing date of his subsequent application for the derivatives. Under the written description/new matter doctrine, the inventor may draft new claims for the new derivative alloys (even though the as-filed claims did not recite that subject matter) if, and only if, the original specification disclosed those alternative formulations. In the terms of the written description doctrine, the applicant may add new claims only if the specification "supports" or "shows possession of" the subject matter in the new claims or amendments. *Vas-Cath Inc. v. Mahurkar*, 935 F.2d 1555, 1563 (Fed. Cir. 1991).

Section 132 expressly states: "No amendment shall introduce new matter into the disclosure of the invention." The CCPA opined that the word "disclosure" might only encompass the descriptive portions of the application instead of the claims. In a surfeit of caution, the CCPA thus decided to use section 112, first paragraph, to prohibit new matter in claims. *In re Ruschig*, 379 F.2d 990, 995–95 (CCPA 1967). Thus, although a separate provision of the Patent Act precludes applicants from introducing new disclosures (including new claims, new amendments to old claims, or new additions to the specification), the CCPA decided to use the "written description" language of § 112 (somewhat out of context) to police priority. The CCPA repeatedly emphasized that its new written description test was "equivalent" to the former new matter test. *In re Rasmussen*, 650 F.2d 1212, 1214 (CCPA 1981). Indeed, the written description requirement appears to be more onerous than enablement. *E.g.*, *In re DiLeone*, 436 F.2d 1404 (CCPA 1971).

B. "Possession" of the Claimed Subject Matter

The test for written description is relatively succinct: there must be adequate disclosure to show possession of the claimed subject matter at the time the application was filed. *See, e.g., Ralston Purina Co. v. Far–Mar–Co, Inc.*, 772 F.2d 1570 (Fed. Cir. 1985). In other words, this test requires "adequate support" in the as-filed application for the later claimed subject matter. The case of *Vas-Cath Inc. v. Mahurkar*, 935 F.2d 1555 (Fed. Cir. 1991) illustrates this test. In that case, Dr. Mahurkar had filed a utility patent on a soft double-lumen catheter that allowed simultaneous insertion and removal of blood. At trial the court encountered prior uses that antedated Mahurkar's filing date. To avoid this prior art, Dr. Mahurkar wished to claim priority back to a design patent containing the same drawings as his later utility patents. The trial court determined that Dr. Mahurkar could not date the utility patents back to the earlier date of the design patent and, thus, had invalidated the patents under § 102(b).

The Federal Circuit reversed and set forth the test for the written description/new matter doctrine: "[T]he applicant must ... convey with reasonable clarity to those skilled in the art that, as of the filing date sought, he or she was in possession *of the invention*." *Id.* at 1563–64 (emphasis original). Because this test depends on a factual analysis of the earlier disclosure in light of the understanding of a person of ordinary skill in the art, the Federal

Circuit remanded. On remand, the trial court determined that the patentee was in possession of the later-claimed subject matter at the time of the design application in part because the "utility application simply lays out the details of what the design drawings show—to be precise, the utility claims narrate what features of the drawings are important, without adding anything." *In re Mahurkar Patent Litigation*, 831 F. Supp. 1354, 1362 (N.D.Ill. 1993), *aff'd*, 71 F.3d 1573 (Fed. Cir. 1995). Dr. Mahurkar then developed his patented invention into a billion-dollar industry.

The written description "possession" test often presents special problems in determining whether disclosure of a genus can show possession of a later-claimed subgenus or species. *See, e.g., In re Smith*, 458 F.2d 1389, 1395–96 (CCPA 1972). In most instances, a broad genus does not adequately describe, or show possession of, a species or subgenus. But if "there are specific facts which lead to a determination that a subgenus is implicitly described," *Ex parte Westphal*, 26 USPQ2d 1858, 1860 (BPAI 1992), the earlier disclosure of the genus may adequately support claims directed solely to a subgenus or species. Conversely, a disclosure of a sufficient number of species may show possession of a genus encompassing those species. *See Utter v. Hiraga*, 845 F.2d 993 (Fed. Cir. 1988).

C. Written Description Unchained

Despite the traditional confines of written description as a doctrine to police priority, the Federal

Circuit has expanded its reach to invalidate claims, even if those claims were part of the as-filed specification. The case that initiated the application of written description as a substantive requirement for patentability was *Regents of the University of California v. Eli Lilly & Co.*, 119 F.3d 1559 (Fed. Cir. 1997). In *Eli Lilly*, the patents generally related to recombinant DNA technology and to microorganisms and plasmids that produce insulin, a treatment for diabetes. The patent was filed in 1977—during the nascency of biotechnology—and described the cDNA (a type of genetic material) sequences found in rats that controlled the chemical pathways to make insulin. The patent's claims recited, *inter alia*, procaryotic microorganisms containing vertebrate insulin-encoding cDNA. Other claims specifically recited human insulin cDNA.

In invalidating the originally filed claims, the Federal Circuit made it clear that the inventor had not enabled the creation of human DNA, only the rat sequence. Yet, rather than invalidate under the traditional disclosure doctrine, the Federal Circuit declared that the applicant had not satisfied the written description doctrine, even though priority was not at stake. Thus, with no explanation for the need to create a new disclosure doctrine, the Federal Circuit set forth a new validity doctrine. *Eli Lilly* emphasized that the new doctrine "requires a precise definition, such as by structure, formula, chemical name, or physical properties." 119 F.3d at 1566 (quoting *Fiers v. Revel*, 984 F.2d 1164, 1171 (Fed. Cir. 1993)).

The rigid *Eli Lilly* test for written description soon encountered problems. In *Enzo Biochem, Inc. v. Gen–Probe Inc.*, 285 F.3d 1013 (Fed. Cir. 2002), the court initially held that a deposit of genetic material could not satisfy the written description requirement. After all, the deposit did not recite the "formula, chemical name, etc." required by the *Eli Lilly* test. Upon petition for rehearing, the panel reversed itself but maintained the viability of the written description doctrine. *Enzo Biochem, Inc. v. Gen–Probe Inc.*, 323 F.3d 956 (Fed. Cir. 2002).

More recently the Federal Circuit has continued its retreat from the stringent *Eli Lilly* formulation of the new written description test. In *Capon v. Eshhar*, 418 F.3d 1349 (Fed. Cir. 2005), the Federal Circuit reformulated the test to vary with the complexity of the technology. Once again, this very general formulation supplied no standard for application of the new doctrine. *See Moba, B.V. v. Diamond Automation, Inc.*, 325 F.3d 1306, 1323 (Fed. Cir. 2003) (Rader, J., concurring) (commenting that juries face the "cumbersome task" of deciding that "the patent's disclosure can enable a skilled artisan to make and practice the entire invention, but still not inform that same artisan that the inventor was in possession of the invention"). After all, this broad generality applies to nearly every patent case and doctrine. The latest trend shows the Federal Circuit beginning to fold its experimental written description doctrine back into the traditional confines of the enablement test for adequate disclosure. In *LizardTech, Inc. v. Earth Resource Mapping,*

Inc., for example, the court noted that the new written description doctrine and enablement "usually rise and fall together." 424 F.3d 1336, 1345 (Fed. Cir. 2005); *see also Moba*, 325 F.3d at 1326 (Rader, J., concurring) ("With some understanding of the difficulties and redundancy of the *Lilly* rule, the Federal Circuit has begun to convert it into the enablement doctrine with a different label."). Although the written description validity doctrine still has considerable "teeth," *Univ. of Rochester v. G.D. Searle & Co.,* 358 F.3d 916 (Fed. Cir. 2004), the move to reunite the Federal Circuit's disclosure doctrines under the traditional enablement test promises to restore some predictability to the tests for adequacy of disclosure.

IV. BEST MODE

A. Purpose

Beyond the requirement for adequate disclosure, the first paragraph of § 112 further requires disclosure of "the best mode contemplated by the inventor of carrying out his invention." This heightened disclosure obligation assists competitors in discovering the most effective implementations of the patented invention. To some extent, best mode attempts to level the playing field between the patentee and his competitors. The best mode requirement prevents a patentee from keeping some valuable aspects of an invention as a trade secret.

B. Two-Part Test

The best mode requirement does not require disclosure of all trade secrets associated with a patented invention. Instead a patentee need only disclose any way of practicing the invention that he considered better than any other at the time of filing. This test has two components: (1) the subjective belief of the inventor of a better method of practicing the claimed invention at the time of filing and (2) concealment (occasionally mere nondisclosure) of that better method. *Chemcast Corp. v. Arco Industries Corp.*, 913 F.2d 923, 927–28 (Fed. Cir. 1990).

1. Inventor's Subjective Belief

The first prong introduces a peculiar subjective test into patent law. For the most part, the Patent Act requires objectivity. The best mode requirement is a notable exception to that general rule. (The intent prong under inequitable conduct is another example, but in that instance, circumstantial evidence often suffices to prove subjective intent. *See* Chapter 14 for a more complete discussion.) Instead of assessing disclosure through the eyes of a hypothetical person of ordinary skill in the art, the best mode requirement assesses the subjective, even idiosyncratic, beliefs of a flesh-and-blood inventor. Accordingly, the best mode test rejects as irrelevant the perception of a person of ordinary skill in the art at the time that the invention could be tweaked to enhance its operability. Only the inventor's perceptions are relevant.

The knowledge of others associated with the inventor, such as his attorneys or coworkers, is not imputed to the inventor. For example, in *Glaxo Inc. v. Novopharm Ltd.*, 52 F.3d 1043 (Fed. Cir. 1995), the court addressed whether claims directed to an anti-ulcer medicament were invalid for failure to disclose the best mode. While the inventor was unaware of an improved process for forming the medicament into a pharmaceutically acceptable composition, even Glaxo's patent attorney knew the better method. Glaxo was the inventor's employer. Without evidence that the inventor shared the rather wide-spread knowledge within Glaxo, the court refused to enforce a best mode prohibition. Instead the court applied the statutory language "contemplated by the inventor" quite literally and thus limited starkly the reach of best mode.

Notably as well, the best mode requirement fixes the inventor's knowledge at the filing date. Subsequent discoveries of preferred embodiments do not create a obligation to update the disclosure with additional best modes. Even continuing applications—including continuations, divisionals, and continuations-in-part—that claim priority to an earlier application do not require an update of the best mode disclosure. For those continuing applications, the best mode disclosure obligation is fixed on the date of the earliest effective filing date. *Transco Prods. Inc. v. Performance Contracting, Inc.*, 38 F.3d 551 (Fed. Cir. 1994).

2. Concealment

Even though the first prong is undoubtedly subjective, the second prong reintroduces some objectivity to determine whether the inventor in fact disclosed his best mode. Whether the inventor concealed his best mode requires a comparison between his subjective belief and the patent's disclosure. This comparison turns on whether a person of ordinary skill in the art at the time would recognize that the inventor disclosed his subjective best mode in the patent as filed.

Although rare (the Federal Circuit has only struck down about a half-dozen patents for failure to disclose a best mode), the case law contains a few examples of clear concealment of a known best mode. For example, in *Chemcast Corp. v. Arco Industries Corp.*, 913 F.2d 923 (Fed. Cir. 1990), the court upheld a judgment that the patentee did not disclose the best mode of his invention, a grommet for attaching material to sheet metal such as securing upholstery to an automobile interior. The record in that case showed that the inventor knew that the locking portion of the grommet should be made from a polyvinyl chloride (PVC) composition sold under the trade name R–4467. R–4467 had a particular hardness measured at 75 on the Shore D scale known in this art. In fact, the inventor knew that 750 man-hours over several months were required to develop R–4467. The inventor had developed a single embodiment of the grommet's locking portion at the time of his application, namely R–4467 with a hardness of 75 Shore D. Yet the inventor did not disclose either R–4467 or its important rigid properties. The inventor disclosed materials with a hardness of 70 Shore A or harder. This disclosure was technically correct, 75 Shore D was much much harder than 70 Shore A, but in fact misleading due to the vast differences between the physical properties of the Shore A and D hardness scales. Furthermore, a generic reference to PVC did not disclose R–4467. Thus, the inventor's disclosure concealed, rather than disclosed, the best mode.

Despite the extreme situation in *Chemcast*, § 112 does not obligate an inventor to highlight what he believes is his best mode. Rather, a patentee may bury the best mode in a list of a large number of less preferable alternatives without offending the best mode requirement. *See, e.g., Randomex Inc. v. Scopus Corp.*, 849 F.2d 585 (Fed. Cir. 1988). Accordingly, inventors often choose the course of including many modes of performing the claimed invention to avert potential best mode challenges.

The invention as claimed generally sets forth the limit of the inventor's best mode disclosure obligation. Although the vast majority of case law, in fact, limits the best mode requirement to features recited in the claims, *see, e.g., DeGeorge v. Bernier*, 768 F.2d 1318 (Fed. Cir. 1985); *Teleflex, Inc. v. Ficosa N. Am. Corp.*, 299 F.3d 1313 (Fed. Cir. 2002), some cases have opened the door to best modes related to features just beyond the explicit recitation of claimed elements. For example, in *Bayer AG v. Schein Pharmaceuticals, Inc.*, the court applied a "material effects" test to expand the reach of the best mode requirement to "aspects of making or using the claimed invention ... [that] materially affected the properties of the claimed invention." 301 F.3d 1306, 1319 (Fed. Cir. 2002). Under this recent and somewhat controversial application of best mode law, an inventor must determine whether unclaimed features "materially affect" the claimed invention. If so, this case would require disclosure of the best modes for any such unclaimed features. Even this articulation of the best mode requirement, however, does not require an inventor to disclose either routine details readily available to a person of ordinary skill in the art or production details relating solely to commercial considerations beyond the quality or nature of the invention as claimed. *Eli Lilly & Co. v. Barr Labs., Inc.*, 251 F.3d 955 (Fed. Cir. 2001); *Young Dental Mfg. Co. v. Q3 Special Prods., Inc.*, 112 F.3d 1137 (Fed. Cir. 1997).

C. Unnecessary Vestige?

Although firmly entrenched in the Patent Act, the best mode requirement is a misfit for a number of reasons. To begin with, best mode is really a "trap for the unwary." *Bayer AG v. Schein Pharms., Inc.*, 301 F.3d 1306, 1325 (Fed. Cir. 2002) (Rader, J., concurring). After all, the best mode requirement is largely self-enforcing. Any inventor with even a passing knowledge of patent law would never fall into the best mode trap because nondisclosure of a critical trade secret within the best mode requirement places the value of the entire patented invention at risk—a risk beyond the requirements of § 112. After all, competitors can, and invariably will, discover the undisclosed trade secret and claim it in a separate patent application. When that application ripens into a patent, the competitor will have a blocking patent capable of compromising the value of the original patent. Therefore, the best mode requirement is unnecessary; an informed patent applicant will never withhold a genuine best mode. Instead informed patent applicants will either disclose the best mode in the original patent's specification (often as a dependent claim) or, if the trade secret is not part of the claimed invention, file a separate patent application on the separate innovation. Because informed patent applicants know to avoid best mode problems, this § 112 requirement is invariably little more than a trap for the uninformed applicant—perhaps a university or independent inventor without corporate legal resources.

In fact, not only universities and garage inventors fall into the best mode trap, but also foreign inventors because the United States is the only country with a best mode requirement. Therefore, a foreign inventor who intends on applying for a patent in his country must include information pertaining to the best mode in his foreign priority application. Although filing in a country without a best mode requirement, the foreign inventor risks losing priority if he changes his application upon entry into the U.S. (A foreign inventor may, of course, supplement his disclosure to conform with the best mode requirement prior to filing in this country; however, he would then not be entitled to priority back to his foreign application under § 119.) United States patent law thus creates extra burdens or traps for foreign applicants.

Because this trade secret relic runs counter to basis patent law policy, commentators have often

recommended dropping this requirement. THE ADVI-
SORY COMMISSION ON PATENT LAW REFORM: A REPORT TO
THE SECRETARY OF COMMERCE 102–03 (1992); *see also*
AIPLA RESPONSE TO THE NATIONAL ACADEMIES REPORT
ENTITLED, "A PATENT SYSTEM FOR THE 21ST CENTURY"
42–44 (2005). The 1992 Commission gave several
compelling reasons to eliminate the best mode requirement. First, best mode is unnecessary because
enablement already compels a full and fair disclosure of a patented invention. Second, a patentee
who intentionally conceals material information already faces penalties under the inequitable conduct
doctrine so best mode is not necessary to remedy
deliberate concealment. Third, the best mode does
not necessarily result in more thorough disclosure
because the inventor has no duty to seek out the
best mode. Rather, the inventor need only disclose
the best mode known to him at the time of the
application. Fourth, where the technology of the
invention rapidly progresses, informing the public
of the best mode at the time of filing will not inform
the public of subsequent improvements made during, for example, the pendency of the application.
Fifth, the best mode requirement only appeared in
1952 suggesting no long-standing, systemic recognition of its importance or necessity.

CHAPTER 10

CLAIMS

I. INTRODUCTION

A. Central Legal Element of a Patent

A patent is, quite simply, the right to exclude others from making, using, selling, offering to sell, or importing inventive technology. But where does that exclusive right begin and end? Before testing for either infringement or validity, patent law requires first a definition of the boundaries of the invention. Claims, which define its boundaries, are therefore a patent's most critical component. In fact, the Federal Circuit has proclaimed, quoting perhaps its most celebrated member, the late Judge Giles S. Rich: "the name of the game is the claim." *In re Hiniker Co.*, 150 F.3d 1362, 1369 (Fed. Cir. 1998). A common metaphor calls the claim the fence around the inventor's property right.

In accordance with their importance, claims are undeniably the most difficult drafting assignment in patent law and maybe even the most difficult drafting assignment in all fields of law. *Topliff v. Topliff*, 145 U.S. 156 (1892). After all, claims must describe and define complex technical subject matter in terms broad enough to foresee and capture future related technology and narrow enough to distinguish all past related technology. The drafter must foresee technological variants and distinguish the technology of the past. At the same time, the drafter must succinctly define the invention's essential features while avoiding any extraneous limits. To further complicate the task, claims are a legal document but must reflect the understanding of a person with ordinary skill in the art, a decidedly scientific point of view. In short, claim drafting puts a premium on technical and legal skill alike, without which the value of the invention decreases dramatically.

Chapter 12 addresses the processes courts use to divine the meaning of claims—a deceptively challenging task on par with claim drafting. This chapter addresses general and specific formats of claims in addition to discussing definiteness, a substantive requirement of patentability.

B. Historical Development

The Patent Act has only required a specific claim for the past century and a quarter. The first Patent Act in 1793, 1 Stat. 318, merely required that an inventor describe the invention in the body of the specification, without delineating its outer bounds. The Act, however, had a similar, even if less exacting, requirement that the inventor provide "a written description of his invention, and of the manner of using, or process of compounding the same, in such full, clear, and exact terms, as to distinguish the same from all other things before known." *In re Barker*, 559 F.2d 588, 592 (CCPA 1977). This aspect of the disclosure, which is the closest ancestor of the modern requirement for claims, served the purpose of:

> put[ting] the public in possession of what the party claims as his own invention, so as to ascertain if he claim anything that is in common use, or is already known, and to guard against prejudice or injury from the use of an invention which the party may otherwise innocently suppose not to be patented. It is, therefore, for the purpose of warning an innocent purchaser, or other person using a machine, of his infringement of the patent; and at the same time, of taking from the inventor the means of practising upon the credulity or the fears of other persons, by pretending that his invention is more than what it really is, or different from its ostensible objects, that the patentee is required to distinguish his invention in his specification.

Evans v. Eaton, 20 U.S. (7 Wheat.) 356, 433–34 (1822). The general description requirement of early U.S. patent law is often referred to as "central claiming."

Although the term "claim" first appeared in the Patent Act of 1836, Chap. 357, 5 Stat. 117, claims did not become a statutory requirement until the Patent Act of 1870, Chap. 230, § 26, 16 Stat. 198. Indeed, section 26 of that Act required that a patentee "shall particularly point out and distinctly claim the part, improvement, or combination which he claims as his invention or discovery." Since then, all patentees must conclude the specification with at least one peripheral claim defining the exclusive right. *See, e.g., McClain v. Ortmayer*, 141 U.S. 419, 424 (1891) (explaining that a patent must describe the exact scope of an invention and its manufacture to "secure to [the patentee] all to which he is entitled, [and] to apprise the public of what is still open to them"). Indeed, "[t]he scope of letters-patent must be limited to the invention covered by the claim, and while the claim may be illustrated it cannot be enlarged by language used in other parts of the specification." *Yale Lock Mfg. Co. v. Greenleaf*, 117 U.S. 554, 559 (1886). This type of claiming is called "peripheral claiming" to distinguish it from its "central claiming" ancestor.

C. Section 112

The 1952 Patent Act, as amended, sets out the standards for claims, in both form as well as substance. As stated by § 112, claims constitute a portion of the specification, even if practitioners colloquially refer to the written description as the sole constituent of the specification. *See In re Dossel*, 115 F.3d 942 (Fed. Cir. 1997) (noting that the statutory structure does not correspond to modern usage). The second through sixth paragraphs of § 112 describe the requirements of claims:

[2] The specification shall conclude with one or more claims particularly pointing out and distinctly claiming the subject matter which the applicant regards as his invention.

[3]   A claim may be written in independent or, if the nature of the case admits, in dependent or multiple dependent form.

[4]   Subject to the following paragraph, a claim in dependent form shall contain a reference to a claim previously set forth and then specify a further limitation of the subject matter claimed. A claim in dependent form shall be construed to incorporate by reference all the limitations of the claim to which it refers.

[5]   A claim in multiple dependent form shall contain a reference, in the alternative only, to more than one claim previously set forth and then specify a further limitation of the subject matter claimed. A multiple dependent claim shall not serve as a basis for any other multiple dependent claim. A multiple dependent claim shall be construed to incorporate by reference all the limitations of the particular claim in relation to which it is being considered.

[6]   An element in a claim for a combination may be expressed as a means or step for performing a specified function without the recital of structure, material, or acts in support thereof, and such claim shall be construed to cover the corresponding structure, material, or acts described in the specification and equivalents thereof.

35 U.S.C. § 112 (numerals added). The second paragraph sets forth the substantive requirement of claims: they must particularly point out and distinctly claim their subject matter. This definiteness

requirement mandates that a patentee sufficiently notify the public (as well as the Patent Office) of the bounds of the invention. The subsequent paragraphs set forth acceptable forms for claims, with paragraphs three through five permitting independent, dependent, and (in limited circumstances) multiple dependent claims. The last paragraph authorizes the use of "means-plus-function" claims. Because the sixth paragraph carries its own special rules (in some ways using features of central claiming in the modern era), skilled practitioners often advise sparing and careful use of this alternative claim format.

Although this chapter serves as an introduction to the basic rules of claims and their format, drafting and prosecuting claims of appropriate scope requires legal skills honed only with experience. Simply put, purely academic study cannot serve as a substitute for exposure to the idiosyncrasies of the Patent Office, the conventions of the patent bar, and the past judicial treatment of claim terms and formats.

II. PARTS OF A CLAIM

At their incipiency, patent practitioners drafted "omnibus" claims in which the patentees claimed the invention "substantially as described" in his description. These claims provided only nebulous boundaries and relied heavily on the drawings and description to define the scope of the invention. Modern practice, however, places a premium on precise claim structure and language.

Each claim, which constitutes the predicate of a single sentence, has three sections: a preamble, a transitional phrase, and a body. Although these parts have varying degrees of significance in each case, each serves a critical legal function. Furthermore, as the statute permits, a claim may depend from—that is, incorporate all the limitations of—another claim.

Consider these hypothetical claims:

What is claimed is:

1. A book for a collection of pictographs comprising a front cover and a plurality of slate pages.

2. A book for a collection of pictographs according to claim 1, wherein the front cover consists of granite.

In claim 1, the independent claim, the preamble is "[a] book for a collection of pictographs"; the transitional phrase uses the legal term of art, "comprising"; and the body of the claim is "a front cover and a plurality of slate pages." Claim 2 depends from claim 1, thus incorporating all the limitations of claim 1, and further defines the claimed book as having a front cover made from granite.

A. One-Sentence Rule

Patent Office guidance makes each claim the predicate of a single sentence that begins with one of the following phrases (or something similar): "I claim"; "The invention claimed is"; or "What is claimed is." Manual of Patent Examining Procedure

§ 608.01(m). Although not a statutory requirement, this form convention falls within the Patent Office's discretion under § 112. *Fressola v. Manbeck*, 36 USPQ2d 1211 (D.D.C. 1995). The *Fressola* court, in fact, lauded the one-sentence rule:

> [T]he one-sentence rule has no impact on the clarity of claims and has fostered the efficient processing of several million patent applications . . . Indeed, the Court believes that the one-sentence rule may even advance these statutory goals by encouraging claims that are generally more succinct than multiple-sentence claims of the same scope.

Id. at 1213–14. And specifically with respect to the statute, the court explained:

> While the statutory language may give the applicant ultimate control over the *substance* of his claim, it does not appear to speak to matters of pure *form*, such as the number of sentences allowed per claim; in other words, since an applicant can . . . make exactly the same claim in one sentence as he could in multiple sentences, the uniform format prescribed by the one-sentence rule does not interfere with his ability to claim whatever he "regards as his invention."

Id. at 1214 (emphasis original).

B. Preamble

The preamble is the initial portion of a claim. The preamble generally states the intended purpose or use of the invention and places it in a general category or field of technology. As a practical benefit, the Patent Office may use this broad categorization in assigning the technology to an appropriate examining group.

Beyond that administrative function, however, a significant conundrum of claim drafting relates to the impact of a preamble on defining the claimed invention. As discussed in Chapter 12, the preamble, as a general rule, does not limit the invention unless the specification indicates that the patent applicant included important defining portions of the claim in the preamble. *Catalina Mktg. Int'l, Inc. v. Coolsavings.com, Inc.*, 289 F.3d 801 (Fed. Cir. 2002). Thus, the hypothetical claim set forth above encompasses any book otherwise meeting the limitations, even a book containing words in lieu of pictographs. In other words, pictographs will not limit the invention of a book with slate pages, absent additional facts and circumstances.

C. Transitional phrase

The transitional phrase connects the preamble to the body of the claim. Beyond that utilitarian function, however, the transition is a legal term of art with great implications for the scope of the claim. In particular, the transitional phrase determines whether the claimed invention is "open"— meaning that the claim reads on any subject matter containing the recited limitations, even if additional, unrecited elements are also present–or "closed"—meaning that the presence of additional, unrecited elements removes subject matter from the scope of the claims. An experienced patent drafter will choose among the well-defined transitional phrases—"comprising," "consisting of," or "consisting essentially of"—to achieve readily discernible and, perhaps more importantly, intended claim scope.

"Comprising," the most common transition, signals an open claim. An open claim encompasses all subject matter that contains each and every limitation recited in the body of the claim. *See, e.g.*, *Genentech, Inc. v. Chiron Corp.*, 112 F.3d 495 (Fed. Cir. 1997). Additional features in the accused product or process do not avoid infringement. Consistent with this fundamental patent rule, structure claimed in the singular using the indefinite article "a" means "at least one" and encompasses a device with multiple structures. *See KCJ Corp. v. Kinetic Concepts, Inc.*, 223 F.3d 1351 (Fed. Cir. 2000). In the above example, this means that a book with a back cover is nonetheless within the scope of claim so long as it has a front cover and slate pages. In a more recent case, a "comprising" claim to a safety razor specifying "a first," "a second," and "a third" blade encompassed as well a razor with four blades. *Gillette Co. v. Energizer Holdings, Inc.*, 405 F.3d 1367 (Fed. Cir. 2005).

"Consisting of," which is less common, is incontrovertibly closed to additional elements. Subject matter is within the scope of a claim reciting "consisting of" as the transitional phrase only if the subject matter contains precisely the identical limitations in the claim–no more and no less. As one court commented, "a drafter uses the phrase 'con-

sisting of' to mean 'I claim what follows and nothing else.' " *Vehicular Techs. Corp. v. Titan Wheel
Int'l, Inc.*, 212 F.3d 1377, 1383 (Fed. Cir. 2000).
This restrictive transitional phrase often appears in
conjunction with other claims having open-ended
transitional phrases. A patent drafter may include a
narrow "consisting of" claim to ensure that this
claim does not ensnare prior art in a crowded field.
To illustrate, a claim that recites, "A composition
consisting of A and B," does not encompass a composition of A, B, and C. In the context of the safety
razor case, if the claim had read "a razor consisting
of first, second, and third blades," it would not have
covered a four-bladed razor. Nevertheless, a "consisting of" claim may encompass a composition consisting of A and B packaged in a container D,
because the container is an aspect unrelated to the
claimed composition. *See Norian Corp. v. Stryker
Corp.*, 363 F.3d 1321 (Fed. Cir. 2004).

Between "comprising" and "consisting of" is a
hybrid transitional phrase, "consisting essentially
of." This phrase also has an established legal meaning: the claim is open to additional elements so long
as those additional elements "do not materially
affect the basic and novel characteristics of the
invention." *PPG Indus. v. Guardian Indus. Corp.*,
156 F.3d 1351, 1354 (Fed. Cir. 1998). This term of
art has an unavoidable factual component—what effect is material? Thus, a wise drafter of a hybrid
claim sets forth in the written description or prosecution history the structural characteristics of a
material effect. *See, e.g., AK Steel Corp. v. Sollac*,

344 F.3d 1234 (Fed. Cir. 2003). To illustrate, a claim that recites, "A composition consisting essentially of A and B," encompasses a composition of A, B, and C only if C does not affect the basic and novel characteristics of the composition. That is, the composition of A, B, and C must be—in effect—insignificantly different than a composition of A and B. Because of its limited openness, savvy patentees prefer "consisting essentially of" over "consisting of" in circumstances where "comprising" is undesirable or unavailable. In the context of the safety razor case, if the claim had read "a razor consisting essentially of first, second, and third blades," it would only cover a four-bladed razor if the fourth blade had no material effect on the razor's shaving performance—an unlikely prospect.

While a patentee may, of course, use other terminology for the transitional phrase, ill-defined legal terms risk imprecision. For example, some phrases are typically open-ended and thus synonyms for "comprising." For instance, "including," "containing," and "characterized by" are generally considered open-ended. Other phrases, however, may have indeterminate legal implications. For instance, "having" may be open, *Crystal Semiconductor Corp. v. TriTech Microelectronics International, Inc.*, 246 F.3d 1336, 1348 (Fed. Cir. 2001), or closed, *Pieczenik v. Dyax Corp.*, 76 Fed. Appx. 293 (Fed. Cir. 2003), depending on the court's reading of the specification and other factors.

Similarly, another transitional phrase without a firm meaning, "composed of," signals a restricted claim on par with either "consisting of" or "consisting essentially of," depending on the circumstances of the case. *AFG Indus., Inc. v. Cardinal IG Co.*, 239 F.3d 1239, 1245 (Fed. Cir. 2001); *In re Bertsch*, 132 F.2d 1014, 1019–20 (CCPA 1942). Accordingly, patentees use transition phrases other than the established conventions at their own peril. Unfamiliar terms invite unintended limits on claim scope.

D. Body

The body must define the invention in clear and concise terms. The body must also set forth the structural or functional relations amongst the features of the invention. For ease of understanding, claims often signal primary limitations by indenting as well as alphanumeric indexing—(a), (b), (c), (1), (2), (3), and so forth. These indentations or alphanumeric labels facilitate prosecution by focusing the examiner on the basic limitations. These indentations also provide the public a simple, step-wise roadmap to understand the scope of the claim. In the example above, the body of the claim could be rewritten more effectively:

1. A book for a collection of pictographs comprising:

    (a) a front cover; and

    (b) a plurality of slate pages.

To define functional relationships, a patentee may claim the interaction between elements. In the above claim, the patentee could claim the connection between elements (a) and (b): "wherein the front cover is disconnectably connected to the plurality of pages." To those experienced in patent law, this language means that the front cover can be easily attached to and unattached from the slate pages.

The vocabulary of claims may seem somewhat anomalous. After all, it is utilitarian prose, not literature. And while the meaning of terms necessarily depends on a complex variety of factors (as discussed in Chapter 12), patent drafters may consult resources to learn the meaning of certain terms in past instances. *See generally* Irwin M. Aisenberg, ATTORNEY'S DICTIONARY OF PATENT CLAIMS (1985).

Each claim, of course, has its own unique body to define the unique invention. Nonetheless, a few general rules inform the claim drafting process. For example, a skilled drafter does not introduce nouns with definite articles, such as "the" or "said." Instead, an indefinite article, such as "a," "an," or "one," or another phrase like "a plurality of" or "several" will typically accompany the first appearance of a noun. After that introduction, definite articles may refer back to a specific limitation already present in the claim. For example, the wherein clause in the last hypothetical claim is a phrase using the definite article "the," and then only to refer back to a limitation, like the front cover, already set forth. A claim term lacking antecedent basis–that is, a term first introduced by a definite article—can make the entire claim indefinite. *But see Energizer Holdings, Inc. v. Int'l Trade Comm'n*, 435 F.3d 1366 (Fed. Cir. 2006).

As mentioned before, a skillful drafter precisely outlines the invented subject matter to capture the correct scope of the invention (and its foreseeable variants) while carving out the prior art and other invalidating subject matter. The body of the claim reflects that skill. Again, resources can assist with claim drafting, *see, e.g.*, Robert C. Faber, LANDIS ON MECHANICS OF PATENT CLAIM DRAFTING (5th ed. 2005), but experience is still the best teacher.

E. Independent and Dependent Claims

The bulk of § 112—paragraphs 3 through 5—sets forth the permissible format of a dependent claim, an abbreviated claim format. To take advantage of this shorthand, a dependent claim must reference an earlier claim and recite at least one additional limitation. In the above example, claim 2 is a typical dependent claim: "2. A book for a collection of pictographs according to claim 1, wherein the front cover consists of granite." This reference thus incorporates all the limitations of claim 1 as well as specifies the additional limitation of a granite cover. Claims 1 and 2 could also provide the bases for a further dependent claim: "3. A book for a collection of pictographs according to claim 1 or 2 further comprising a back cover." Claim 3 is a multiple dependent claim, which is permissible because it refers to other, non-multiple dependent claims in the alternative. For example, the statute prohibits the following claim: "4. A book for a collection of pictographs according to claim 1, 2, or 3, wherein the book has a mass no greater than 10 kilograms."

Claim 4, a multiple dependent claim, cannot depend from claim 3, another multiple dependent claim.

Astute patent drafters often include many dependent claims. Dependent claims are, by definition, more limited and specific than independent claims. These claims thus help ensure that the invention can more likely survive unforeseen invalidity attacks based on either unknown (or even unknowable) prior art or inadequate disclosure of the claimed subject matter. Broad independent claims are desirable to capture as much infringing behavior as possible, but the broader claim could encompass prior art as well. Thus, broad claims run a greater risk of invalidity. With these principles in mind, a patentee will seek the broadest independent claims that the Patent Office will allow, but at the same time successively narrow the claimed invention in a series of dependent claims to the most valuable embodiment at the time of prosecution.

In this way, claim drafters visualize claim scope as a pyramid. The broadest claim sits at the foundation of the claim pyramid and supports a series of sequentially narrower claims with the most preferred embodiment at the peak. The claims of intermediate scope capture a wider range of subject matter but reduce as well the risk of invalidation. For example, the following set of claims shows this narrowing culminating in two peaks, yet with varying degrees of intermediate claims:

1.   A book for a collection of pictographs comprising a front cover and a plurality of slate pages.

2. A book for a collection of pictographs according to claim 1, wherein the front cover comprises a rock.

3. A book for a collection of pictographs according to claim 2, wherein the rock is an igneous rock.

4. A book for a collection of pictographs according to claim 3, wherein the igneous rock is granite.

5. A book for a collection of pictographs according to claim 2, wherein the rock is gneiss.

Aside from narrowing claims to minimize the invalidity risk, a patentee may also use dependent claims to change the form of the claim. For instance, if claim 1 recites a complex chemical compound requiring a full page to depict all substitutable active groups, a patentee may reference that claim in a method of treatment claim, reciting "A method of treating hair loss comprising administering the compound of claim 1 to a mammal in need thereof."

III. SPECIAL CLAIM FORMATS

Although all claims must follow the one-sentence rule and typically contain a preamble, transitional phrase, and body, some claim formats–means-plus-function, product-by-process, Jepson, and Markush–deserve special attention. A functional claim, also known as a means-plus-function or § 112, ¶ 6, claim, recites a "means" for accomplishing function as set forth in the specification. A product-by-process claim, as the name suggests, claims a product made from the process steps recited in the claim. A Jepson claim recites a specific improvement over the prior art. Lastly, a claim with a Markush group recites alternatives cabined by a certain format.

A. Means–Plus–Function

1. Section 112, Paragraph 6

The Patent Act expressly authorizes a functional claim format: "An element in a claim for a combination may be expressed as a means or step for performing a specified function without the recital of structure, material, or acts in support thereof." 35 U.S.C. § 112, sixth paragraph. No other claim format gets an express statutory endorsement. This express endorsement, however, does not come without a price. The second clause of the same paragraph instructs that a means-plus-function claim "shall be construed to cover the corresponding structure, material, or acts described in the specification and equivalents thereof." *Id.*

The history of functional claiming begins long before § 112 became part of Title 35 in 1952. One of the earliest and most famous patent cases in the United States involved a functional claim. In the seminal case of *O'Reilly v. Morse*, 56 U.S. (15 How.) 62 (1854), Samuel Morse claimed the "use of [electricity] . . . for marking or printing intelligible characters." With this language, Morse really sought approval of a single means claim—now clearly forbidden under § 112 which requires "that the enabling disclosure of the specification be commensurate in scope with the claim." *In re Hyatt*, 708 F.2d 712, 714 (Fed. Cir. 1983) (citing *O'Reilly*, 56 U.S. at 112). At the one point that distinguished the invention from the prior art, Morse used sweeping functional language that could encompass innumerable ways to use electricity to print letters. The Supreme Court rejected the claim because its breadth encompassed far more than the telegraph machine Morse had in fact invented. *See O'Reilly*, 56 U.S. at 112–13.

After the famous *O'Reilly* case, however, functional claims began to serve the important role of allowing claim drafters to encompass many potential prior art elements in a combination claim. Claim drafters could relate aspects of the claim to the other features in the invention. For instance, a functional claim element could be used to designate a connection between two important features in a combination A and B. In the prior art, there could be many ways to connect A to B. But because the connector was a known component, the drafter would not want to include a claim specifying each separate "connecting means." The functional claim element resolved this problem by encompassing all prior art performing that function. Functional claims served this classical purpose for many years without difficulty.

The Supreme Court confronted again the breadth of functional claiming ninety years after *O'Reilly*. In 1946, the Supreme Court prohibited use of functional claims at the exact point of novelty in a combination claim. *See Halliburton Oil Well Ce-*

menting Co. v. Walker 329 U.S. 1 (1946). The Supreme Court foresaw that functional language could embrace every conceivable way of performing a function, thus claiming more than the inventor had invented or claiming subject matter already available to the public. To prevent "the broadness, ambiguity, and overhanging threat of the functional claim," *Halliburton*, 329 U.S. at 12, the Supreme Court prohibited inventor Walker's functional claim.

Patent drafters perceived *Halliburton* as a threat to the classical use of functional claims. Thus, a few years later, acknowledging the utility of the functional format to embrace conveniently a wide variety of ways to perform an element of a combination, Congress authorized means-plus-function claims. "This new language permits a patent applicant to express an element in a combination claim as a means for performing a function. The applicant need not recite structure, material, or acts in the claim's means-plus-function limitation." *Valmont Indus., Inc. v. Reinke Mfg. Co.*, 983 F.2d 1039, 1042 (Fed. Cir. 1993). In this respect, the 1952 Act overruled *Halliburton*. *See In re Donaldson Co.*, 16 F.3d 1189 (Fed. Cir. 1994) (*en banc*). In statutorily reversing the *Halliburton* decision, the new section 112 addressed the concern that a functional claim might be overbroad by limiting its meaning to the structures disclosed in the specification and their equivalents. *See In re Fuetterer*, 319 F.2d 259 (CCPA 1963).

2. Practical Significance

A simple example from a more recent patent case reveals the implications of the functional claim. The case involved a patent on a method of displaying non-prescription eyeglasses on racks. *See Al–Site Corp. v. VSI Int'l, Inc.*, 174 F.3d 1308 (Fed. Cir. 1999). The invention placed the eyeglasses on a tag and suspended the tag from a rack. The tag was attached to eyeglasses with a loop that encircled the nose bridge of the glasses. The claim defined that hanger mechanism as a "fastening means in engagement with said extension [of the tag] to maintain said loop closed." Under the statute, this claim points to the specification for the structure corresponding to fastening function. At that point, the specification could list innumerable alternative ways to fasten the loop. In fact, the specification listed only two means–buttons to close the loop and rivets to make the same attachment. Thus, this claim language ensures that the invention as claimed encompasses each of these embodiments and their equivalents. *See, e.g., Versa Corp. v. Ag–Bag Int'l Ltd.*, 392 F.3d 1325 (Fed. Cir. 2004). This claim format thus provides a convenient way to claim all fastening structures (and their equivalents) that are known to the inventor and listed in the specification without reciting those structures in the body of the claim. Section 112 therefore creates a convenient claim format. This claim format, however, receives different treatment from other claims.

For many years after enactment of the 1952 Act, functional claims received different treatment in administrative proceedings to acquire a patent than in litigation proceedings to enforce a patent. The PTO reasoned that claims should receive their "broadest reasonable interpretation" during prosecution (the standard process for evaluating claims at the PTO), *In re Prater*, 415 F.2d 1393, 1404–05 (CCPA 1969), and refused to apply § 112, ¶ 6 during examination. Thus, the PTO read means-plus-function claims according to their plain meaning–to cover all possible means for performing the recited function. The PTO did not confine means claims to the structure described in the specification and equivalents thereof. Thus, the PTO rejected more functional claims than the language of section 112 required. Meanwhile, courts enforcing patents applied the statutory language, limiting functional claims to the disclosed structure and equivalents.

This disharmony between PTO practice and the statute came before the Federal Circuit in the case of *In re Donaldson Co.*, 16 F.3d 1189 (Fed. Cir. 1994) (*en banc*). In simple terms, the invention was a dust collector with flexible diaphragm-like walls. To clean the collector, the operator reversed the air pressure causing the walls to flex in the opposite direction and dislodge caked dust into a bin below. The application claimed: "means, responsive to pressure increases in said chamber caused by said cleaning means, for moving particulate matter in a downward direction." The PTO rejected this claim over the Swift prior art reference. Swift also cleaned dust collectors by reversing air pulses. In Swift, however, the dust collector walls were sloped, not flexible. The PTO nonetheless reasoned that sloped walls were a means responsive to air pressure for moving dust downward. The PTO refused to consult the structure in the specification which recited flexible walls as the claimed means. Therefore, the PTO rejected the application as obvious in light of the prior art, particularly the Swift reference.

On appeal, the Federal Circuit, in very insistent tones, instructed the PTO to follow § 112, ¶ 6: "Per our holding, the 'broadest reasonable interpretation' that an examiner may give means-plus-function language is that statutorily mandated in paragraph six. Accordingly, the PTO may not disregard the structure disclosed in the specification corresponding to such language when rendering a patentability determination." *Donaldson*, 16 F.3d at 1194–95. Following this instruction, the Federal Circuit construed the means clause as limited to the flexible walls disclosed in the application's specification and equivalents thereof. Because the Swift reference did not teach or suggest flexible walls, the court reversed the PTO's obviousness determination.

Of course, the significance of § 112, ¶ 6, for the examination of, as well as the enforcement of, patents prompts the inevitable question: What precise set of words invokes the procedures and limitations of § 112? This question has troubled both examiners at the PTO and courts enforcing exclusive rights. Therefore, the Federal Circuit has devised some guidelines for determining that particular language in a claim invokes this unusual treatment:

> Specifically, if the word "means" appears in a claim element in combination with a function, it is presumed to be a means-plus-function element to which § 112, ¶ 6 applies. Nevertheless, according to its express terms, § 112, ¶ 6 governs only claim elements that do not recite sufficient structural limitations. Therefore, the presumption that § 112, ¶ 6 applies is overcome if the claim itself recites sufficient structure or material for performing the claimed function.

> Although use of the phrase "means for" (or "step for") is not the only way to invoke § 112, ¶ 6, that terminology typically invokes § 112, ¶ 6 while other formulations generally do not. Therefore, when an element of a claim does not use the term "means," treatment as a means-plus-function claim element is generally not appropriate. However, when it is apparent that the element invokes purely functional terms, without the additional recital of specific structure or material for performing that function, the claim element may be a means-plus-function element despite the lack of express means-plus-function language.

Al-Site Corp. v. VSI Int'l, Inc., 174 F.3d 1308, 1318 (Fed. Cir. 1999) (citations omitted). Thus, a claim including the word "means" is presumptively a means-plus-function claim; a claim without the word "means" is presumptively not a functional claim.[6]

As mandated by the statute, an alleged infringement does not fall within the scope of the claims unless the accused device contains the disclosed structure or its equivalent. The crux of almost all infringement cases, however, is not the disclosed structure; rather, the dispute typically centers on whether an undisclosed structure in the accused device qualifies as an equivalent. The eyeglasses case mentioned above confronted that very question. In *Al-Site*, the patentee claimed a device for displaying a pair of eyeglasses on a rack that permits a customer to test the fit and look of the eyewear without removing the display hanger. 174 F.3d at 1315. In particular, the claim recited a "fastening means" for connecting the hanger portion to the pair of eyeglasses. Because the specification disclosed only mechanical structures—a rivet and a button—as the structure corresponding to the fastening means, the court properly instructed the jury that the claim was limited to those structures (and their equivalents). The accused device used an adhesive to adjoin a loop securing the hanger to the eyewear. Although mechanical fasteners might seem very different from chemical adhesives, the trial record established that adhesives, rivets, and staples were equivalent—that is, insubstantially different—to a person having ordinary skill in the art.

6. The court's reference to step-plus-function claims is based on the statute, which recognizes such claims. Due to their infrequency, step-plus-function claims remain an enigma. *Cf. Seal–Flex, Inc. v. Athletic Track & Court Constr.*, 172 F.3d 836 (Fed. Cir. 1999) (Rader, J., concurring).

The court, under the very deferential treatment accorded to jury verdicts, upheld the verdict of infringement.

Furthermore, the patentee must provide disclosure in the specification that corresponds to the means-plus-function limitation, and clearly links the functional language to that structure. Indeed, "structure disclosed in the specification is 'corresponding' structure only if the specification or prosecution history clearly links or associates that structure to the function recited in the claim. This duty to link or associate structure to function is the *quid pro quo* for the convenience of employing § 112, ¶ 6." *B. Braun Med., Inc. v. Abbott Labs.*, 124 F.3d 1419, 1424 (Fed. Cir. 1997). In fact, a failure to disclose the structure may render the claim indefinite. *See, e.g., Budde v. Harley–Davidson, Inc.*, 250 F.3d 1369 (Fed. Cir. 2001). Indeed, a specification cannot simply recite that a claimed function be performed by known methods or using known equipment and satisfy the definiteness requirement for a means-plus-function element; some structure must be disclosed. *Biomedino, LLC v. Waters Techs. Corp.*, 490 F.3d 946 (Fed. Cir. 2007).

3. Equivalents Under Section 112, Paragraph 6, and the Doctrine of Equivalents

The doctrine of equivalents, which prohibits infringers from using technology that is insubstantially different from the claimed invention (as discussed more fully in Chapter 13), and equivalents of a limitation in means-plus-function format are, unsurprisingly, closely related, but with some important differences. To begin with similarities between the related concepts, the doctrine of equivalents and § 112, ¶ 6 equivalents both use a similar evaluation methodology. Both test for "insubstantial differences" between the claimed and accused products or processes for the doctrine of equivalents or between the structures in the specification defining the means and prior art structures (when the PTO examines for patentability) or accused structures (when a court tests for infringement) for § 112, ¶ 6. *See Valmont Indus., Inc. v. Reinke Mfg. Co.*, 983 F.2d 1039, 1043 (Fed. Cir. 1993).

The related concepts share another similarity. Both the doctrine and structural equivalents apply on an element-by-element basis for infringement. *See Warner–Jenkinson Co., Inc. v. Hilton Davis Chem. Co.*, 520 U.S. 17 (1997). This element-by-element application, however, requires a clarification that initiates an examination of the differences.

One important difference between the related concepts involves the effect of prior art. The prior art constrains the range of permissible equivalents under the doctrine of equivalents. *See Wilson Sporting Goods Co. v. David Geoffrey & Assoc.*, 904 F.2d 677 (Fed. Cir. 1990). The Federal Circuit has indicated that this principle does not apply to equivalency under § 112, ¶ 6:

Although under the doctrine of equivalents prior art restricts the extent to which patent protection can be equitably extended beyond the claims to cover an accused device, the policies underlying that concept are not served by restricting [§ 112,6] claim *limitations* in the same manner. Claim limitations may, and often do, read on the prior art, particularly in combination patents.

Intel Corp. v. U.S. Int'l Trade Comm'n, 946 F.2d 821, 842 (Fed. Cir. 1991) (emphasis in original) (internal citations omitted).

A second difference relates to assessment of function. As discussed above, § 112, ¶ 6 requires identity of function, not simply the substantially similar function permitted under the doctrine of equivalents. *Chiuminatta Concrete Concepts, Inc. v. Cardinal Indus., Inc.*, 145 F.3d 1303 (Fed. Cir. 1998). Thus, while lack of an identical function prevents infringement of a § 112, ¶ 6 claim term, it will not necessarily preclude infringement under the doctrine.

The most important difference, however, is the timing of the assessment of equivalence under the doctrine and under § 112, ¶ 6. Section 112 specifies a procedure under which a "claim shall be construed." This difference flows from the elemental principle that a claim's meaning is set at the time of filing. *Phillips v. AWH Corp.*, 415 F.3d 1303 (Fed. Cir. 2005) (*en banc*). Thus, the literal meaning of a means-plus-function claim element must be set upon filing, meaning that any structural equivalents must be known and in place at the time of filing. Because claim scope may not vary after filing, structural equivalents would not include what the

Supreme Court called "after-arising equivalents." These "after-arising equivalents" are substitutes for claim terms known to those of skill in the art that arise due to technological advances after patent filing.

In contrast, the inquiry for infringement under the doctrine of equivalents takes place at the time of infringement. *See Warner–Jenkinson*, 520 U.S. at 37. Thus, the doctrine of equivalents, unlike structural equivalents under § 112, ¶ 6, embraces "after-arising equivalents":

> One important difference between § 112, ¶ 6 and the doctrine of equivalents involves the timing of the separate analyses for an "insubstantial change." As this court has recently clarified, a structural equivalent under § 112 must have been available at the time of the [filing] of the claim. An equivalent structure or act under § 112 cannot embrace technology developed after the issuance of the patent because the literal meaning of a claim is fixed upon its issuance. An "after arising equivalent" infringes, if at all, under the doctrine of equivalents.... Furthermore, under § 112, ¶ 6, the accused device must perform the identical function as recited in the claim element while the doctrine of equivalents may be satisfied when the function performed by the accused device is only substantially the same.

Al-Site, 174 F.3d at 1320–21.

This explanation offers a good opportunity to return to the "fastening means" in the eyeglasses display rack case. The patentee claimed "means for fastening" and described rivets and buttons in the specification. Suppose Velcro® fasteners were invented a few years after the patent issued. Would those Velcro fasteners literally infringe the "fastening means" language and thus qualify as structural equivalents? The Federal Circuit answered that question in *Al-Site*:

A proposed equivalent must have arisen at a definite period in time, i.e., either before or after patent [filing]. If before, a § 112, ¶ 6 structural equivalents analysis applies and any analysis for equivalent structure under the doctrine of equivalents collapses into the § 112, ¶ 6 analysis. If after, a non-textual infringement analysis proceeds under the doctrine of equivalents.

Id. at 1320 n.2. Thus, the Velcro® will not literally infringe the means language, but it may infringe under the doctrine of equivalents. It will not infringe literally because the meaning of the claim is fixed from the time of issuance and cannot embrace "after-arising technology." The doctrine of equivalents, however, can embrace "after-arising technology."

Another important difference between the doctrine of equivalents and structural equivalents under § 112 is the relevant structure (material or acts as well) to which equivalents apply. Section 112 refers, of course, to the structure in the specification, while the doctrine refers to the structure in the claims. In sum, the doctrine of equivalents and structural equivalents are related concepts, albeit with non-trivial differences in terms of timing, scope, and purpose.

4. International Treatment

The United States is alone in its unique treatment of functional claims. Until amendments in 1996, Japan often restricted functional claims to the specific exemplified embodiments. The prior statute required that claims set forth the indispensable features of the invention, but Article 36, Paragraph 5, now states: "The applicant has to state, claim by claim, all the features which he considers necessary for identifying the invention for which a patent is sought." Furthermore, the European Patent Office permits functional rather than structural claim limitations if the invention cannot be defined structurally without restricting the scope of the invention.

B. Product-by-Process

1. Purpose

Before the advent of sophisticated reverse engineering and analytical technology, product-by-process claims served an important function. In some circumstances, an inventor could create a product (usually a new molecular structure) without knowing its precise structure or characteristics. The inventor thus did not have any way to precisely claim the product's structure. In that instance, the law permitted the inventor to claim the product in the only way possible—by claiming the product made according to the inventor's fabrication process.

In more modern practice, of course, an inventor can practically always claim a product according to its structure. A product claim is very strong and desirable because it protects that claimed structure however made or used. Thus, if another innovator makes the same product by a new process (even a more efficient process), the first inventor of the structure retains the exclusive right to that structure. To illustrate with a hypothetical, an inventor could make an excellent new shoe polish out of a petroleum byproduct and obtain a product patent on the new entity. If another innovator finds a cheaper way to make the patented polish out of timber byproducts, the first inventor still has the exclusive right to the new product. The second innovator may obtain a patent on the timber by-product fabrication process, but not a patent on the existing structure.

Similarly, if another innovator finds a new use of the structure, the first inventor still has an exclusive right to the product for all of its uses, even those he did not invent himself. In our hypothetical, another innovator learns that the shoe polish composition grows hair when applied to human skin. Again, the second innovator gets a process patent on a method of using the old product (to grow hair), but the first inventor still has an exclusive right to the product for all of its uses.

As noted earlier, a product patent is more valuable than a process patent because it gives the patentee an exclusive right to the new structure however made or used. Moreover a product can usually be made by many processes. A mere change in the order of the steps or slight alterations in starting materials or catalysts can constitute a new process (sometimes with more efficient results). Thus a process patent can often be circumvented with a new process to reach the same result, but a product patent is not so easily avoided.

Returning to the product-by-process format, this type of claim is a product claim. Therefore, it gives the patentee entitlement to the structure however made or used. Nonetheless the claim itself recites no structure but only a fabrication process. Thus, with a claim to a single process, the applicant has received exclusive rights to the product even if made by a variety of other methods. Accordingly, this claim form has created some difficulties for courts in determining its precise reach and scope.

As noted above, this claim format had its genesis in assisting an applicant who could not describe a new product other than by the method of its fabrication. More recently, however, some applicants have sought protection not only on the structure of, for example, a chemical compound but also on the process of making the structure. In this second case, the patentee may seek a product-by-process claim as a fall-back, providing protection of the product even if his understanding of the structure later turns out to be inaccurate or erroneous. After all, this alternative product claim could cover that product without regard to its manufacture, even though the claim specifically recites a step-wise procedure. *See SmithKline Beecham Corp. v. Apotex Corp.*, 439

F.3d 1312 (Fed. Cir. 2006); *Scripps Clinic & Research Found. v. Genentech, Inc.*, 927 F.2d 1565 (Fed. Cir. 1991).

Construing a product-by-process claim in this manner, however, contradicts the historical justification for the claim format. The claim format was developed in a prior era lacking the sophisticated analytical equipment able to detect structures, which are available to modern scientists. For example, in deciding an infringement case with an early version of a product-by-process claim, the Supreme Court held that the same chemical produced by a different process did not infringe: "Every patent for a product or composition of matter must identify it so that it can be recognized aside from the description of the process for making it, or else nothing can be held to infringe the patent which is not made by that process." *Cochrane v. Badische Anilin & Soda Fabrik*, 111 U.S. 293, 310 (1884). Nearly a century later, courts continued to recognize that product-by-process claims were limited by the claimed process. *In re Hughes*, 496 F.2d 1216 (CCPA 1974). Indeed, in *Atlantic Thermoplastics Co. v. Faytex Corp.*, 970 F.2d 834 (Fed. Cir. 1992), the court examined the history of product-by-process claims and held that, contrary to the one-year old *Scripps Clinic* decision, product-by-process claims cannot be construed to ignore the recited process limitations.[7]

7. The holdings of *Scripps Clinic* and *Atlantic Thermoplastics* remain somewhat irreconcilable. *See SmithKline Beecham Corp. v. Apotex Corp.*, 453 F.3d 1346 (Fed. Cir. 2006) (Rader, J., dissenting from denial of the suggestion for rehearing *en banc*). Although some uncertainty may exist, prudent patentees reasonably assume that product-by-process claims are process specific.

2. International Treatment

The United States is not alone in recognizing product-by-process claims. For example, the Guidelines for Examination in the European Patent Office explain:

Claims for products defined in terms of a process of manufacture are allowable only if the products as such fulfil the requirements for patentability, i.e. inter alia that they are new and inventive. A product is not rendered novel merely by the fact that it is produced by means of a new process (see T 150/82, OJ 7/1984, 309). A claim defining a product in terms of a process is to be construed as a claim to the product as such. The claim may for instance take the form "Product X obtainable by process Y". Irrespective of whether the term "obtainable", "obtained", "directly obtained" or an equivalent wording is used in the product-by-process claim, it is still directed to the product per se and confers absolute protection upon the product (see T 20/94, not published in OJ).

Part C, Chapter III, Paragraph 4.7b. Furthermore, Japanese law allows the use of product-by-process claims in limited circumstances. EXAMINATION GUIDELINES FOR PATENT AND UTILITY MODEL IN JAPAN, Part I, Chap. 1, § 2.2.2.1(7). *See also Kirin Amgen v. Hoechst Marion Carousel Ltd.*, [2005] 1 All ER 667.

C. Jepson

A Jepson claim expressly recites in the claim the prior art (usually in the preamble) and then specifies and claims an improvement on that prior art. *See* 37 C.F.R. § 1.75(e). For example, the following is a Jepson claim: "A book for a collection of pictographs comprising a front cover and a plurality of slate pages, *wherein the improvement* comprises the front cover consisting of granite." The underscored phrase, or the use of something similar, alerts the Patent Office and the public that the patentee admits everything preceding that phrase, that is, everything in the preamble, is prior art. 37 C.F.R. § 1.75(e)(3). Once admitted, the preamble may form a basis of an obviousness rejection, even if it was erroneously designated prior art. *In re Fout*, 675 F.2d 297 (CCPA 1982); *but see Reading & Bates Constr. Co. v. Baker Energy Res. Corp.*, 748 F.2d 645 (Fed. Cir. 1984) (holding that an inventor's own work in the preamble of a Jepson claim may not be treated as an admission of prior art). Due to the perils of using this claim format, skilled patent drafters avoid it unless necessary to obtain a patent in a crowded field. In Europe, on the other hand, the EPO often insists on the use of this format.

D. Markush

Named for a onetime patent applicant, *Ex Parte Markush*, 1925 C.D. 126 (Comm'r Pat. 1925), claims reciting a Markush group permit a patentee to aggregate substitutable limitations and claim them in the alternative. The following is an example: "A book for a collection of pictographs comprising a front cover and a plurality of slate pages, wherein the front cover comprises a rock *selected from the group consisting of granite, sandstone, and gneiss.*"

The underscored phrase is the Markush group. Thus, the claim encompasses front covers made from any of those rocks. That is, the claimed genus of rocks includes the species of granite, sandstone, and gneiss. The only formatting requirement is that the group be closed—"consisting of" or a similarly closed term must introduce the group. The only substantive requirement is that the named species share a common property that explains their grouping. Although not constrained to specific subject matter, Markush groups are commonplace in claiming a chemical invention. Within the chemical practice, a claim will often recite variables, such as R, R^1, X, X^1, or the like, which are later defined by Markush groups.

This claiming technique is not unique to the United States—in fact, German chemists and their patent agents initially used variables to tabulate similar compounds, and this practice, which later morphed into Markush groups, traveled stateside when these applications were translated and filed in the United States. In modern times, the European Patent Office permits these claims as well:

Where a single claim defines (chemical or non-chemical) alternatives, i.e. a so-called "Markush grouping", unity of invention should be considered to be present if the alternatives are of a similar nature (see III, 3.7).

When the Markush grouping is for alternatives of chemical compounds, they should be regarded as being of a similar nature where:

(i) all alternatives have a common property or activity, and

(ii) a common structure is present, i.e. a significant structural element is shared by all of the alternatives, or all alternatives belong to a recognised class of chemical compounds in the art to which the invention pertains.

GUIDELINES FOR EXAMINATION IN THE EUROPEAN PATENT OFFICE, Part C, Chapter III, Paragraph 4.7b. Similarly, Japan similarly allows the use of Markush claims in limited circumstances. *See* EXAMINATION GUIDELINES FOR PATENT AND UTILITY MODEL IN JAPAN, Part I, Chap. 1, §§ 2.2.2.1(4), 2.2.3.1(2).

IV. DEFINITENESS

A. Test

The Patent Act requires that the "claims particularly point[ ] out and distinctly claim[ ] the subject matter which the applicant regards as his invention." 35 U.S.C. § 112, paragraph 2. The claims, which appear at the end of the specification, must define the invention. These "particular" and "distinct" boundaries notify the public and the Patent Office of the scope of the invention. Accordingly, if the claims are too vague, indecipherable, or impenetrable, they do not meet a substantive requirement for patentability: definiteness.

The basic rule is that a person of ordinary skill in the art must be able to understand the claims when read in light of the specification. *Orthokinetics, Inc. v. Safety Travel Chairs, Inc.*, 806 F.2d 1565 (Fed.

Cir. 1986). In *Orthokinetics*, the patentee claimed a collapsible wheelchair that could be inserted into a car. The trial court ruled that, as a matter of law, the claims were invalid as indefinite because the patentee did not specify the dimensions of the wheelchair necessary to fit different makes and models of cars—a Checkers cab or a Hummer certainly has a different geometry than a Volkswagen bug. The Federal Circuit reversed, specifically noting that testimony showed that a person of ordinary skill in the art would understand and potentially adapt the claimed invention to fit vehicles of various sizes. This result makes sense because otherwise the applicant would have needed to draft a different claim for every type of automobile. Moreover, as the court observed, the necessary variations to accommodate different automobile models would be easily obtained by one of ordinary skill in this art in light of the patent's disclosures. Of course, this particular invention also lies in a rather predictable field of technology.

The amount and quality of claim detail necessary to satisfy the definiteness requirement varies with the scope of the claims, the complexity of the subject matter, and the level of ordinary skill in the art. *Miles Labs., Inc. v. Shandon Inc.*, 997 F.2d 870 (Fed. Cir. 1993). Courts examine and determine the scope of the claims as a matter of law, but review the other two definiteness variables as questions of fact. *See, e.g., BJ Servs. Co. v. Halliburton Energy Servs., Inc.*, 338 F.3d 1368 (Fed. Cir. 2003). Nevertheless, "[i]ndefiniteness is also a legal determination arising out of the court's performance of its duty construing the claims." *Id.* at 1372. In fact, the Federal Circuit has commented that difficult questions of claim construction do not render claims indefinite:

> Under a broad concept of indefiniteness, all but the clearest claim construction issues could be regarded as giving rise to invalidating indefiniteness in the claims at issue. But we have not adopted that approach to the law of indefiniteness. We have not insisted that claims be plain on their face in order to avoid condemnation for indefiniteness; rather, what we have asked is that the claims be amenable to construction, however difficult that task may be. If a claim is insolubly ambiguous, and no narrowing construction can properly be adopted, we have held the claim indefinite.

Exxon Research & Eng'g Co. v. United States, 265 F.3d 1371, 1375 (Fed. Cir. 2001) (citations omitted). Thus, the standard for indefiniteness requires a near impossibility of discerning the meaning of the claims. And even where, for example, a patentee coins a term—by definition, it lacks a commonly understood meaning by persons of ordinary skill in the art—without also defining the new term in the specification, the claims do not lack definiteness if the constituents of the new term allow a person of ordinary skill in the art to reasonably infer a meaning. *Bancorp Servs., L.L.C. v. Hartford Life Ins. Co.*, 359 F.3d 1367 (Fed. Cir. 2004).

B. Relative Terminology & Words of Approximation

The definiteness requirement also comes into play with claim terms like "substantially" or "about" or "approximately." Wary of the strict limits of absolute specificity, patentees often define their inventions with relative terminology or words of approximation. Although commonly encountered, the definiteness inquiry remains the same: if a person of ordinary skill in the art would understand (even with great difficulty) the scope of the invention, relative claim terms such as "close proximity" are not indefinite. *Rosemount, Inc. v. Beckman Instruments, Inc.*, 727 F.2d 1540, 1547 (Fed. Cir. 1984).

Nevertheless, words of approximation—pejoratively called "weasel words"—cause greater concern due to their ubiquity in claims. Their ubiquity, though, is tolerated when they accommodate minor variations within the scope of the invention in accordance with the exactness demanded by the technological field and by the prior art. *Andrew Corp. v. Gabriel Elecs., Inc.*, 847 F.2d 819 (Fed. Cir. 1988). For example, in *Verve, LLC v. Crane Cams, Inc.*, 311 F.3d 1116 (Fed. Cir. 2002), the court reversed a judgment that claims reciting "a substantially constant wall thickness" were indefinite because the trial court improperly failed to consider the understanding of a person of ordinary skill in the art. Similarly, other words, such as "about" and "approximately," are permissible to provide some leeway in avoiding an unforgiving (and unnecessary) numerical limitation. In some circumstances, however, the claimed subject matter requires precision at odds with words of approximation, particularly where the prior art abuts against the imprecise limitation. *See Amgen, Inc. v. Chugai Pharm. Co.*, 927 F.2d 1200 (Fed. Cir. 1991). Thus, each circumstance must be evaluated on its own terms, even if words of degree or approximation routinely provide a discernable claim scope in most circumstances.

CHAPTER 11

ISSUES IN PATENT ACQUISITION

I. INTRODUCTION

As discussed in Chapter 2, an inventor must apply for a patent with the Patent Office, which examines the inventor's application for compliance with both formal and substantive requirements. Various issues may arise in connection with patent acquisition, including correct inventorship, inequitable conduct, and double patenting.

Specifically, only an inventor may apply for a patent. In the event that a patent has multiple inventors, this simple requirement becomes more complex. For instance, even if an inventor only contributes to a single claim in a patent with many claims, that "lesser" inventor is not "lesser" under the law and instead enjoys co-ownership of the entire patent.

During the application process, a patent applicant also has a duty of candor. Under that duty, the applicant must disclose various forms of relevant information to the Patent Office. If an applicant intentionally withholds relevant information, the patentee can lose the right to enforce the entire patent.

Finally, an inventor may only receive a single patent for each invention (or obvious variants of the invention). Thus, if an applicant attempts to claim the same invention in different applications, the doctrine of double patenting prevents the inventor from using this device to undeservedly extend the patent term.

II. INVENTORSHIP

Under U.S. law, only the actual inventor (or set of inventors) receives a patent on the invention. Although a simple proposition, declaration of the inventors often gives rise to disputes in patent litigation. To avoid these problems, the application must name all of the true inventors—and only the true inventors. Even if the application lists incorrect inventors at the time of filing, the declaration of inventorship must be corrected upon discovery of the erroneous list. In fact, 35 U.S.C. § 102(f) establishes that only a true inventor is entitled to a patent. A patent derived from someone other than the named inventor is invalid.

A. Test for Inventorship

The Patent Act expressly requires that only true inventors may file for a patent. 35 U.S.C. § 111(a). In the case of multiple inventors, they must jointly apply for a patent, "even though (1) they did not physically work together or at the same time, (2) each did not make the same type or amount of contribution, or (3) each did not make a contribution to the subject matter of every claim of the patent." 35 U.S.C. § 116. Even though their contributions need not be concurrent, qualitatively equivalent, or quantitatively equivalent, the timing of their contributions is pivotal. Each inventor must contribute to the conception of the invention as claimed.

As discussed in Chapter 7, conception—not reduction to practice—is the touchstone of inventorship. Consider for a moment a research team led by an eminent scientist. The scientist may originate an idea and then instruct his assistants to make the idea work. The assistants would generally use well-known research or experimental techniques to comply with the instructions. These technicians help to reduce the invention to practice, but do not qualify as inventors. Even the talented technician who supplements the inventor's work with significant research skills does not become an inventor. On the other hand, the talented technician may also modify the invention during the work. That modification, reflected in the claims, makes the assistant a joint inventor. In other words, to invent, the technician or assistant must actually conceive of some part of the invention.

These conception rules mean that an inventor must contribute to the conception of the claimed subject matter, not merely to the disclosure of the patent. The Federal Circuit applied these principles in *Board of Education of Florida State University v. American Bioscience, Inc.*, 333 F.3d 1330 (Fed. Cir. 2003). In that case, a group of researchers worked together on related projects. A smaller part of the team conceived of a new chemical compound. The full team then worked to produce the new product. None of the team members beyond the small inventive group were inventors. None of the rest contributed to the conception of the claimed invention. The claims recited a chemical compound. Therefore, no one beyond the originators conceived of the compound with all of its components, a requirement for conception in the chemical field. Even though several others had specific parts of the claimed compounds in mind at the time, they had not conceived of or contributed to the entire invention. *See* Chapter 7.

Once a patent issues, the law creates a presumption that the named inventors are the correct and only inventors. *Hess v. Advanced Cardiovascular Sys., Inc.*, 106 F.3d 976 (Fed. Cir. 1997). This presumption discourages frivolous inventorship disputes. In *Hess*, for instance, a laboratory assistant simply implemented the invention as conceived by another.

If the wrong inventor files and prosecutes the patent, the correct inventors may petition the Patent Office to issue a certificate of correction naming the proper inventors. 35 U.S.C. § 256. Alternatively, an omitted inventor may request that a court, under the same statutory provision, order the Patent Office to correct the patent's inventorship. Similar to proving inventorship elsewhere, an allegedly omitted inventor must corroborate any claims of conception with contemporaneous documents, oral testimony, or other circumstantial evidence. *See* Chapter 7. Notably, if inventorship can be corrected under either one of the provisions of § 256, the patent is not invalid.[8]

B.   Consequences of Incorrect Inventorship

Even though not invalidating, incorrect inventorship can render a patent practically worthless. The default rule, in fact, provides that "each of the joint owners of a patent may make, use, offer to sell, or sell the patented invention within the United States, or import the patented invention into the United States, without the consent of and without accounting to other owners." 35 U.S.C. § 262. Even though this section refers to "owners" and not inventors, an inventor is the first owner of a patent. That inventor may, of course, assign his rights in a patent (or a patent application) to another, 35 U.S.C. § 261, but "an invention presumptively belongs to its creator." *Teets v. Chromalloy Gas Turbine Corp.*, 83 F.3d 403, 407 (Fed. Cir. 1996). And a contributor to even one claim of a patent is a co-inventor on the whole patent; there is no such creature as a partial inventor on a patent—a person is either a full-fledged inventor or not. 35 U.S.C. § 116. A contributor to a single claim, therefore, can effectively erase the benefits of the entire patent to the primary inventor.

Ethicon, Inc. v. United States Surgical Corp., 135 F.3d 1456 (Fed. Cir. 1998), tells the chilling story of an inventing relationship gone awry. As is often the

8. A change in inventorship under § 256 may also affect inventorship for a nondomestic patent application, such as a PCT application. *See Chou v. Univ. of Chicago*, 254 F.3d 1347 (Fed. Cir. 2001).

case with inventorship issues, this case featured an eminent scientist and an assistant. The eminent scientist, Dr. InBae Yoon, was a physician and noted leader in the field of surgical devices. Yoon already had many patents on trocars, the sharp instruments that open a small hole for endoscopic surgery. Yoon hired an assistant, Young Jae Choi, to help with the mechanics of a new safety trocar that would detect penetration past tough muscle tissue and prevent stab wounds to the organs beyond. Choi, an electronics technician without even a college degree, collaborated with Yoon on the safety trocars. Choi and Yoon worked together for about a year and a half before Choi left the relationship. Soon thereafter Yoon filed a patent application disclosing and claiming safety trocars with himself as the sole inventor.

Yoon and his exclusive licensee asserted two claims of the patent against U.S. Surgical. Meantime U.S. Surgical obtained a license from Choi (for a relatively small fee) and asserted that Choi was a co-inventor of the safety trocars. The district court, with the Federal Circuit's concurrence, found that Choi contributed to a few limitations in two claims (out of the patent's 55) that Yoon did not even assert against U.S. Surgical. Choi corroborated his contributions to those few claims with some contemporaneous sketches depicting the subject matter. Due to Choi's inventive contribution (no matter how nominal), he shared ownership of the entire patent with Yoon. As a co-owner, Choi was free to license the invention to U.S. Surgical. Yoon could not maintain the lawsuit against U.S. Surgical. Effectively, Yoon was deprived of the core patent right—the ability to exclude another from making, using, or selling the patented technology—because he omitted Choi, the co-inventor of some subject matter, from the patent. Yoon, of course, could have avoided this devastating consequence by requiring Choi, upon entering his employ, assign to Yoon the rights to all inventions arising from the collaboration.

III. INEQUITABLE CONDUCT

A. Purpose

Although just two entities—the applicant and the Patent Office—take part in prosecution of a patent application, the grant of a patent affects the public as a whole. And because patent prosecution is *ex parte*, the interested public, particularly the applicant's competitors, has no input during the acquisition of the patent right. Furthermore, the Patent Office has no laboratories, no test facilities, no dedicated scientists, and no economists to evaluate the assertions of a patent applicant relating to the characteristics or commercial success of embodiments of the claimed subject matter. In other words, absent compelling circumstances, such as a violation of immutable laws of physics giving rise to a rejection under § 101, the Patent Office does not challenge the veracity of a patent applicant's statements or declarations.

Because the system relies on the truthfulness of its participants, it imposes a duty of candor on the patent applicant. The applicant thus has a duty to disclose all material information to the patent examiner. This requirement manifests itself not in a statute-based condition for patentability but in inequitable conduct—an equitable doctrine that carries many of the implications of a regulatory condition. This duty of candor, furthermore, extends beyond the patent applicant or patentee and includes the prosecuting attorney, "because the knowledge and actions of applicant's attorney are chargeable to applicant." *FMC Corp. v. Manitowoc Co.*, 835 F.2d 1411, 1415 n.8 (Fed. Cir. 1987).

At one time, the prevalence of charges of inequitable conduct during litigation caused the Federal Circuit to lament that "the habit of charging inequitable conduct in almost every major patent case has become an absolute plague." *Burlington Indus., Inc. v. Dayco Corp.*, 849 F.2d 1418, 1422 (Fed. Cir. 1988). The plague continues today; alleged infringers invariably seek out even the slenderest factual support for asserting inequitable conduct for strategic and tactical reasons. The strategy is simple: a charge of inequitable conduct permits the alleged infringer to paint the patentee as unscrupulous and undeserving of its patent (thus offsetting to some degree the presumption of validity), provides an opportunity to obtain discovery into otherwise privileged or immune documents (especially the prosecuting attorney's papers), and creates satellite litigation focused on the patentee's conduct and credibility.

Due to the allure of even marginally justified claims of inequitable conduct, defendants often assert this charge as a matter of course. For this reason, the Federal Circuit has attempted to curtail its application by requiring that the factual underpinnings be proven by clear and convincing evidence. This heightened burden of proof, however, does not eliminate the benefits, whether perceived or real, in allegations of inequitable conduct. Just as importantly, though, this heightened burden of proof also does not concomitantly reduce any incentive to fully disclose any prior art that is relevant to the claimed subject matter.

Notably, inequitable conduct renders an entire patent—not just the affected claims—unenforceable. *Kingsdown Med. Consultants, Ltd. v. Hollister Inc.*, 863 F.2d 867 (Fed. Cir. 1988). Indeed, inequitable conduct occurring in the prosecution of one application can, in certain circumstances, infect the descendents of that application's family. *See, e.g.*, *Consolidated Aluminum Corp. v. Foseco Int'l Ltd.*, 910 F.2d 804 (Fed. Cir. 1990); *but see Baxter Int'l, Inc. v. McGaw, Inc.*, 149 F.3d 1321 (Fed. Cir. 1998). Furthermore, a patent applicant may "cure" any inequitable conduct that may have occurred during prosecution only by expressly notifying the Patent Office of the misrepresentation and correcting that misrepresentation during prosecution. In such a case, however, there are three steps that the applicant must take:

The first requirement ... is that he expressly advise the PTO of ... [the misrepresentation], stating specifically wherein it resides. The second requirement is that, if the misrepresentation is of one or more facts, the PTO be advised what the actual facts are, the applicant making it clear that further examination in light thereof may be required if any PTO action has been based on the misrepresentation. Finally, on the basis of the new and factually accurate record, the applicant must establish patentability of the claimed subject matter.... It does not suffice that one knowing of misrepresentations in an application or in its prosecution merely supplies the examiner with accurate facts without calling his attention to the untrue or misleading assertions sought to be overcome, leaving him to formulate his own conclusions.

Rohm & Haas Co. v. Crystal Chem. Co., 722 F.2d 1556, 1572 (Fed. Cir. 1983).

B. Test for Inequitable Conduct

Inequitable conduct combines two elements: nondisclosure of material information and intent to deceive the Patent Office. These two prongs are factual and must be proven by clear and convincing evidence. *See, e.g., Kingsdown Med. Consultants, Ltd. v. Hollister Inc.*, 863 F.2d 867 (Fed. Cir. 1988). The materiality prong includes, but is not limited to, the standard set forth in 37 C.F.R. § 1.56 (requiring disclosure of any information considered worthy of disclosure by a reasonable examiner). The intent prong requires proof, usually circumstantial proof, of an intent to deceive the Patent Office. Furthermore, these separate elements counterbalance each other: the higher the materiality of nondisclosed information, the lower the quantum of proof necessary to establish intent and vice versa. In the end, inequitable conduct weighs all the circumstances surrounding the patent prosecution to ascertain whether the applicant was culpable enough to render the patent unenforceable. *See, e.g., Dayco Prods., Inc. v. Total Containment, Inc.,* 329 F.3d 1358 (Fed. Cir. 2003).

1. Materiality

The traditional standard for materiality required a showing that "a reasonable examiner would have considered such prior art important in deciding whether to allow the parent application." *Driscoll v. Cebalo,* 731 F.2d 878, 884 (Fed. Cir. 1984). This standard arose in part from the administrative rule establishing the duty of candor then applicable for patent applicants. *See* 37 C.F.R. § 1.56(a) (1991). The Patent Office, however, amended this rule in 1992, setting forth a more specific set of criteria for materiality:

[I]nformation is material to patentability when it is not cumulative to information already of record or being made of record in the application, and:

(1) It establishes, by itself or in combination with other information, a prima facie case of unpatentability of a claim; or

(2) It refutes, or is inconsistent with, a position the applicant takes in:

(i) Opposing an argument of unpatentability relied on by the Office, or

(ii) Asserting an argument of patentability.

37 C.F.R. § 1.56(a). This amended rule, however, has not apparently replaced or supplanted the prior definition of materiality. *Digital Control Inc. v. Charles Machine Works*, 437 F.3d 1309 (Fed. Cir. 2006). Regardless, the pre–1992 Rule 56 and the current Rule 56 are not markedly different. *See, e.g.*, *Ulead Sys., Inc. v. Lex Computer & Mgmt. Corp.*, 351 F.3d 1139 (Fed. Cir. 2003). Furthermore, all patent applicants should follow the basic counsel to disclose anytime materiality seems even remotely possible. *See LaBounty Mfg. v. U.S. Int'l Trade Comm'n*, 958 F.2d 1066 (Fed. Cir. 1992).

For example, the Federal Circuit upheld a decision rendering two patents—the '563 patent and its relative, the '410 patent—unenforceable for nondisclosure of a single reference, Wagenseil. *Molins PLC v. Textron, Inc.*, 48 F.3d 1172 (Fed. Cir. 1995). Although disclosed during foreign prosecution, Wagenseil was not disclosed to the Patent Office during prosecution of the '563 patent. Upon realizing this error, the patentee filed a prior art statement disclosing the Wagenseil reference under 37 C.F.R. § 1.501, which permits entry of a list of relevant art into the publicly available prosecution history for any enforceable patent. Furthermore, the PTO even considered the undisclosed reference during a reexamination and declined to reject any claims. Even though the patent survived reexamination, the court held that it was indeed material. After all, Wagenseil taught claimed elements that were only available in separate references and taught claimed elements that were not disclosed by any other reference. Furthermore, the patentee abandoned several foreign applications in the face of the anticipatory Wagenseil reference. In ruling, the court emphasized that a particular examiner's failure to reject the claims over a reference is not dispositive: the test focuses whether a reasonable examiner would have considered the reference important. Ultimately the trial court found, and the Federal Circuit upheld, that the applicant had intended to deceive the PTO. As evidence of intent, the Federal Circuit put great weight on the applicant's admission of the significance of Wagenseil in many foreign prosecutions while not disclosing the reference to the PTO. Even though years had passed and the patentee had tried to correct the misrepresentation, the Federal Circuit found the patent unenforceable.

A patentee may oppose a finding of materiality by showing that a reference is cumulative. A reference is cumulative if it repeats the disclosure of a subject already disclosed to the PTO. In fact, "a patentee has no obligation to disclose an otherwise material reference if the reference is cumulative or less material than those already before the examiner." *Halliburton Co. v. Schlumberger Tech. Corp.*, 925 F.2d 1435, 1440 (Fed. Cir. 1991). Nonetheless an affirmative statement, such as an affidavit, that misleads, distorts, or omits crucial facts can never be merely cumulative over other information. *Refac Int'l, Ltd. v. Lotus Dev. Corp.*, 81 F.3d 1576 (Fed. Cir. 1996). In holding statements in a patent's written description as material, the Federal Circuit clarified: "[A]ffirmative misrepresentations by the patentee, in contrast to misleading omissions, are more likely to be regarded as material." *Hoffman-La Roche, Inc. v. Promega Corp.*, 323 F.3d 1354, 1367 (Fed. Cir. 2003).

Most inequitable conduct cases concern acts or omissions during prosecution, but the doctrine applies as well to post-issuance activities that affect the patentability or enforceability of the patent. For instance, one patentee may have lost the right to enforce its patent for falsely asserting small entity status in payment of maintenance fees. *Ulead Sys., Inc. v. Lex Computer & Mgmt. Corp.*, 351 F.3d 1139 (Fed. Cir. 2003). Furthermore, the duty of candor applies also to statements in a petition for a certificate of correction. *Cf. Winbond Elecs. Corp. v. Int'l Trade Comm'n*, 262 F.3d 1363 (Fed. Cir. 2001).

2. Intent

After a finding of materiality, the inequitable conduct inquiry moves on to the intent prong. Even in the face of undisclosed material references, the patent is only unenforceable if the patentee also intended to mislead the Patent Office by intentionally withholding the material information. In other words, the intent prong weighs the patentee's conduct in light of all evidence, including evidence of good faith, to assess the culpability of the nondisclosure (or disclosure). Like any other inquiry into subjective intent, a case rarely presents a "smoking gun," or direct evidence of intent to mislead. *See Ristvedt–Johnson, Inc. v. Brandt, Inc.*, 805 F.Supp. 549, 554–55 (N.D. Ill. 1992). Instead a court must usually infer intent from circumstantial evidence, such as evidence that the patentee knew, or should have known, the materiality of the withheld information. *See Brasseler, U.S.A. I, L.P. v. Stryker Sales Corp.*, 267 F.3d 1370 (Fed. Cir. 2001). With a highly material reference, even nominal intent evidence may suffice. In other words, "where withheld information is material and the patentee knew or should have known of that materiality, he or she can expect to have great difficulty in establishing subjective good faith sufficient to overcome an inference of intent to mislead." *Bristol-Myers Squibb Co. v. Rhone–Poulenc Rorer, Inc.*, 326 F.3d 1226, 1239 (Fed. Cir. 2003).

In the modern case setting the proper standard for intent—*Kingsdown Medical Consultants, Ltd. v. Hollister Inc.*, 863 F.2d 867 (Fed. Cir. 1988) (*en banc* in part)—the Federal Circuit evaluated a very evident error in the prosecution process. In a patent with many claims, the PTO examiner had rejected claim 50 as indefinite. The applicant then amended that defective claim. In an effort to obtain other claims, the applicant filed a continuation application. In the continuation, the applicant mistakenly included again the rejected, not the amended, claim with a new number, 43. The patent issued with the new claim that had been once rejected as indefinite. The trial court found inequitable conduct with intent shown by either the prosecuting attorney's gross negligence or the circumstances evincing deceptive intent. On appeal, the Federal Circuit noted that the record showed that the prosecuting attorney was unaware of the error until the litigation. The error was ministerial oversight. Although refusing to condone inattention to detail, the court referred to the "relative ease with which others also overlooked the differences in the claims" as evidence of no deceptive intent. *Id.* at 873. The *en banc* court also clarified gross negligence cannot satisfy the deceptive intent requirement. Even this grossly negligent error, the Federal Circuit explained was not intent because "the involved conduct, viewed in light of all the evidence, including evidence indicative of good faith, must indicate sufficient culpability to require a finding of intent to deceive." *Id.* at 876.

Kingsdown also stands for another very interesting principle. The applicant had intentionally drafted claims to read on the infringer's device that was already in the marketplace. Thus, the applicant crafted the continuation to capture a product already available to consumers. As long as the claims comply with all applicable rules and laws, the Federal Circuit explained, "there is nothing improper, illegal or inequitable in filing a patent application for the purpose of obtaining a right to exclude a known competitor's product from the market." *Id.*

at 874. Moreover this aspect of the prosecution had no relevance for the inequitable conduct inquiry.

A violation of the duty of candor can have implications beyond rendering a patent unenforceable. In a concurring opinion, the late Judge Helen Nies explained that more culpable conduct can bring more severe consequences:

> [T]hree standards [govern the penalties for] misconduct by a patentee ... : (1) misconduct which makes a patent unenforceable (which we have termed "inequitable conduct"); (2) misconduct which is sufficient to make a case "exceptional" under 35 U.S.C. § 285 so as to warrant, in the discretion of the trial judge, an award of attorneys fees; and (3) misconduct which rises to the level of common law fraud and which will support an antitrust claim. As a litigant moves from a purely defensive position, to a recoupment request, to an affirmative claim for damages, it is reasonable to impose more stringent requirements.

Argus Chem. Corp. v. Fibre Glass–Evercoat Co., 812 F.2d 1381, 1387 (Fed. Cir. 1987) (Nies, J., additional views). Thus, culpable misconduct can result in a fee award. In really egregious cases, the attempt to enforce a patent known to be invalid or unenforceable can expose a litigant to the treble damages of antitrust law. *See Walker Process Equip., Inc. v. Food Mach. & Chem. Corp.*, 382 U.S. 172 (1965). The extreme forms of misconduct require more proof of culpable intent.

C. International Treatment

Foreign patent regimes do not rely on inequitable conduct or an equivalent to ensure candor during prosecution. Instead, these regimes rely on other mechanisms to elicit the best prior art and eliminate improper patents. For example, competitors may often oppose an application by submitting prior art during prosecution or may bring some form of "nullity" action to cancel an issued patent. A specialized patent tribunal, with some similarities to the administrative Board of Patent Appeals and Interferences at the PTO, often hear and resolve these challenges to patent validity. At the turn of the 21st Century, the United States enacted a similar procedure—*inter partes* reexamination—which has much of the same function, even if not widely used.

IV. DOUBLE PATENTING

A. Purpose

The Patent Act only permits one patent for each invention:

> Whoever invents or discovers any new and useful process, machine, manufacture, or composition of matter, or any new and useful improvement thereof, may obtain *a patent* therefor, subject to the conditions and requirements of this title.

35 U.S.C. § 101 (emphasis added). In other words, an inventor may not file a second application claiming again a patented invention. Although not perfectly clear in the statute's language, this intuitive requirement makes sense. Without a prohibition on

double patenting, a patentee could extend an exclusive right beyond the statutory term by filing a series of patent applications on identical (or nearly identical) inventions. As discussed in Chapter 7, the novelty-defeating provisions of § 102—most notably § 102(e)—restricts prior art to the activities of another. Therefore, the inventor's own activities bar patentability under § 102(b), but not § 102(e). An unscrupulous applicant could game the patent system by repeatedly applying for a patent on the same invention within the one-year grace period. Obviously this stratagem would effectively yield an indefinite term and defeat the limited term of patent protection. The double patenting prohibition thus preserves the limited patent term.

B.   Two Types

1.   Same Invention or Statutory

Same invention double patenting—also called "statutory" double patenting due to its basis in the statute—applies when an applicant claims a single invention in two separate applications. Because the claims define an invention, statutory double patenting applies when the two applications share at least one claim of identical scope. As a matter of procedure, a court applying this double patenting rule must first construe the applications' claims and then compare them. In making this comparison, the court must realize that variations in verbiage do not necessarily cause variations in claim scope. For example, changing "suitcase" to "portable, semi-rigid traveling bag" may not change the scope of the claimed subject matter.

The imprecision of claim construction makes application of the double patenting rule difficult. The predecessor to the Federal Circuit observed that a "good test, and probably the only objective test, for 'same invention,' is whether one of the claims could be literally infringed without literally infringing the other. If it could be, the claims do not define identically the same invention." *In re Vogel*, 422 F.2d 438, 441 (CCPA 1970). For example, in *Vogel*, the court noted the difference between claims related to sausage-making: "The patent claims are limited to pork. Appealed claims 7 and 10 are limited to meat, which is not the same thing. . . . Claim 11 is limited to beef. Beef is not the same thing as pork." *Id.* at 442. Thus, a sausage maker could infringe claims in the later application without also infringing claims in the issued patent. Accordingly, the applicant was not claiming the same invention.

If, however, an application or patent claims the same invention twice, the latter set of claims are invalid for statutory double patenting under § 101. Unlike the second type—"obviousness-type" double patenting–a terminal disclaimer cannot overcome invalidity for same invention double patenting.

2. "Obviousness–Type" or Nonstatutory

Because even a slight differential in claim scope avoids statutory double patenting, the Federal Circuit's predecessor created "obviousness-type" or nonstatutory double patenting to close the loophole.

This judge-made rule shares the same policy as statutory double patenting: an inventor may not unduly extend the term of his exclusive right by filing a series of applications claiming only marginally different subject matter.

The more accurate label for this doctrine is probably nonstatutory double patenting because obviousness-type double patenting does not entail an obviousness analysis under § 103. After all, obviousness compares the claimed invention with actual prior art references, whereas nonstatutory double patenting compares the scope of a claim with the scope of an earlier claim. Obviousness also often requires evidence of a motivation to combine or modify the prior art, whereas nonstatutory double patenting does not. Lastly, obviousness requires examination into secondary considerations tending to establish nonobviousness, whereas nonstatutory double patenting again does not. *Geneva Pharms., Inc. v. GlaxoSmithKline PLC*, 349 F.3d 1373 (Fed. Cir. 2003).

Although sharing the misleading "obviousness" moniker, obviousness-type double patenting shares more in common with statutory double patenting than with obviousness. The test for obviousness-type double patenting hinges on differences in the claim scope. Merely marginal, negligible variants do not qualify for a separate patent. Nonstatutory double patenting is thus largely an equitable judgment turning on the qualitative differences between two claims. In making this judgment, the application's disclosure does not apply beyond information relevant to construing its respective claim. Nonetheless a disclosed embodiment within the scope of a claim may assist in determining whether one claim is an obvious variant of another. *In re Vogel*, 422 F.2d 438 (CCPA 1970). For example, in *Vogel*, the court determined that claim 11, which recited beef not pork, was not an obvious variant due to the differences in beef and pork characteristics. The court, however, ruled that the claims reciting meat not pork were obvious variants because pork is a type of meat, and thus allowing a claim on meat "would therefore extend the time of monopoly as to the pork process." 422 F.2d at 442. Because no terminal disclaimer cured this instance of nonstatutory double patenting, the claims reciting meat were invalid.

Furthermore, where a second claim reads on an inherent, natural result of an earlier claim, the claims are not patentably distinct. In *Eli Lilly & Co. v. Barr Laboratories, Inc.*, 251 F.3d 955 (Fed. Cir. 2001), the court held a claim reciting a method of blocking the uptake of serotonin by brain neurons in animals by administering fluoxetine hydrochloride was invalid for nonstatutory double patenting in light of an earlier patent claiming a method of treating anxiety in a human by administering an effective amount of fluoxetine or a pharmaceutically acceptable salt thereof. In particular, evidence showed that administering fluoxetine inherently, inevitably, and necessarily blocks the uptake of serotonin, regardless of whether in administered in the treatment of anxiety.

In contrast to the "one-way" test for obviousness-type double patenting set forth in *Vogel*, a "two-way" test may be appropriate in limited circumstances. For example, in *In re Braat*, 937 F.2d 589 (Fed. Cir. 1991), the court encountered commonly assigned inventions related to optical storage technology. Due to delays in the Patent Office, the later-filed application (with subject matter similar to the first-filed application) issued as a patent before the first-filed application. Although complementary, the first-filed application dominated the later-filed application—that is, the later-filed application claimed a combination of the subject matter claimed in the first-filed application and additional, new subject matter. Due to the inequity of punishing an inventor for circumstances beyond his control, the court applied a "two-way" test: Each patent's claims must have been an obvious variant of the other patent to show nonstatutory double patenting.

When the Patent Office does not cause the delay in the issuance of a second claim, a "two-way" test does not apply. For example, where an applicant chooses to obtain or prosecute narrower claims before seeking broader coverage, a "one-way" test prevails. *In re Goodman*, 11 F.3d 1046 (Fed. Cir. 1993).

C. Terminal Disclaimer

Importantly, an applicant may separately claim subject matter nearly identical to an earlier filing so long as a terminal disclaimer disclaims any patent term beyond the expiration of the first patent. In other words, a terminal disclaimer may overcome obviousness-type, but not same invention, double patenting. The Patent Act authorizes this practice:

> Whenever, without any deceptive intention, a claim of a patent is invalid the remaining claims shall not thereby be rendered invalid. A patentee, whether of the whole or any sectional interest therein, may, on payment of the fee required by law, make disclaimer of any complete claim, stating therein the extent of his interest in such patent. Such disclaimer shall be in writing and recorded in the Patent and Trademark Office, and it shall thereafter be considered as part of the original patent to the extent of the interest possessed by the disclaimant and by those claiming under him.

35 U.S.C. § 253. Under a terminal disclaimer, the term of the obvious variant of the initial patent expires concurrently with the term of the initial patent. A terminal disclaimer, however, only remains effective if the patents remain commonly owned throughout their terms. 37 C.F.R. § 1.321(c).

Because it compares claim scope to claim scope, nonstatutory double patenting is inherently ambiguous. In any event, the frequency of nonstatutory double patenting is likely to decrease with the change in patent term from 17 years from issuance to 20 years from the effective filing. Patent applications claiming priority to an earlier patent can obtain no longer term, even without a terminal disclaimer. In other words, terminal disclaimers will only be needed to insure common ownership of the later patent with the earlier one.

V. INTERNATIONAL PROSECUTION

To adequately protect an invention in the international marketplace, a patent attorney must work with foreign, as well as domestic, patent laws. Despite harmonization and cooperation efforts, international agreements—such as the Paris Convention, the Patent Cooperation Treaty, and the World Trade Organization's TRIPS agreement—have left differences in patent practice across the globe. Of these, the two most critical, for prosecution purposes, are the Paris Convention and the PCT. Chapter 16 provides an overview of the domestic implications of these international agreements.

CHAPTER 12

CLAIM CONSTRUCTION

I. INTRODUCTION

When granted a patent, an inventor receives an official copy of the patent, complete with an elaborate cover having the seal of the United States Patent and Trademark Office. The patent also proclaims that the "requirements of law have been complied with, and it has been determined that a patent on the invention shall be granted under the law." This proclamation includes the promise that the inventor now possesses rights under the Patent Act. These rights, however, cannot extend beyond the scope of the patented invention. Thus, the key to patent rights (and validity) depends on the interpretation of the patent claims.

In this respect, the patent is like a deed to real property; it demarcates the limits of the property. *See, e.g., Motion Picture Patents Co. v. Universal Film Mfg. Co.*, 243 U.S. 502 (1917). A deed informs a prospective purchaser of the property's boundaries, which enables that purchaser to visit, survey, and assess the property before buying or renting. The deed also notifies potential trespassers of the boundaries of the property.

Similarly a patent contains signposts signaling the contours of the patentee's property: claims. A claim defines the patentee's property right. In one respect, however, claims differ from real property deeds. Deeds demarcate boundaries with mathematical precision down to the fraction of an inch. Patent claims, on the other hand, attempt to define new products or processes in old language—a task that defies precision. Moreover interpretation of language defining new technology—a step removed from the drafting task—can be even more difficult.

The law professes to construe claims according to the understanding of a person of ordinary skill in the art at the time of invention. This simple rule belies the complexity of the process. Even this simple linguistic framework has two key aspects—a technological aspect and a temporal aspect. Each aspect presents a court with challenges in discerning claim meaning. With these governing aspects in mind, a court—the ultimate arbiter of claim meaning—will use various sources to construe a disputed claim:

- the claim language itself;
- the written description, also called the specification;
- the prosecution history, or
- the public record of the discourse with the Patent Office during acquisition of the patent;
- dictionaries, treatises, and encyclopedias (preferably, but not always, technical); expert

testimony; and prior art references (such as scientific articles).

In the search for the understanding of a skilled artisan at the time of invention, these sources vary in relative importance from one technology and patent to the next. Nevertheless, in an effort to impose some predictability on claim construction, courts (and most important the Federal Circuit) have articulated a hierarchy among these sources preferring intrinsic evidence unique to the patent—that is, the claim language, the specification, and the prosecution history—over extrinsic evidence. In particular, courts express skepticism about expert testimony as a key to claim interpretation.

The importance of claim construction predominates during patent enforcement proceedings. Before determining whether an activity trespasses on the patented property, the court (or even attorney offering an opinion on infringement) must set the boundaries of the exclusive right. Patent infringement receives detailed treatment in Chapter 13. Claim construction, however, is not only an infringement doctrine; it precedes almost every analysis in patent law. For example, the Patent Office must construe claims during the process of deciding whether a patent meets the substantive requirements for patentability. Indeed, the first step in any validity-related determination—regardless of whether during the prosecution or enforcement phase—is claim construction. A court would have quite a difficult time determining, for example, whether the claimed invention had previously been described in a printed publication without an articulation of the invention at hand.

Claims, therefore, play a critical role in notifying the public, including a patentee's competitors and potential competitors, of the scope of the patentee's exclusive rights. As empirical evidence of claim construction's heightened importance, the Federal Circuit has revisited the claim construction process *en banc* three times over the last decade and produced scores upon scores of panel opinions as well. In sum, any patent practitioner simply must acquire some confidence in accurately construing claim language. A prosecuting attorney (patent drafter and legal expert in PTO administrative procedures) must be able to choose language that effectively protects an invention. A litigating attorney must be able to craft winning interpretations and effective defenses during trials on claim infringement or validity. A counseling attorney (an advisor for businesses on the legal implications of market activity) must be able to evaluate the scope of patent rights and the implications of market activities. A transactional attorney (a deal maker for license agreements or cooperative research agreements between commercial entities) must be able to formulate language that withstands litigation challenges. At the heart of every facet of patent work is claim construction.

II. CLAIM CONSTRUCTION

The Patent Act requires that a patentee's or applicant's "specification ... conclude with one or more claims particularly pointing out and distinctly claiming the subject matter which the applicant regards as his invention." 35 U.S.C. § 112, paragraph 1. As discussed in Chapter 10, claims appear at the end of a patent as sequentially numbered predicates that set forth the peripheries of an invention. The meaning of the words in a claim is a challenging inquiry rivaled in patent law only by the difficulty of an obviousness determination.

A.   Challenges of Claim Construction

A patentee has only words and grammatical constructs to demark technological advance. Words, by their very nature as symbols, are fraught with ambiguity and multiple meanings. Philosophers have struggled for centuries with the implications of communication with symbols. Plato, in his famous *Allegory of the Cave*, pictured humanity as trapped in a cave watching shadows dance on the opposite wall cast by a fire that is out of sight. The shadows cast by the real figures moving around the fire are humanity's only (obviously imperfect) contact with reality. Thus, the symbols provide a common experience, but an experience often distant and distorted from reality. The allegory illustrates that each observer focuses on a different aspect of the dancing shadow and potentially derives a different meaning from the symbol. Words thus unite and divide humanity.

Similarly Ludwig Wittgenstein, perhaps the greatest philosopher of the 20th century, devoted his life to the mystery of meaning. He posited in his writings that meaning was a product of social conditioning and context. Every human learns the meaning of symbols, including words, from his own unique experience. Because each individual learns from distinct experiences and cultures, they are conditioned to perceive symbols differently. Even if symbols could precisely represent reality, each human would perceive them differently. Sadly Wittgenstein died in seclusion after retreating in despair over the impossibility of genuine human communication.

Returning from philosophy to patent law, words are necessarily vague at the margins. Sometimes, they are vague by design. Other times, through no fault of their user, words simply cannot convey intent with accuracy. Open any dictionary. Almost every word has a plethora of definitions. Inversely, every thought, feeling, and description may be expressed with an almost infinite number of different word configurations. At this reality, the poet rejoices, but the patent lawyer shudders. These linguistic options impede precise meaning. For instance, in commenting on the process of statutory interpretation–an exercise corresponding in many respects with claim construction–Justice Frankfurter commented:

> [Words] are symbols of meaning. But unlike mathematical symbols, the phrasing of a document, especially a complicated enactment, seldom attains more than approximate precision. If individual words are inexact symbols, with shifting

variables, their configuration can hardly achieve invariant meaning or assured definiteness.

Autogiro Co. of Am. v. United States, 384 F.2d 391, 396 (Ct. Cl. 1967) (quoting Frankfurter, *Some Reflections on the Reading of Statutes*, 47 COL. L. REV. 527, 528 (1947)).

The technological content of patent claims further complicates expression. The intricate moving parts of a carburetor, the complex reactions in a chemical process, or the topology of a computer chip do not find easy expression in words. As one court commented, "[t]hings are not made for the sake of words, but words for things." *Autogiro*, 384 F.2d at 397. Moreover, by definition, the patent drafter describes something new, something never before described.

To compensate for this problem, courts allow inventors to invent new words or phrases for their claiming task. Thus, the inventor may define, either explicitly or implicitly through usage, claim terms in ways inconsistent with ordinary and customary meanings. In other words, patentees may be their own lexicographers by changing the art-specific meaning of preexisting terms or by coining new ones. The flexibility to define and redefine terms, however, comes with its own set of problems. For example, what is the scope of the new definition? Will old words adequately convey a new meaning? When does an old symbol carry novel meaning and when does it simply carry its common meaning?

Despite the inherent imprecision of words, courts insist that a patent give competitors notice of the scope of the exclusive right. Without proper notice, competitors cannot adjust their conduct to avoid infringement. Indeed, a reasonable competitor should be able to make prudent commercial decisions after reading the patent. This notice imperative requires predictability, an objective at odds with the inherent inexactness of claim terms. The law nonetheless strives for this predictability by tying the meaning of the patentee's words to the understanding of one having ordinary skill in the art at the time of the invention.

B. Claim Construction in the Federal Circuit Era: *Markman*

The objective of the Federal Circuit's creation in 1982 was primarily to bring predictability and uniformity to patents. And as the court began fulfilling those goals, the amount of patent litigation markedly increased, including an increase in patent cases tried before a jury. These lay juries typically displayed a limited ability to comprehend and resolve intricate scientific questions and interpret the technical terms of a patent claim. *See, e.g., Markman v. Westview Instruments, Inc.*, 52 F.3d 967 (Fed. Cir. 1995) (*en banc*), *aff'd*, 517 U.S. 370 (1996) (jury misreads simple term "inventory" and trial judge overrules jury); *McGill Inc. v. John Zink Co.*, 736 F.2d 666 (Fed. Cir. 1984) (holding that the jury's implicit interpretation of the term "recovered liquid hydrocarbon absorbent" was inconsistent with other claim language, the patent's specification and file

history, and expert testimony). Indeed, a jury's un-
bridled discretion in interpreting a patent's claims
threatened to undo much of the predictability
achieved through the unification of patent appeals
into a single court. Recognizing the problem, the
Federal Circuit attacked it head on. In one of its
most important cases, the Federal Circuit withdrew
claim construction from the jury. By making claim
construction a question of law within the sole prov-
ince of the trial judge, the Federal Circuit ruled that
the Seventh Amendment did not require a jury trial
on those issues.

In *Markman*, the Federal Circuit also took the
opportunity to set forth its approach to construing
claims. This approach endorsed a hierarchical analysis to resolve disputes over claim meaning. The
court assigned the highest value, when construing a
claim, to the language of the claim itself. Where the
language and context of the claim itself adequately
defines the invention, the patentee's chosen language governs. The Federal Circuit also gave special
priority to evidence from other sources intrinsic to
the patent: the specification and the prosecution
history. Nonetheless, the court stated that, absent
an express definition, "[t]he written description
part of the specification itself does not delimit the
right to exclude [because] [t]hat is the function and
purpose of claims." 52 F.3d at 980 Similarly, "[a]l-
though the prosecution history can and should be
used to understand the language used in the claims,
it too cannot enlarge, diminish, or vary the limitations in the claims." *Id.* (quotation omitted). Thus,

the Federal Circuit appropriately emphasized the preeminence of the claims themselves. After all, these are the words the applicant chose and the PTO accepted as the limits of the exclusive right. Invariably, however, these terms may contain technical nuances not apparent on their face. For that reason, the court gave priority to the contemporaneous writings in the specification and prosecution history to provide the context for construing those words.

For the same reason, the court acknowledged that extrinsic evidence derived from sources outside the patent and its prosecution history may on occasion have relevance. In particular, the court stated:

> Extrinsic evidence consists of all evidence external to the patent and prosecution history, including expert and inventor testimony, dictionaries, and learned treatises. This evidence may be helpful to explain scientific principles, the meaning of technical terms, and terms of art that appear in the patent and prosecution history. Extrinsic evidence may demonstrate the state of the prior art at the time of the invention. It is useful to show what was then old, to distinguish what was new, and to aid the court in the construction of the patent.

Markman, 52 F.3d at 980 (quotation omitted). As a caution, however, the court advised that extrinsic evidence serves to help in "understanding of the patent, not for the purpose of varying or contradicting the terms of the claims." *Id.* at 981. And upon consideration of all the relevant evidence (intrinsic and extrinsic), the court will divine the meaning of the disputed terms as a matter of law.

The *Markman* case involved an invention to prevent the loss of clothing at the dry cleaners. The invention claimed an inventory control and reporting system. Upon receiving an item of clothing, the shopkeeper attached a bar code. Then as the clothing passes different points in the dry cleaning process, a computer system reads the bar code and monitors its progress and position. The parties disputed the meaning of the claim term "inventory." The patentee wanted to read the term broadly to embrace dollars and invoices. Thus, Markman wanted the patent to cover computer systems that monitor finances for a dry cleaner. The defendant wanted to limit "inventory" to only articles of clothing.

The jury found for the patentee, but the trial judge and the Federal Circuit read the specification and the prosecution history to limit "inventory" to articles of clothing. In reaching this conclusion, the Federal Circuit rejected the patentee's attempts to alter this meaning through self-serving inventor testimony or expert testimony from a patent attorney. Instead the court rejected this evidence as testimony on the ultimate legal question reserved for the court.

The Supreme Court's *Markman* decision primarily focused on the role of the jury. The Seventh Amendment states: "In Suits at common law, where the value in controversy shall exceed twenty dollars, the right to a trial by jury shall be preserved." U.S. CONST., AMDT. 7. Under Seventh Amendment jurisprudence, however, a right to a jury arises only for factual issues decided by a jury at common law in 1790—that is, at the date of the amendment's adoption. A review of patent adjudication before 1790 disclosed no analogue to modern claim construction. This result was not surprising, as patent claims first appeared in 1836 and did not gain their modern importance until 1870. Without a pre–1790 analogue, the Supreme Court resolved the Seventh Amendment issue on the basis of practical considerations: judges could do the job better than juries.

In removing claim construction from the jury, the Supreme Court did not adopt the Federal Circuit's characterization of the issue as purely legal. Instead, the Court acknowledged that claim construction involves the "mongrel practice" of deriving a legal conclusion after the consideration of evidence. In particular, the Court explained that the "fact/law distinction at times has turned on a determination that, as a matter of the sound administration of justice, one judicial actor is better positioned than another to decide the issue in question." *Markman v. Westview Instruments, Inc.*, 517 U.S. 370, 388 (1996) (quotation omitted). Accordingly, the Court opted for judicial claim constructions.

Thus, the Federal Circuit, with help from the Supreme Court, embarked on a plan to improve patent adjudication by removing claim construction from juries. This advance, however, brought a different form of procedural uncertainty. Adopting the fiction that claim construction does not involve fact finding, the Federal Circuit reviews claim construction *de novo*, without giving any deference to the district court judge.[9] *Cybor Corp. v. FAS Techs., Inc.*, 138 F.3d 1448 (Fed. Cir. 1998) (*en banc*).

Reviewing claim constructions without deference, the Federal Circuit has reversed those rulings at a high rate, with assessments ranging from approximately one-third to somewhere approaching one-half. *See* Christian Chu, *Empirical Analysis of the Federal Circuit's Claim Construction Trends*, 16 BERK. TECH. L. J. 1075 (2001); Kimberly Moore, *Are District Court Judges Equipped to Resolve Patent Cases?*, 15 HARV. J.L. TECH. 1 (2001). This high reversal rate, in turn, causes criticism that the parties in patent cases tend to discount the trial court's interpretation as merely the "first act" in a

9. Claim construction undeniably includes fact-based inquiries into the state of technology and technological expression at a particular point in time (the time of invention). Indeed, the ultimate claim construction standard examines the understanding of a person of ordinary skill in the art at the time of invention—another factual inquiry. Without acknowledging the factual component of claim construction, a court need not accept one party's arguments over another, but may set forth an independent meaning as a matter of law. *See Exxon Chem. Patents, Inc. v. Lubrizol Corp.*, 64 F.3d 1553 (Fed. Cir. 1995). Still the Federal Circuit insists that it "begin[s] with and carefully consider[s] the trial court's work." *Key Pharms. v. Hercon Labs. Corp.*, 161 F.3d 709, 713 (Fed. Cir. 1998). In other words, the appellate court is more inclined to affirm a thorough claim construction than a cursory one. Even without deferential review, the reasoning of the trial court holds persuasive value.

play that culminates at the Federal Circuit. *Cybor*, 138 F.3d at 1476 (Rader, J., dissenting). Thus, the non-deferential standard of review, in effect, "postpone[s] the point of certainty to the end of the litigation process, at which point, of course, every outcome is certain anyway." *Id.* Accordingly, this standard of review frustrates early certainty of claim meaning. Moreover, if a trial court cannot avoid a jury trial before receiving a definitive claim construction, it risks having to conduct a second trial if the Federal Circuit reverses.

To avoid this last predicament, trial judges seek to convert claim construction hearing into a mandatory summary judgment hearing. Usually this conversion works because the litigants desire early finality and the claim construction issue largely resolves infringement and validity. Indeed in the post-*Markman* era, most patent cases arrive at the Federal Circuit after a grant of summary judgment or the issuance of a consent judgment.

With claim construction as a pure issue of law, the trial judges also enjoy vast discretion over the procedural aspects of claim construction. Thus, patent litigants occasionally bemoan the lack of uniformity in claim construction practices. In most cases, the trial court will wait until the parties conduct some discovery and narrow the number of relevant claim terms for construction. Then the trial court will often hold a hearing and accept arguments and evidence regarding the meaning of those terms. As with all procedural or docket-management issues, the trial court enjoys a wide discretion on the timing as well as the form of this so-called *Markman* hearing. *See, e.g., Sofamor Danek Group, Inc. v. DePuy–Motech, Inc.*, 74 F.3d 1216 (Fed. Cir. 1996). Accordingly, the trial court has no obligation to construe the claims before trial or even hear live testimony on claim meaning. Moreover, a trial court is free to revisit the initial claim construction once additional facts or arguments come to light. *Utah Med. Prods., Inc. v. Graphic Controls Corp.*, 350 F.3d 1376 (Fed. Cir. 2003).

Moreover no party may immediately appeal an adverse claim construction as a matter of right. *Nystrom v. TREX Co.*, 339 F.3d 1347 (Fed. Cir. 2003). Instead, to reach the Federal Circuit for a "binding" claim construction, one of four scenarios must occur: the trial court must rule on all pending issues, either summarily or through a trial; the trial court must dismiss any pending claims without prejudice; the trial court must direct a judgment of fewer than all pending claims under Federal Rule of Civil Procedure 54(b); or the appellant must seek the trial court's and the appellate court's permission for an interlocutory appeal under 28 U.S.C. § 1292(c). The Federal Circuit has consistently declined to accept interlocutory appeals to review claim construction on a premature record. *See Bayer AG v. Biovail Corp.*, 279 F.3d 1340 (Fed. Cir. 2002).

C. Sources of Claim Meaning

Acutely aware of a growing dissatisfaction with the high reversal rate and the uncertainty of claim construction procedure and results, the Federal Circuit convened another *en banc* proceeding on the issue. *Phillips v. AWH Corp.*, 415 F.3d 1303 (Fed. Cir. 2005). *Phillips*, like *Markman*, involved quite simple technology. The invention claimed modular security walls that might be used for a prison. Because the internal support structures, or "baffles," of one side of the walls do not extend to the other side, these modular panels insulate against fire and noise. The patent also depicted these "baffles" at angles that would deflect bullets and prevent them from passing through the walls. Based on those depictions, the trial court (and the original Federal Circuit panel) limited the contested claim term "baffle" to an angled structure that would serve to deflect bullets. The accused structure had baffles disposed at right angles from the outer wall surfaces, thus reducing the chance that the baffle would serve the bullet deflection function. The district court had entered summary judgment for the defendant, AWH, because Phillips could not prove infringement under a claim construction requiring baffles with acute or obtuse angles. The *en banc* court, however, declined to limit the broad term "baffle" to the projectile-deflecting embodiments in the specification.

The claim language recited "internal steel baffles extending inwardly." The *en banc* court placed the primary emphasis on the claim language itself that did not limit the baffles to any specific angled configuration. The court then relied on the intrinsic evidence to support that reading:

The intrinsic evidence confirms that a person of skill in the art would understand that the term "baffles," as used in the '798 patent, would have that generic meaning.... The fact that the written description of the '798 patent sets forth multiple objectives to be served by the baffles recited in the claims confirms that the term "baffles" should not be read restrictively to require that the baffles in each case serve all of the recited functions.... Accordingly, we conclude that a person of skill in the art would not interpret the disclosure and claims of the '798 patent to mean that a structure extending inward from one of the wall faces is a "baffle" if it is at an acute or obtuse angle, but is not a "baffle" if it is disposed at a right angle.

415 F.3d at 1325–27.

As in *Markman*, the Federal Circuit in *Phillips* reiterated its commitment to a hierarchy of evidentiary sources for claim construction. The claim language itself is preeminent in importance. Additional intrinsic evidence occupies the next level of importance. The court observed that the best context for the claim language comes from the patentee's own words and descriptions in the contemporaneous specification and prosecution history. Finally, extrinsic evidence has a more limited role in the process. The court expressed wariness about the possibility of litigation-induced evidence in this category: "extrinsic evidence consisting of expert reports and testimony is generated at the time of and for the purpose of litigation and thus can suffer from bias . . . ." *Id.* at 1318. In claim construction proceedings, a court may pursue an iterative process that consults the intrinsic evidence then relevant extrinsic evidence then intrinsic evidence again, all the while focusing on the claim language. Again, the understanding of a person having ordinary skill in the art at the time of the invention provides the standard that informs the entire process.

1. The Claim Language

The court in *Phillips* restated the "bedrock principle of patent law that the claims of a patent define the invention." *Id.* at 1312 (citations omitted). Thus, the claim language governs the process of ascertaining the scope of the invention and not, for example, the patentee's commercial embodiment. *See Zenith Labs., Inc. v. Bristol–Myers Squibb Co.*, 19 F.3d 1418 (Fed. Cir. 1994). Indeed, "the claim construction inquiry, therefore, begins and ends in all cases with the actual words of the claim." *Renishaw plc v. Marposs Societa' per Azioni*, 158 F.3d 1243, 1248 (Fed. Cir. 1998).

The Federal Circuit also expressed that "the words of a claim are generally given their ordinary and customary meaning." *Phillips*, 415 F.3d at 1312 (citations omitted); *see also Johnson Worldwide Assocs., Inc. v. Zebco Corp.*, 175 F.3d 985 (Fed. Cir. 1999) (discussing a "heavy presumption" that the claim terms receive their ordinary meaning). This shorthand, however, is not an invitation to divorce the terms from their proper technological and temporal context. Indeed the Federal Circuit has emphasized that the "customary meaning" refers to the customary meaning in the art. *Home Diagnostics, Inc. v. LifeScan, Inc.*, 381 F.3d 1352 (Fed. Cir. 2004). An entertaining passage in a Federal Circuit opinion illustrated this principle:

The word "normal" that appears in this case has a different "customary" meaning to a psychiatrist in a mental hospital (where "normal" refers to a sane mental state) than to a pharmacist seeking proper dosages (where "normal" doses would vary with body weight and other factors), than to a marriage counselor (where a "normal" marriage probably means an average marriage, i.e., one perpetually in danger of divorce), than to an oil well driller in a pump technology.

Ferguson Beauregard/Logic Controls, Div. of Dover Res., Inc. v. Mega Sys., LLC, 350 F.3d 1327, 1347–48 (Fed. Cir. 2003) (Rader, J., concurring). In sum, the meaning of a word varies according to its context and the technological understanding at the time of the invention sets that context.

The "ordinary and customary meaning" may guide claim construction "generally" and "frequently," *Phillips*, 415 F.3d at 1312, but the Federal Circuit has explained reasons to depart from this principle:

First, the claim term will not receive its ordinary meaning if the patentee acted as his own lexicographer and clearly set forth a definition of the disputed claim term in either the specification or prosecution history. Second, a claim term will not carry its ordinary meaning if the intrinsic evidence shows that the patentee distinguished that term from prior art on the basis of a particular embodiment, expressly disclaimed subject matter, or described a particular embodiment as important to the invention.

Third, ... a claim term also will not have its ordinary meaning if the term chosen by the patentee so deprives the claim of clarity as to require resort to the other intrinsic evidence for a definite meaning. Last, as a matter of statutory authority, a claim term will cover nothing more than the corresponding structure or step disclosed in the specification, as well as equivalents thereto, if the patentee phrased the claim in step-or means-plus-function format.

CCS Fitness, Inc. v. Brunswick Corp., 288 F.3d 1359, 1366–67 (Fed. Cir. 2002) (citations and quotations omitted). In this list, the first two departure categories distill down to a single concept: Is there something in the specification or the prosecution history that would reasonably lead a person of ordinary skill in the art to believe that the patentee's words do not carry their customary meaning? These categories accordingly encompass express lexicography and express or implicit disclaimers. The third, somewhat amorphous, category relates to the ambiguity of the words present in the claim itself. In other words, the ordinary meaning must be clear and apparent to take effect. The fourth and final category acknowledges the statute. A claim invoking

35 U.S.C. § 112, paragraph 6, is limited to the structure disclosed in the specification and the equivalents of that structure. *See* Chapter 13.

The "ordinary and customary meaning" principle carries a warning. Strict adherence to the words in the claim as understood by a person of ordinary skill in the art at the time of the invention may result in a claim scope that the patentee did not in all likelihood intend. For example, in *Chef America, Inc. v. Lamb–Weston, Inc.*, 358 F.3d 1371 (Fed. Cir. 2004), the patentee claimed a process for making dough products with a light, flaky, and crispy texture when later heated in an oven or microwave. But the words of the claim recited a step of "heating the ... dough *to* a temperature in the range of about 400°F to 850°F." *Id.* at 1372 (emphasis added). Thus, the claim recited a process that heated the dough itself to a temperature of at least 400°F. At that temperature, of course, the dough would become an unusable charcoal briquet. No doubt the claim drafter meant that the dough ought to be baked in an oven *at* a temperature in the range of about 400°F to 850°F for a brief time. The claim did not, however, use the proper preposition. The Federal Circuit simply lacked the power to redraft the claims: "Even a nonsensical result does not require the court to redraft the claims of the ... patent.... Where, as here, the claim is susceptible to only one reasonable construction, ... we must construe the claims based on the patentee's version of the claim as he himself drafted it." *Id.* at 1374.

In reaching its conclusion, the *Chef America* court disregarded an affidavit reflecting the understanding of a person of ordinary skill in the art, because that evidence did not show that the claim language had a different meaning. Instead that evidence merely confirmed that a person of ordinary skill in the art would have recognized that the claimed process was inoperable and that the patentee likely intended to use different words. That is, the testimony reinforced that the claim drafter committed an error. Thus, an inventor must choose claim language with care. U.S. courts will not correct claim drafting errors.

2. The Specification

A claim, however, is only one part of a patent. In the words of the Federal Circuit, "[t]he claims, of course, do not stand alone. Rather they are part of a fully integrated written instrument, consisting principally of a specification that concludes with the claims. For that reason, claims must be read in view of the specification of which they are a part." *Phillips*, 415 F.3d at 1315 (internal citations deleted). This pithy statement does not disclose the entire complicated relationship between the written description and the scope of the claims.

As a starting point, the specification provides the context for a proper understanding of the claims. After all, the specification is a contemporaneous document drafted to explain the invention. *See, e.g., Vitronics Corp. v. Conceptronic, Inc.*, 90 F.3d 1576 (Fed. Cir. 1996). In *Phillips*, the Federal Circuit invoked a commentary from its predecessor, the Court of Claims, that characterized the specification " 'as a concordance for the claims,' based on the statutory requirement that the specification 'describe the manner and process of making and using' the patented invention." *Phillips*, 415 F.3d at 1315 (quoting *Autogiro Co. of Am. v. United States*, 384 F.2d 391, 397–98 (Ct. Cl. 1967)). By the same token, this strong language does not mean that the claimed invention is limited to any embodiment or embodiments described in the specification. The claims, after all, define the invention. The specification has a different role, namely describing the fabrication and use of the invention. To fulfill its function, the specification need not describe every permutation or combination of the invention. The *Phillips* court itself did not limit the "baffle" claim to the angled embodiment prominently and repeatedly described in the specification. Instead, the Circuit applied the correct practice of examining the specification to determine whether, either implicitly or explicitly, the patentee had limited the scope of the claim language.

In general, the claimed invention is not limited to a preferred embodiment, even if the specification does not describe any other embodiment. For example, in *Teleflex, Inc. v. Ficosa North America Corp.*, 299 F.3d 1313 (Fed. Cir. 2002), the court rejected an argument that a claim reciting a clip—a component of a two-piece shift cable in an automobile—was limited to the sole embodiment disclosed in the specification. In examining the specification for any restriction on the broad ordinary meaning, the court explained that "the number of embodiments disclosed in the specification is not determinative of the meaning of disputed claim terms." *Id.* at 1327. Because the intrinsic record was devoid of any clear statements of manifest restriction, the court accorded "clip" its full range of meaning. Indeed, "the specification need not present every embodiment or permutation of the invention and the claims are not limited to the preferred embodiment of the invention." *Netword, LLC v. Centraal Corp.*, 242 F.3d 1347, 1352 (Fed. Cir. 2001). In other words, "limitations from the specification are not to be read into the claims," even though claims must be read in light of the specification. *Comark Commc'ns, Inc. v. Harris Corp.*, 156 F.3d 1182, 1186 (Fed. Cir. 1998). While numerous opinions echo that guideline, a complete picture of claim construction law suggests that the specification very often does impose constraints on claim scope.

When a patentee repeatedly emphasizes a feature or function of an invention, that emphasis often converts into a constraint on claim scope. For example, in *SciMed Life Systems, Inc. v. Advanced Cardiovascular Systems, Inc.*, 242 F.3d 1337 (Fed. Cir. 2001), the patents claimed balloon dilatation catheters for coronary angioplasty. Each claim recited a general "lumen" configuration. The specification reiterated over and over that the invention comprised only a coaxial—and not a side-by-side—lumen configuration:

At various points, the common specification of the three patents indicates that the claimed invention uses coaxial, rather than side-by-side lumens, i.e., that the guide wire lumen is contained within the inflation lumen and that the inflation lumen is annular. Read together, these portions of the common specification lead to the inescapable conclusion that the references in the asserted claims to an inflation lumen "separate from" the guide wire lumen must be understood as referring to coaxial lumens, and thus that the asserted claims read only on catheters having coaxial lumens.

Id. at 1342. Thus, repetition and emphasis resulted in a limitation on the general claim term "lumen."

This case also illustrates another instance when specification descriptions will almost invariably limit broader claim terms, namely when the specification expressly defines the entire invention in terms of the narrower embodiment or configuration. In *SciMed*, the specification expressly defined "all embodiments of the present invention":

It is difficult to imagine how the patents could have been clearer in making the point that the coaxial lumen configuration was a necessary element of every variant of the claimed invention. Moreover, there is no suggestion that the patentee made that statement unaware of the alternative dual lumen configuration, because earlier in the patent the patentee had distinguished the dual lumen configuration used in prior art devices as having disadvantages that the coaxial lumens used in the patented invention had overcome. *Id.* at 1344.

The difficulty, however, arises when the specification repeatedly emphasizes a feature, but includes a statement or two endorsing a broader reading or when the specification does not explicitly apply a narrower description to the entire invention, but nonetheless suggests the narrower reading. For instance, in the case about safety razors, the specification described the claim in terms of a "three-bladed" configuration approximately thirty times. *Gillette Co. v. Energizer Holdings, Inc.*, 405 F.3d 1367 (Fed. Cir. 2005). Yet in one passage, the specification also referred to a "plurality of blades" that could encompass more than three blades. The Federal Circuit, in that instance, relied on a broader reasonable reading of the claims themselves. Nonetheless, repeated usage of a single term in accordance with a single meaning often indicates that that term has only that single meaning. In other words, "when a patentee uses a claim term throughout the entire patent specification, in a manner consistent with only a single meaning, he has defined that term 'by implication.' " *Bell Atl. Network Servs., Inc. v. Covad Commc'ns Group, Inc.*, 262 F.3d 1258, 1271 (Fed. Cir. 2001). On the other hand, where the patentee varies the use of a claim term, that varied usage indicates that that term has a broader meaning encompassing at least all of those usages. *See, e.g., Johnson Worldwide*

Assocs., Inc. v. Zebco Corp., 175 F.3d 985 (Fed. Cir. 1999).

In sum, the relationship between the specification and claim scope is very complex. The claims must be read "in view of the specification, of which they are a part," *Markman v. Westview Instruments, Inc.*, 52 F.3d 967, 979 (Fed. Cir. 1995) (*en banc*), but never to the point of "read[ing] a limitation from the specification into the claims." *Liebel-Flarsheim Company v. Medrad, Inc.*, 358 F.3d 898, 904 (Fed. Cir. 2004). The Federal Circuit has not been able to articulate a neutral principle that distinguishes between these potentially conflicting guidelines. In *Liebel-Flarsheim*, the Federal Circuit expressed confidence that a careful reading of the claims from the vantage point of the skilled artisan would usually put the specification into its proper context. In general terms, a court must consult the specification during every claim construction, but the specification descriptions do not limit broader claim language, unless the specification clearly indicates, either expressly or implicitly, that the invention is narrower than the scope of the claim language.

3. The Prosecution History

As the third intrinsic source for claim meaning, the written record created during the administrative process culminating in the patent's grant—also known as the prosecution history or file wrapper—also forms an important source for claim meaning. As discussed in Chapter 2, the prosecution history contains the correspondence between the inventor and the Patent Office during acquisition of the patent. In this back-and-forth set of negotiations, an examiner typically issues rejections or objections regarding the claims, and the applicant rebuts those rejections or objections by making legal or factual arguments, amending the claims, or both. This record becomes publicly available upon issuance of the patent. Therefore, applicants cannot argue before the Patent Office that claims are very narrow to avoid prior art and obtain allowance then later argue before a court that the claims are very broad to prove infringement. *See, e.g., Southwall Techs., Inc. v. Cardinal IG Co.*, 54 F.3d 1570 (Fed. Cir. 1995).

The Federal Circuit in *Phillips* endorsed prosecution history as part of the claim construction process: "In addition to consulting the specification, we have held that a court 'should also consider the patent's prosecution history, if it is in evidence.'" *Phillips*, 415 F.3d at 1317 (quoting *Markman*, 52 F.3d at 980). At the same time, the Circuit recognized the limitations of this claim construction tool: "Yet because the prosecution history represents an ongoing negotiation between the PTO and the applicant, rather than the final product of that negotiation, it often lacks the clarity of the specification and thus is less useful for claim construction purposes." *Phillips*, 415 F.3d at 1317. The Circuit might have also observed that prosecution histories are often sketchy and incomplete.

The administrative record of allowance is not evidence of the patentee's subjective intent; intent is irrelevant. Instead, the prosecution history is an objective record that the public may rely upon when discerning the scope of the invention. *See Biogen, Inc. v. Berlex Labs., Inc.*, 318 F.3d 1132 (Fed. Cir. 2003). Besides incompleteness, the administrative record, of course, includes many arguments and amendments that were not in fact necessary to obtain allowance. *Elkay Mfg. Co. v. Ebco Mfg. Co.*, 192 F.3d 973 (Fed. Cir. 1999). Furthermore, comments in the prosecution history of related applications—regardless of whether ancestors or descendents—also affect the scope of a patent. *See Microsoft Corp. v. Multi–Tech Sys., Inc.*, 357 F.3d 1340 (Fed. Cir. 2004).

A patent's prosecution history, therefore, may inform the proper construction of a claim, although its importance—similar to the importance of the specification—varies according to the completeness and relevance of the record. If, for example, the patentee's statements are ambiguous, reasonably amenable to multiple interpretations, or at best inconclusive, the Federal Circuit will not rely on passing commentary to narrow the claims. *See N. Telecom Ltd. v. Samsung Elecs. Co.*, 215 F.3d 1281 (Fed. Cir. 2000). In addition, the case law holds that blatantly erroneous comments do not restrict the meaning of the claims, so long as a person of ordinary skill in the art would readily identify the comments as mistaken. *See, e.g., Biotec Biologische*

Naturverpackungen GmbH v. Biocorp, Inc., 249 F.3d 1341 (Fed. Cir. 2001).

Some prosecution histories may evince the applicant's unambiguous surrender of subject matter. In that case, the claim scope will be limited, even though the claim language may not also reflect that surrender of subject matter. For instance, in *Omega Engineering, Inc. v. Raytek Corp.*, 334 F.3d 1314 (Fed. Cir. 2003), the court considered whether the patentee made a "clear and unmistakable" disclaimer with respect to the term "to visibly outline." After considering the prosecution history in its entirety, the court determined that the patentee narrowed the meaning of the claim by repeatedly distinguishing the prior art: "Since the patentee offered a narrower construction of the verb 'to visibly outline' in the disputed function, it has clearly and unmistakably disclaimed the territory between the full ordinary meaning of the claim language and the asserted new meaning." *Id.* at 1327.

The applicant's characterization of the invention in the prosecution history can, as shown by *Omega*, narrow claim scope. In some instances, however, a patentee will attempt to manipulate the proceedings before the Patent Office in an attempt to alter the scope of the invention. Courts, though, are loath to accept a litigation-induced, self-serving attempt to modify the meaning of a term, particularly one that is inconsistent with the remainder of the intrinsic evidence. Indeed, where the specification defines a term (either implicitly or expressly), the prosecution history cannot broaden that definition. *Multiform Desiccants, Inc. v. Medzam, Ltd.*, 133 F.3d 1473 (Fed. Cir. 1998).

4. Extrinsic Evidence

In addition to the intrinsic evidence, which a court must consider during claim construction, extrinsic evidence may also factor into the court's determination. Extrinsic evidence is, as its name suggests, any evidence external to the patent and the prosecution history—including, for example, dictionaries, treatises, encyclopedias, expert testimony, and prior art references. Although not forming a part of the public record, this category is important to frame the inquiry within its proper technological and temporal context. In other words, extrinsic evidence can provide the background knowledge or understanding of a person or ordinary skill in the art at the time of the invention. *See, e.g., Markman v. Westview Instruments, Inc.*, 52 F.3d 967 (Fed. Cir. 1995) (*en banc*).

In *Phillips*, the Federal Circuit "authorized district courts to rely on extrinsic evidence," 415 F.3d at 1317, but with considerable cautionary comments. For instance, extrinsic evidence, the court observed, "is less significant than the intrinsic record in determining the legally operative meaning of claim language." *Id.* (internal citation omitted). Thus, if an analysis of the intrinsic evidence yields an unambiguous definition for a disputed claim term, extrinsic evidence may not alter that definition. The primary role for extrinsic evidence, as suggested by the Federal Circuit, may lie in "educat[ing] the court regarding the field of the invention and ... help[ing] the court determine what a person of ordinary skill in the art would understand the claim terms to mean." *Id.* at 1319.

The Federal Circuit also advises that extrinsic evidence "may be used only to help the court come to the proper understanding of the claims; it may not be used to vary or contradict the claim language." *Vitronics Corp. v. Conceptronic, Inc.*, 90 F.3d 1576, 1584 (Fed. Cir. 1996). Despite this somewhat restricted application, patent litigation often features considerable wrangling over extrinsic evidence. The cautions about this form of evidence require some additional examination of its various categories.

a) Dictionaries, Treatises, and Encyclopedias

At first blush, these publicly available resources might seem to provide an excellent objective source of claim meaning. After all, these resources are independent of influence from the pressures of litigation and may provide context for a claim's customary meaning in the art at the time of the invention. Indeed, at one point, the Federal Circuit began to place heavy reliance on dictionary definitions:

Dictionaries, encyclopedias and treatises ... may be the most meaningful sources of information to aid judges in better understanding both the tech-

nology and the terminology used by those skilled
in the art to describe the technology.

Texas Digital Sys., Inc. v. Telegenix, Inc., 308 F.3d
1193, 1202–03 (Fed. Cir. 2002). When this reliance
on a form of extrinsic evidence began to trump
intrinsic evidence, the Federal Circuit stepped in
and offered a correction. This dictionary dalliance
away from the importance of intrinsic evidence,
therefore, was brief. The *Phillips* case was the
vehicle to correct the line of cases that gave "greater emphasis to dictionary definitions" and a "less
prominent role to the specification and the prosecution history." 415 F.3d at 1319.

The Federal Circuit explained its reasons for
skepticism about according dictionaries precedence
over the specification:

> The main problem with elevating the dictionary
> to such prominence is that it focuses the inquiry
> on the abstract meaning of words rather than on
> the meaning of claim terms within the context of
> the patent.... [H]eavy reliance on the dictionary
> divorced from the intrinsic evidence risks trans-
> forming the meaning of the claim terms to the
> artisan into the meaning of the term in abstract,
> out of its particular context, which is the specifi-
> cation.

415 F.3d at 1321. The Federal Circuit then proceeded to describe the potential problem in more specific
terms:

> The problem is that if the district court starts
> with the broad dictionary definition in every case

and fails to fully appreciate how the specification implicitly limits that definition, the error will systematically cause the construction of the claim to be unduly expansive.

Id. The *en banc* court also noted that dictionaries, even technical dictionaries, present multiple definitions. Moreover different dictionaries and even different editions of the same dictionary can present further variance in term meaning, all divorced from the specific context of the patent.

After discounting these extrinsic sources, the Circuit nonetheless reaffirmed "the appropriate use of dictionaries." *Id.* at 1322. These sources are particularly useful to "assist in understanding the commonly understood meaning of words," as opposed to the technical usage of terms in the context of particular art at the particular time of invention. *Id.* In sum, these sources remain available, but in a more confined role.

b) Expert Testimony

Because claim construction requires the understanding of a person of ordinary skill in the art at the time of the invention, expert testimony may also provide context for construing claims. Indeed, a technical expert may aid a court's understanding with respect to the state of the art, the disclosure of the prior art, or even the meaning of a claim term. Similarly, an inventor's testimony—even though from the perspective of a person having "extraordinary" skill in the art—may also have relevance for the meaning of a term in limited circumstances.

Above all, however, a court must treat this evidence carefully to prevent any manipulation to expand claim scope beyond the reach specified in intrinsic evidence.

The Federal Circuit offered some guidance in *Phillips* on the role of expert testimony:

> [E]xpert reports and testimony [are] generated at the time of and for the purpose of litigation and thus can suffer from bias that is not present in intrinsic evidence. The effect of that bias can be exacerbated if the expert is not one of skill in the relevant art or if the expert's opinion is offered in a form that is not subject to cross-examination.

415 F.3d at 1318. Thus, the trial court has, with expert testimony in particular, a "considerable task of filtering the useful extrinsic evidence from the fluff." *Id.*

Indeed, this advice did not originate with *Phillips*; the Federal Circuit has consistently singled out expert testimony for careful scrutiny by district court judges. In a very influential case following *Markman*, the Circuit advised that expert testimony on the proper construction of a disputed claim term should "rarely, if ever, occur." *Vitronics Corp. v. Conceptronic, Inc.*, 90 F.3d 1576, 1585 (Fed. Cir. 1996). Later the Federal Circuit backed off that strong admonition to grant trial judges more discretion to take relevant evidence from experts, but retained its warnings about relying on experts to vary from the intrinsic record. *Pitney Bowes, Inc. v. Hewlett–Packard Co.*, 182 F.3d 1298 (Fed. Cir.

1999). In its proper context, the Federal Circuit itself has relied on expert testimony. For instance, expert testimony assisted recognition that the term "acid" in pharmacology (and not general chemistry) includes salts of that acid. *See, e.g., Merck & Co. v. Teva Pharms. USA, Inc.,* 347 F.3d 1367 (Fed. Cir. 2003).

Inventor testimony, a special form of expert testimony, intensifies the potential for non-credible testimony. After all, the inventor certainly has a stake in the outcome of the litigation. Nonetheless, the "inventor is a competent witness to explain the invention" as well as "background information, including explanation of the problems that existed at the time the invention was made and the inventor's solution to these problems." *Voice Techs. Group, Inc. v. VMC Sys., Inc.,* 164 F.3d 605, 615 (Fed. Cir. 1999). In light of the potential for self-serving testimony, however, courts will typically only permit the inventor's testimony to restrict—and not expand— the meaning of a disputed claim term. *See Jonsson v. Stanley Works,* 903 F.2d 812 (Fed. Cir. 1990).

c) Prior Art References and Scientific Articles

Less controversial than expert testimony and less frequently cited than dictionaries, prior art references and scientific articles may help establish the knowledge within the art at the time of invention, regardless of whether reported to the Patent Office during prosecution. *Arthur A. Collins, Inc. v. N. Telecom Ltd.,* 216 F.3d 1042 (Fed. Cir. 2000). In particular, prior art references may aid in the definition of a term beyond its normal function of protecting the public domain. In *Kumar v. Ovonic Battery Co.*, 351 F.3d 1364 (Fed. Cir. 2003), the court disregarded dictionary definitions in favor of a prior art definition extensively discussed during prosecution.

D. Guidelines for Claim Construction

Although loose language in case law occasionally recites "rules" for claim construction, the process is not amenable to rules. The so-called canons of claim construction are more accurately characterized as guidelines rather than immutable truths. *Renishaw plc v. Marposs Societa' per Azioni*, 158 F.3d 1243 (Fed. Cir. 1998). A "rule" for one case may have no application in the next. Thus, a proper claim construction avoids rote regurgitation "rules" without a thorough analysis based on the relevant evidence informing the likely perception of a person of ordinary skill in the art at the time of the invention. Nevertheless, the following list attempts to organize the guiding principles from strongest to weakest:

1. The ordinary and customary meaning of claim language enjoys a heavy presumption of accuracy.

2. Where intrinsic evidence unambiguously delineates claim scope, it controls.

3. For intrinsic evidence, a claim term should be read with reference to the specification, but never to the extent of importing a

limitation from the specification into the claim.

4. To determine ordinary meaning, a court may rely on general and technical dictionary definitions.

5. A claim, if possible, should be construed to encompass a disclosed embodiment of the invention and a reading that excludes the preferred embodiment is rarely correct.

6. Claims may be construed to uphold their validity, but construction must precede a validity determination and should not prevent a clear interpretation that renders the claim invalid.

7. Claim differentiation, strongest for dependent claim relationships, may be overcome by intrinsic or even relevant extrinsic evidence.

8. Extrinsic evidence, though relevant, may not contradict intrinsic evidence.

E. Practical Problems

The process of construing claims presents some recurrent difficulties. Some of these difficulties include whether a preamble limits the scope of the invention, whether construing a claim in light of the specification violates the prohibition against importing limitations from the specification, whether the accused device has a role in claim construction, and whether a claim construction may change within the same case.

1. Preamble

As discussed in Chapter 10, a claim's preamble has the purpose of setting forth the subject matter of the invention. Although a preamble may be simple like "a method," it may also recite more information like "a method for curing colon cancer." Courts often struggle to decide whether that additional information—often an intended use—limits the scope of the claim. The answer to that question usually hinges on the importance of the preamble information to give meaning to the rest of the claim. *Pitney Bowes, Inc. v. Hewlett–Packard Co.*, 182 F.3d 1298 (Fed. Cir. 1999). Stated differently, a preamble has the significance that the rest of the claim dictates. *Bell Commc'ns Research, Inc. v. Vitalink Commc'ns Corp.*, 55 F.3d 615 (Fed. Cir. 1995).

In *Catalina Marketing International, Inc. v. Coolsavings.com, Inc.*, 289 F.3d 801 (Fed. Cir. 2002), the Federal Circuit expounded on this general rule about the preamble as a limitation:

> For example, this court has held that Jepson[10] claiming generally indicates intent to use the preamble to define the claimed invention, thereby limiting claim scope. Additionally, dependence on a particular disputed preamble phrase for antecedent basis may limit claim scope because it indicates a reliance on both the preamble and claim body to define the claimed invention. Likewise, when the preamble is essential to under-

10. A Jepson claim, a specific type of claim that recites an improvement, is examined more fully in Chapter 10.

stand limitations or terms in the claim body, the preamble limits claim scope.

Further, when reciting additional structure or steps underscored as important by the specification, the preamble may operate as a claim limitation.

Moreover, clear reliance on the preamble during prosecution to distinguish the claimed invention from the prior art transforms the preamble into a claim limitation because such reliance indicates use of the preamble to define, in part, the claimed invention. Without such reliance, however, a preamble generally is not limiting when the claim body describes a structurally complete invention such that deletion of the preamble phrase does not affect the structure or steps of the claimed invention. Thus, preamble language merely extolling benefits or features of the claimed invention does not limit the claim scope without clear reliance on those benefits or features as patentably significant.

Moreover, preambles describing the use of an invention generally do not limit the claims because the patentability of apparatus or composition claims depends on the claimed structure, not on the use or purpose of that structure.

Id. at 808–09 (citations and quotations omitted) (footnote added). Distilled down, this test depends on whether the intrinsic record elevates the preamble beyond a statement of intended or general use.

2. Construing Claims in Light of the Specification Versus Impermissibly Importing a Limitation from the Specification

A court must, of course, consult a patent's written description in construing claims. Because the claims and specification have different purposes in the patent document, the specification cannot in all cases be coextensive with the scope of the claims. By the same token, an applicant may limit the scope of the invention expressly or implicitly through the written description. Claim construction practices have not effectively articulated a rule for determining the specification's role—mere informant or scope constraint. In fact, these competing roles are a microcosm for the larger issue of claim construction. *See, e.g., Liebel-Flarsheim Co. v. Medrad, Inc.,* 358 F.3d 898 (Fed. Cir. 2004).

Indeed, the *Texas Digital* case placed undue emphasis on dictionaries to prevent the cardinal patent law "sin" of pulling a limitation from the specification into the claims. *Phillips,* 415 F.3d at 1320. When *Phillips* undertook to restrict the application of dictionaries, the Federal Circuit acknowledged this purpose of the dictionary cases and the difficult distinction between "using the specification to interpret the meaning of a claim and importing limitations from the specification into the claim." 415 F.3d at 1323. The Federal Circuit thought that the distinction was manageable "if the court's focus remains on understanding how a person of ordinary skill in the art would understand the claim terms." *Id.* "In particular," the court continued, "we have expressly rejected the contention that if a patent describes only a single embodiment, the claims of the patent must be construed as limited to that embodiment." *Id.* In another case, the Federal Circuit explained:

[T]his court recognizes that it must interpret the claims in light of the specification, yet avoid impermissibly importing limitations from the specification. That balance turns on how the specification characterizes the claimed invention. In this respect, this court looks to whether the specification refers to a limitation only as a part of less than all possible embodiments or whether the specification read as a whole suggests that the very character of the invention requires the limitation be a part of every embodiment. For example, it is impermissible to read the one and only disclosed embodiment into a claim without other indicia that the patentee so intended to limit the invention. On the other hand, where the specification makes clear at various points that the claimed invention is narrower than the claim language might imply, it is entirely permissible and proper to limit the claims.

Alloc, Inc. v. Int'l Trade Comm'n, 342 F.3d 1361, 1370 (Fed. Cir. 2003) (citations omitted).

3. Construing Claims to the Extent Necessary Versus Construing Claims in Light of the Accused Device

A court should construe only those claim terms "in controversy, and only to the extent necessary to resolve the controversy." *Vivid Techs., Inc. v. Am. Sci. & Eng'g, Inc.*, 200 F.3d 795, 803 (Fed. Cir. 1999). This sensible statement stems from the nature of our judicial system, which only resolves actual controversies. The problem, however, arises with respect to determining the claim terms "in controversy." To frame the dispute, a court usually needs some information about the accused device.

Nonetheless the law ignores the accused device once the parties identify the truly disputed terms. In this way, the law ensures that the second step of infringement—comparing the accused device to the properly construed claims–remains separate from the first—construing the claims. Indeed, "claims are not construed 'to cover' or 'not to cover' the accused device. That would make infringement a matter of judicial whim. It is only *after* the claims have been *construed without reference to the accused device* that the claims, as so construed, are applied to the accused device to determine infringement." *SRI Int'l v. Matsushita Elec. Corp. of Am.*, 775 F.2d 1107, 1118 (Fed. Cir. 1985) (*en banc*) (emphasis original). In other words, the court may not construe the claims with an eye to the outcome.

Beyond that proscription on result-oriented claim construction, however, the trial court retains broad discretion to consult the accused product or process for the context of the dispute. The Federal Circuit explained:

The rule [against construing a claim with reference to the accused device], however, does not

forbid awareness of the accused product or process to supply the parameters and scope of the
infringement analysis, including its claim construction component. In other words, the "reference" rule accepted in *Pall Corp.*, *Multiform Desiccants*, and *Scripps Clinic* does not forbid any
glimpse of the accused product or process during
or before claim construction. In light of these
principles, if the litigants cannot themselves inform a trial court of the specific issues presented
by the infringement inquiry—that is, issues of the
breadth of the claim construction analysis and
the most useful terms to facilitate that defining
process—then a trial court may refer to the accused product or process for that context during
the process.

Wilson Sporting Goods Co. v. Hillerich & Bradsby,
442 F.3d 1322, 1326–27 (Fed. Cir. 2006).

4. Evolving Claim Construction

On occasion, litigants will seek—and the trial
court may issue—a ruling on claim construction
before all issues in the case have crystallized. A
court must often construe the claims to resolve a
preliminary injunction issue. To prevail on a motion
for preliminary relief, the patentee must show a
reasonable likelihood of success on the merits,
which in turn requires proof of likely infringement.
At this preliminary stage, the full issues of claim
construction are not fully the case may not be fully
developed. The discovery process may be just underway. In this setting, the district court's claim con-

struction is tentative. The law, in fact, does not prohibit a trial court from "engag[ing] in a rolling claim construction, in which the court revisits and alters its interpretation of the claim terms as its understanding of the technology evolves." *Jack Guttman, Inc. v. Kopykake Enters., Inc.*, 302 F.3d 1352, 1361 (Fed. Cir. 2002).

The Federal Circuit has itself construed the same claim differently between an initial appeal on a preliminary injunction and an appeal on the final judgment. *CVI/Beta Ventures, Inc. v. Tura LP*, 112 F.3d 1146, 1160 n.7 (Fed. Cir. 1997) (commenting that "unlike the earlier appeal, this appeal required us to construe the asserted claims based upon the final and complete record in the case"). Moreover, a trial court has the discretion to revisit or reconsider an earlier claim construction ruling, even if not initially issued in connection with a preliminary injunction. For example, in *Utah Medical Products, Inc. v. Graphic Controls Corp.*, 350 F.3d 1376 (Fed. Cir. 2003), the court upheld a claim construction that was modified in light of additional arguments misreading the first attempt at construing the claims. The appellate court, in fact, commended the trial court's correction: "Recognizing the shortcomings of its original attempt to define the scope of the claims, the district court admirably amended its construction to supply a better definition before trial." *Id.* at 1382.

F.   Claim Construction at the Patent Office

While the same sources of claim meaning affect the meaning of claims during prosecution before the

Patent Office, the pre-issuance standard for claim construction features a slightly different perspective than enforcement proceedings. In simple terms, claim construction during enforcement requires firm and discernible boundaries on the exclusive right. During prosecution, on the other hand, the process of setting claim scope is still underway. That process often requires the applicant to amend or modify the definition of the invention.

During prosecution, therefore, the Patent Office accords claims their "broadest reasonable interpretation consistent with the specification" and the understanding of one of ordinary skill in the art at the time of prosecution. *In re Bond*, 910 F.2d 831, 833 (Fed. Cir. 1990) (citation omitted). This standard expands claim scope to minimize the likelihood that the claims will acquire an undeserved breadth. Furthermore, "[c]onstruing claims broadly during prosecution is not unfair to the applicant ... , because the applicant has the opportunity to amend the claims to obtain more precise claim coverage." *In re Am. Acad. of Sci. Tech Ctr.*, 367 F.3d 1359, 1364 (Fed. Cir. 2004). Accordingly, any ambiguity in the scope of the claims results in an expanded, not constricted, interpretation during prosecution.

CHAPTER 13

INFRINGEMENT

I. INTRODUCTION

Anyone who makes, uses, sells, offers to sell, or imports a patented invention (without the owner's consent) infringes. Infringement falls in two general categories: direct and indirect. Direct infringement further subdivides into literal infringement and non-textual infringement under the doctrine of equivalents. Direct infringement depends primarily on the construction of the claims. Any product or process that includes each and every limitation directly infringes that claim.

Indirect infringement, also called vicarious infringement, subdivides into contributory infringement and inducement. These subcategories hold accountable individuals who supply a component of the invention or direct another's infringement.

Aside from these fundamental categories, the Patent Act creates a few special categories of infringement. For example, a unique enforcement scheme governs generic pharmaceuticals seeking approval from the Food and Drug Administration. Moreover, the Patent Act extends infringement to extraterritorial activities in some specific situations. Similarly, the Act forbids importation of a product made from a patented process outside the United States.

Lastly, in some special circumstances, courts excuse actions that might otherwise be infringing. A patentee may have—even unintentionally—granted the alleged infringer an implied license or exhausted his patent rights by already selling the good. Moreover, a party has the right to repair a licensed good, without, however, reconstructing it. Any party, furthermore, may use a patent for idle curiosity without fear of infringing.

II. LITERAL INFRINGEMENT

The right to exclude extends beyond the traditional categories of "making, using, or selling." In whole, § 271(a) provides: "Except as otherwise provided in this title, whoever without authority makes, uses, offers to sell, or sells any patented invention, within the United States or imports into the United States any patented invention during the term of the patent therefor, infringes the patent." This section sets forth an inventor's core rights.

Infringement entails a two-step analysis: first, the court construes the claims; and second, the finder of fact compares those construed claims to the accused product or process. *See, e.g.*, *Markman v. Westview Instruments, Inc.*, 52 F.3d 967 (Fed. Cir. 1995) (*en banc*). The first step of claim construction dominates the inquiry. Once the scope of the exclusive right is known, the second step is often a foregone conclusion. Thus, the prior chapter on claim construction was really an analysis of the requirements for literal infringement which vary from patent to patent and claim to claim.

Only the patentee may make, use, sell, offer for sale, or import patented subject matter. Without a license, any others simply infringe. Notably, an "offer for sale" infringes only if the sale will occur before expiration of the patent. 35 U.S.C § 271(i). With that sole exception, these rights are straightforward, even if nuanced. For example, the sale of equipment for performing a process is not a sale of the process itself. *Joy Techs., Inc. v. Flakt, Inc.*, 6 F.3d 770 (Fed. Cir. 1993). This provision's complexity, furthermore, lurks in requirements created by case law, such as territorial restrictions or other unstated exceptions.

III. THE DOCTRINE OF EQUIVALENTS— NON–TESTUAL INFRINGEMENT

A. Purpose

In sharp contrast with the simple two-step process for literal infringement, the doctrine of equivalents extends the exclusive right beyond the literal scope of the claims. In other words, an entity may nevertheless infringe a patent even though its accused product or process practices subject matter outside the literal scope of the claims. Counterintuitive at first blush, judicial opinions strive to justify this judge-made doctrine. For instance, courts have postulated that strict adherence to literal claim scope would diminish the value of patents and foster "unscrupulous copyists":

> [T]o permit imitation of a patented invention which does not copy every literal detail would be to convert the protection of the patent grant into a hollow and useless thing. Such a limitation would leave room for—indeed encourage—the unscrupulous copyist to make unimportant and insubstantial changes and substitutions in the patent which, though adding nothing, would be enough to take the copied matter outside the claim, and hence outside the reach of law.

Graver Tank & Mfg. Co. v. Linde Air Prods. Co., 339 U.S. 605, 607 (1950).

This "unscrupulous copyist" justification, however, cannot carry the entire weight of the doctrine of equivalents (DOE). In the first place, DOE applies even in cases of inadvertent use of the invention. Thus, the doctrine is not limited to intentional infringement, let alone "unscrupulous copying" (whatever that means). Moreover this justification supplies no neutral standard for distinguishing between designing around (evading the claims by designing an improvement for one or more features of the invention—a laudatory form of "copying" encouraged by the patent system) and infringing behavior. The "unscrupulous copyist" justification also has some of the weaknesses of the following justifications.

Courts have also justified DOE as a doctrine that ameliorates the inherent difficulties of defining an inventive idea in words. In fact, the Supreme Court recently commented:

> Unfortunately, the nature of language makes it impossible to capture the essence of a thing in a patent application.... The language in the patent claims may not capture every nuance of the invention or describe with complete precision the range of its novelty.

Festo Corp. v. Shoketsu Kinzoku Kogyo Kabushiki Co., 535 U.S. 722, 731 (2002). Again this justification cannot alone support DOE. Patent law already has several rules to accommodate the purely linguistic impediments in claim drafting. For instance, the drafter has the option to coin new terms under the lexicographer rule. The patent owner may even use reissue proceedings and continuation practices to expand unintentionally narrow claims. With these tools to assist in fashioning claim language, this justification poses another question: Should the DOE rescue a claim drafting mistake? In other words, claim drafting and correction tools should allow a careful claim drafter to clothe the invention adequately in language; thus, when literal language does not capture a variant that the drafter should have foreseen and covered, should DOE be available to compensate for the drafter's error? The straightforward answer is probably not, but courts have on occasion allowed DOE to compensate for claiming insufficiencies. *See, e.g., Primos, Inc. v. Hunter's Specialties, Inc.*, 451 F.3d 841 (Fed. Cir. 2006).

Lastly, the doctrine accommodates the enforcement of the patent against after-arising technology—that is, subject matter that was unknowable at the time the patent issued. *Sage Prods., Inc. v. Devon Indus., Inc.*, 126 F.3d 1420 (Fed. Cir. 1997). A dissent-in-part from the Federal Circuit's subsequently overruled *en banc Festo* opinion explains this justification:

Without a doctrine of equivalents, any claim drafted in current technological terms could be easily circumvented after the advent of an advance in technology. A claim using the terms "anode" and "cathode" from tube technology would lack the "collectors" and "emitters" of transistor technology that emerged in 1948. Thus, without a doctrine of equivalents, infringers in 1949 would have unfettered license to appropriate all patented technology using the out-dated terms "cathode" and "anode."

Festo Corp. v. Shoketsu Kinzoku Kogyo Kabushiki Co., 234 F.3d 558, 619 (Fed. Cir. 2000) (*en banc*) (Rader, J., concurring-in-part, dissenting-in-part). This objective test grounded in foreseeability places a premium on drafting patent applications describing and claiming all subject matter known to a person of ordinary skill in the art. But even here, the application of the doctrine of equivalents is not restricted solely to unforeseeable technology.

B. Test(s)

Although the doctrine of equivalents attempts to mitigate the unfairness of holding a patentee to the precisely defined limitations in the claims, the doctrine might, if taken to an extreme, endanger the notice function of claims. Indeed, a competitor should be able to recognize—and thus reasonably rely upon—the boundaries of a patent. Thus the vague and unspecified scope of non-textual infringement would unnecessarily restrict legitimate innovation and competition. For this reason, courts have sought over time to define DOE restrictively. At present, courts use two phraseologies to capture the same, amorphous idea: function-way-result and insubstantial differences.

The Supreme Court, for example, used the function-way-result test in *Graver Tank:* "[A] patentee may invoke this doctrine to proceed against the producer of a device if it performs substantially the same function in substantially the same way to obtain the same result." 339 U.S. 605, 608 (quotations omitted). The Court further explained "that if two devices do the same work in substantially the same way, and accomplish substantially the same result, they are the same, even though they differ in name, form or shape." *Id.* In addition, the Court noted that although not a formulaic inquiry, the doctrine may depend on whether a person of ordinary skill in the art would recognize the interchangeability between the claimed subject matter and the alleged equivalent. This factual determination can be informed by any number of evidentiary sources, including expert testimony, articles, texts, and treatises, and prior art. Based on this test, the *Graver Tank* Court held that silicates of manganese were equivalent to the silicates of alkaline earth metals (such as magnesium) recited in the claimed welding composition.

The Federal Circuit had fashioned another test, the insubstantial differences analysis. *Hilton Davis Chem. Co. v. Warner-Jenkinson Co.*, 62 F.3d 1512 (Fed. Cir. 1995) (*en banc*). The Supreme Court accepted both semantic formulations of the test:

> In our view, the particular linguistic framework used is less important than whether the test is probative of the essential inquiry: Does the accused product or process contain elements identical or equivalent to each claimed element of the patented invention? Different linguistic frameworks may be more suitable to different cases, depending on their particular facts.

Warner-Jenkinson Co. v. Hilton Davis Chem. Co., 520 U.S. 17, 40 (1997). And the alternative insubstantial differences test captures the same concept, fittingly, where the inflexibility of language impedes the determination at hand. In *Warner-Jenkinson*, for example, the Court remanded for a determination whether a purification process operated at a pH of 5.0 is insubstantially different from a nearly identical process operated at a pH of 6.0.

C. Limitations

Courts, in particular the Federal Circuit, recognized, however, the impossibility of defining amorphous terms like "insubstantial" or even "equivalent." These formulations are always a matter of degree. Yet, without some definition, DOE would threaten the notice function of claims. Because a confining definition proved elusive, the Federal Circuit moved as well to adopt confining limitations on DOE. If it could not define the doctrine, it would confine it.

The most frequent confining rules are prosecution history estoppel and the all-elements rule. The Federal Circuit, however, also acknowledges that the scope and content of the prior art as well as the scope and content of the patentee's disclosure may limit the reach of DOE.

1. Prosecution History Estoppel

Just as a claim amendment or argument informs the proper construction of a claim, an amendment or statement during prosecution may inform, and often defeat, a claim of equivalency.[11] Prosecution history estoppel thus "preclud[es] a patentee from regaining, through litigation, coverage of subject matter relinquished during prosecution of the application for the patent." *Wang Labs., Inc. v. Mitsubishi Elecs. Am., Inc.*, 103 F.3d 1571, 1577–78 (Fed. Cir. 1997). Notably, a patentee relinquishes subject matter in a narrowing amendment "when either (1) a preexisting claim limitation is narrowed by amendment or (2) a new claim limitation is added by amendment." *Honeywell Int'l Inc. v. Hamilton Sundstrand Corp.*, 370 F.3d 1131, 1140 (Fed. Cir. 2004). Although on its face relatively straightfor-

---

11. Prosecution disclaimer when construing claims differs in name from prosecution history estoppel when confining equivalents. Nonetheless the same standard applies to both doctrines for using prosecution history to limit claim coverage. *See Omega Eng'g, Inc. v. Raytek Corp.*, 334 F.3d 1314, 1326 n.1 (Fed. Cir. 2003).

ward, the legal framework belies this intuitive concept.

In *Warner-Jenkinson*, the Court introduced the foundation of a series of steps for analyzing whether an applicant amended a claim for a reason related to patentability, thus invoking prosecution history estoppel. The Court explained that a patentee has the burden of establishing the reason for amendment and that, in the absence of a justification, the presumption arose that the reason was related to patentability. This presumption generated great debate, which the Supreme Court revisited five years later in *Festo Corp. v. Shoketsu Kinzoku Kogyo Kabushiki Co.*, 535 U.S. 722 (2002). In that case, the Court set forth three categories that rebut the presumption of prosecution history estoppel once a claim has been narrowed:

> The equivalent may have been unforeseeable at the time of the [amendment]; the rationale underlying the amendment may bear no more than a tangential relation to the equivalent in question; or there may be some other reason suggesting that the patentee could not reasonably be expected to have described the insubstantial substitute in question.

Id. at 740–41.

Upon remand, the Federal Circuit aggregated the steps necessary to apply prosecution history estoppel in light of *Warner-Jenkinson* and *Festo*:

> The first question in a prosecution history estoppel inquiry is whether an amendment filed in the

Patent and Trademark Office ("PTO") has narrowed the literal scope of a claim. If the amendment was not narrowing, then prosecution history estoppel does not apply.... [T]he second question is whether the reason for that amendment was a substantial one relating to patentability....

[T]he third question in a prosecution history estoppel analysis addresses the scope of the subject matter surrendered by the narrowing amendment. At that point *Festo* imposes the presumption that the patentee has surrendered all territory between the original claim limitation and the amended claim limitation. The patentee may rebut that presumption of total surrender by demonstrating that it did not surrender the particular equivalent in question according to the [three] criteria....

Festo Corp. v. Shoketsu Kinzoku Kogyo Kabushiki Co., 344 F.3d 1359, 1366–67 (Fed. Cir. 2003) (*en banc*) (citations omitted). While the three rebuttal criteria—foreseeability, tangentiality, and some other reason—are unsettled, the court did provide some guidance. For example, foreseeability imposes on claim drafters to expressly claim technology that was foreseeable at the time of the amendment and precludes DOE from capturing that foreseeable technology. Foreseeability is an objective criterion driven by the knowledge of a person of ordinary skill in the art at the time of the amendment, a fact-based inquiry. *Smithkline Beecham Corp. v. Excel Pharms., Inc.*, 356 F.3d 1357 (Fed. Cir. 2004).

The foreseeability principle (perhaps the best justification for DOE overall) has its origins in efforts "to reconcile the preeminent notice function of claims with the protective function of the doctrine of equivalents. The reconciling principle is simple: the doctrine of equivalents does not capture subject matter that the patent drafter reasonably could have foreseen during the application process and included in the claims." *Johnson & Johnston Assoc. Inc. v. R.E. Service Co., Inc.*, 285 F.3d 1046, 1056 (Fed. Cir. 2002) (Rader, J., concurring).

Tangentiality, on the other hand, refers to amendments that do not pertain or relate to the disputed element in the accused device. *Primos, Inc. v. Hunter's Specialties, Inc.*, 451 F.3d 841 (Fed. Cir. 2006). The Federal Circuit has determined that this is a very narrow category. *Festo*, 344 F.3d at 1369–70. At least one Federal Circuit opinion has noted that the vague tangentiality factor "run[s] counter" to principles of public notice that enable designing around. *Cross Med. Prods., Inc. v. Medtronic Sofamor Danek, Inc.*, 480 F.3d 1335, 1347 (Fed. Cir. 2007) (Rader, J., concurring). The last category is a catchall and, as such, has a narrow applicability, such as where the limitations of language prevent drafting a claim to include the equivalent subject matter. *Amgen Inc. v. Hoechst Marion Roussel, Inc.*, 457 F.3d 1293 (Fed. Cir. 2006).

2. All-Elements Rule

Even if accompanied by a less complicated framework, the all-elements rule provides another potent restraint on the reach of the doctrine of equivalents. In emphasizing the vitality of the all-elements rule, the Supreme Court noted:

Each element contained in a patent claim is deemed material to defining the scope of the patented invention, and thus the doctrine of equivalents must be applied to individual elements of the claim, not to the invention as a whole. It is important to ensure that the application of the doctrine [of equivalents], even as to an individual element, is not allowed such broad play as to effectively eliminate that element in its entirety.

Warner-Jenkinson, 520 U.S. at 29. This restraint—that is, application of equivalency on a limitation-by-limitation basis—is firmly entrenched in case law. After all, if a device wholly lacks a claim element, it could not infringe under the doctrine of equivalents without vitiating that part of the claim. *See, e.g.*, *Pennwalt Corp. v. Durand–Wayland, Inc.*, 833 F.2d 931 (Fed. Cir. 1987) (*en banc*).

The all-elements rule, however, contains an inherent inconsistency. On the one hand, DOE applies to find infringement when the claim does not literally cover the accused process or product, i.e., when a claim limitation is literally missing. On the other hand, the all-elements rule limitation precludes application of DOE when a claim limitation is literally missing. No neutral standard determines when a missing limitation compels infringement under DOE or precludes DOE under the all-elements rule. As a matter of practice, the all-elements rule probably applies when the court decides that the missing element creates a substantial (rather than insubstantial) difference from the literal claim language. In other words, the all-elements rule in reality just reapplies the test for DOE itself. Thus, the all-elements rule may in fact just be a way that the Federal Circuit can reach a determination of equivalency (usually a matter of fact for the jury) as a question of law for the court.

The case of *Corning Glass Works v. Sumitomo Electric U.S.A., Inc.*, 868 F.2d 1251 (Fed. Cir. 1989), illustrates the difficulty of deciding when a missing claim limitation invokes DOE or precludes DOE under the all-elements rule. In that case, the patent claimed a fiber optic cable with inner core layer and an outer cladding around the core. The claim called for doping the core to make its index of refraction greater than the index of refraction for the outer cladding. Because the core has a different refractive index, light would follow the course of the cable. This invention was the advent of fiber optics.

The accused device did not, however, positively dope the core as required in the claims; rather, it negatively doped the cladding. The result was the same: the differences in the indices of refraction caused the light to follow the cable. The Federal Circuit could easily determine that the assertion of DOE vitiated the express claim limitation requiring a doped core. On the other hand, the Federal Circuit could also easily determine that DOE applied to overcome an insubstantial difference despite the missing limitation. In holding that the doped core layer limitation was not vitiated, the Federal Circuit remarked that it "has not set out in its precedent a definitive formula for determining equivalency between a required limitation or combination of limitations and what has been allegedly substituted therefor in the accused device. Nor do we propose to adopt one here." *Corning Glass*, 868 F.2d at 1260.

3. Prior Art

Another intuitive limitation on the doctrine of equivalents prevents the doctrine from extending the exclusive right to encompass the prior art. In other words, a court may not permit a patentee to prevent another from using subject matter that belongs to the public. This subject matter, of course, includes not only anticipatory subject matter but also obvious subject matter. In other words, an equivalent cannot solely comprise unpatentable subject matter. Accordingly, this analytical construct requires not only a hypothetical claim but also a hypothetical validity analysis.

The court in *Wilson Sporting Goods Co. v. David Geoffrey & Associates*, 904 F.2d 677 (Fed. Cir. 1990), applied this analytical construct to prohibit the scope of enforcement from reaching the accused golf balls. The patent at issue claimed a golf ball with a particular configuration of dimples determined by dividing the surface area of the ball into 80 triangles. These 80 triangles defined six equatorial circumferences—that is, intersecting circles that each passed around the widest portion of the ball. These "great" circles each defined a axis of symmetry, along which there were no dimples. The prior art contained balls also having six great circles, although these great circles had dimples intersecting them. In holding that the accused golf balls were not equivalents to the claimed balls, the court explained:

Whether prior art restricts the range of equivalents of what is literally claimed can be a difficult question to answer. To simplify analysis and bring the issue onto familiar turf, it may be helpful to conceptualize the limitation on the scope of equivalents by visualizing a *hypothetical* patent claim, sufficient in scope to *literally* cover the accused product. The pertinent question then becomes whether that hypothetical claim could have been allowed by the PTO over the prior art. If not, then it would be improper to permit the patentee to obtain that coverage in an infringement suit under the doctrine of equivalents. If the hypothetical claim could have been allowed, then *prior art* is not a bar to infringement under the doctrine of equivalents.

Id. at 684 (emphasis original). With that framework in hand, the court held that because the accused balls would have been obvious in light of the prior art, they did not infringe under the doctrine of equivalents. Although not mandatory in every case, this framework can be helpful in some instances to limit the range of equivalents. Indeed, it prevents a patentee from gaining through equivalency subject matter that could not have been gained during prosecution. *See Key Mfg. Group, Inc. v. Microdot, Inc.*, 925 F.2d 1444 (Fed. Cir. 1991).

The hypothetical claim analysis, however, is itself not unbounded; a patentee may not use it to narrow a claim in some aspects while at the same time broadening it in other aspects. In other words, a "hypothetical claim analysis is not an opportunity to freely redraft granted claims," because "[t]hat opportunity existed in the PTO, where the submitted claims were examined for patentability." *Streamfeeder, LLC v. Sure–Feed Sys., Inc.*, 175 F.3d 974, 983 (Fed. Cir. 1999).

4. Public Dedication

In certain circumstances, a patentee loses the opportunity to assert DOE because of failure to draft claims to encompass equivalent subject matter. Although this evokes unforeseeability as a requirement for infringement by equivalency, the public dedication limitation requires something more specific: a manifest showing of the patentee's knowledge of an equivalent. In particular, a patentee who discloses an alternative embodiment in the specification, yet fails to claim it, dedicates that subject matter to the public. In *Johnson & Johnston Associates Inc. v. R.E. Service Co.*, 285 F.3d 1046 (Fed. Cir. 2002) (*en banc*), the Federal Circuit determined that a patentee could not assert that claims reciting an aluminum device covered a steel device as an equivalent because the specification expressly mentioned, but did not claim, the stainless steel embodiment. But the patentee, the court clarified, was not without recourse:

> A patentee who inadvertently fails to claim disclosed subject matter, however, is not left without remedy. Within two years from the grant of the original patent, a patentee may file a reissue application and attempt to enlarge the scope of the original claims to include the disclosed but previously unclaimed subject matter. 35 U.S.C. § 251. In addition, a patentee can file a separate application claiming the disclosed subject matter under 35 U.S.C. § 120. Notably, Johnston took advantage of the latter of the two options by filing two continuation applications that literally claim the relevant subject matter.

Id. at 1055.

D. Means-Plus—Function Claims

As discussed in Chapter 10, a patent claim in means-plus-function format covers literally the corresponding structure in the specification as well as that structure's equivalents. *See* 35 U.S.C. § 112, paragraph 6. This statutory clause incorporates insubstantially different subject matter into the literal scope of the claim. *See, e.g., Al-Site Corp. v. VSI Int'l, Inc.*, 174 F.3d 1308 (Fed. Cir. 1999). Does this mean that a structural equivalent (a literal part of the claim) could itself have an equivalent under DOE, thus creating an equivalent of an equivalent? No, the timeframe of application of these various tests for equivalents precludes an equivalent of an equivalent. Because the meaning of claim language must be established at the time of filing (otherwise it is invalid for indefiniteness), a means-plus-function claim only includes those structural equivalents known at the time of filing. An equivalent under the doctrine of equivalents, on the other hand, applies to subject matter (usually unforeseeable) that arises after the patent's issuance. *See, e.g., Chiuminatta Concrete Concepts, Inc. v. Cardinal Indus., Inc.*, 145 F.3d 1303 (Fed. Cir. 1998). Thus, a proposed equivalent will either arise before filing and fall under § 112, paragraph 6, or arise after filing and invoke DOE. *Al-Site*, 174 F.3d at 1320 n.2.

E.   Reverse Doctrine of Equivalents

Just as the doctrine of equivalents provides a patentee with exclusive rights over subject matter outside the literal claim scope, it may provide an infringer with an additional defense to literal infringement. In other words, literally infringing activities may be outside the scope of enforcement. The reverse doctrine of equivalents applies ''where a device is so far changed in principle from a patented article that it performs the same or similar function in a substantially different way, but nevertheless falls within the literal words of the claim.'' *Graver Tank & Mfg. Co. v. Linde Air Prods. Co.*, 339 U.S. 605, 609 (1950). While this equitable doctrine exists, courts have serious doubts about its continued viability. *See, e.g., Tate Access Floors, Inc. v. Interface Architectural Res., Inc.*, 279 F.3d 1357 (Fed. Cir. 2002).

F. Indirect Infringement

Aside from direct infringement, the Patent Act sets forth two categories of vicarious infringement. The first, inducement of infringement, arises under § 271(b):

Whoever actively induces infringement of a patent shall be liable as an infringer.

And the second, contributory infringement, arises from the next subsection, § 271(c):

Whoever offers to sell or sells within the United States or imports into the United States a component of a patented machine, manufacture, combination, or composition, or a material or apparatus for use in practicing a patented process, constituting a material part of the invention, knowing the same to be especially made or especially adapted for use in an infringement of such patent, and not a staple article or commodity of commerce suitable for substantial noninfringing use, shall be liable as a contributory infringer.

Although different, these types of indirect infringement complement one another. A contributory infringer, for example, also induces infringement. Moreover, both types share three elements:

1. The indirect infringer acted knowingly or intentionally in either inducing infringement or selling a material component that has no substantial noninfringing uses.

2. The indirect infringer's actions culminated in another's direct infringement.

3. The indirect infringer's actions took place during the patent's term.

See, e.g., Hewlett-Packard Co. v. Bausch & Lomb Inc., 909 F.2d 1464, 1469 (Fed. Cir. 1990). Although direct infringement is an obvious prerequisite, the focus must remain on what the allegedly indirect infringer did and when he did it. *See, e.g. Standard Oil Co. v. Nippon Shokubai Kagaku Kogyo Co.*, 754 F.2d 345 (Fed. Cir. 1985).

Inducement of infringement and contributory infringement, however, are not the same. Inducement more flexibly encompasses a greater number of situations, including those that involve subject matter with noninfringing as well as infringing uses or that involve encouragement of the use of certain subject matter.

1. Inducement of Infringement

Although the statute does not explicitly set forth that inducement requires knowledge, judicial gloss has firmly entrenched this requirement. To begin with, the alleged indirect infringer "must have actual or constructive knowledge of the patent." *Insituform Techs., Inc. v. Cat Contracting, Inc.*, 161 F.3d 688 (Fed. Cir. 1998). In addition to that knowledge, the patentee must show that the alleged indirect infringer intended the infringing acts. *See, e.g., C.R. Bard, Inc. v. Advanced Card. Sys., Inc.*, 911 F.2d 670 (Fed. Cir. 1990). The Federal Circuit has clarified that the indirect infringer's intent must be specific—that is, an intent (knowing of the patent) to cause the infringement. *DSU Med. Corp. v. JMS*

Co., 471 F.3d 1293 (Fed. Cir. 2006) (*en banc* in relevant part). Specifically, the Federal Circuit overruled the general intent standard for inducement in *Hewlett-Packard Co. v. Bausch & Lomb Inc.*, 909 F.2d 1464, 1469 (Fed. Cir. 1990) (holding that "proof of actual intent to cause the acts which constitute the infringement is a necessary prerequisite to finding active inducement."). Instead the *en banc* opinion endorsed the specific standard of intent in *Manville Sales Corp. v. Paramount Systems, Inc.*, 917 F.2d 544, 553 (Fed. Cir. 1990) (holding that the alleged indirect infringer must "possess[ ] specific intent to encourage another's infringement" and that "the alleged infringer's actions induced infringement acts *and* that he knew or should have known his actions would induce actual infringements.") (emphasis original).

This requisite intent or knowledge manifests itself in various circumstances, all of which require facilitating, encouraging, or aiding another's infringement. For example, a sale of an infringing business may in some circumstances indirectly infringe. *Compare Water Techs. Corp. v. Calco, Ltd.*, 850 F.2d 660 (Fed. Cir. 1988) *with Hewlett-Packard Co. v. Bausch & Lomb, Inc.*, 909 F.2d 1464 (Fed. Cir. 1990). Similarly, instructing another—for example, by providing directions on how to infringe a method claim—would also suffice. *See, e.g., Warner-Lambert Co. v. Apotex Corp.*, 316 F.3d 1348 (Fed. Cir. 2003). And not infrequently, a company's officers or directors may incur personal liability for inducing the company's infringement, at least in limited circumstances. *See, e.g., Sensonics, Inc. v. Aerosonic Corp.*, 81 F.3d 1566 (Fed. Cir. 1996).

2. Contributory Infringement

Although requiring knowledge of the patent, contributory infringement applies in narrower circumstances than inducement. In particular, this remedy requires a sale, offer for sale, or importation of only a portion of the patented invention in addition to a lack of substantial noninfringing uses for that component. In other words, a contributory infringer must know of the patent and provide another with a nonstaple component (that is, a component whose only use is in a patented combination). *See, e.g., Aro Mfg. Co. v. Convertible Top Replacement Co.*, 377 U.S. 476 (1964); *Dawson Chem. Co. v. Rohm & Haas Co.*, 448 U.S. 176 (1980).

Notably, the Patent Act exempts from contributory infringement certain activities, when done by the patentee, that could otherwise amount to misuse under § 271(d). *See* Chapter 14. Specifically, a patentee may, without misusing his patent rights, ''(1) derive[ ] revenue from acts which if performed by another without his consent would constitute contributory infringement of the patent [and] (2) license[ ] or authorize[ ] another to perform acts which if performed without his consent would constitute contributory infringement of the patent.'' 35 U.S.C. § 271(d). Counter-intuitively then, contributory infringement is relevant to determining permissible uses of patent rights.

IV. TERRITORIAL SCOPE

As a general matter, the right to exclude granted by a United States patent may only preclude activities within U.S. borders. That is, domestic patent law cannot reach purely extraterritorial activities. *See, e.g., Waymark Corp. v. Porta Sys. Corp.*, 245 F.3d 1364 (Fed. Cir. 2001). The globalization of markets and the ease of transferring portions of an enterprise abroad, however, have influenced this general rule. In a famous recent case, the Federal Circuit had to determine if an "electronic mail system" with one component located in Canada (the BlackBerry® system) infringed a domestic patent as a "use" under § 271(a). The court decided that the "control and beneficial use" of the patented system occurred within the borders of the United States. Therefore, even though one claimed feature lay outside U.S. borders, the court upheld the jury verdict of infringement. *NTP, Inc. v. Research in Motion, Ltd.*, 418 F.3d 1282 (Fed. Cir. 2005).

Another relatively recent section of the Patent Act has also expanded the reach of domestic patent law. Before 1984, an entity could manufacture and export the unassembled components of a patented combination without infringing. In *Deepsouth Packing Co. v. Laitram Corp.*, 406 U.S. 518 (1972), for example, the Court permitted the defendant to continue manufacturing all the components of a patented shrimp peeler domestically and ship them—unassembled, of course—abroad for assembly and usage. In the words of the Supreme Court, "[t]he statute makes it clear that it is not an infringement to make or use a patented product outside of the United States." *Id.* at 527. Section 271(f)—enacted in 1984—partially overruled this decision.

Moreover, before 1988, the extraterritorial manufacture of a good followed by importation of that good would not infringe a patent reading on that product. That is, method patents could not prevent processes performed abroad, even if the product of that process later entered the United States. *See, e.g., United States v. Studiengesellschaft Kohle, m.b.H*, 670 F.2d 1122 (D.C. Cir. 1981). Section 271(g) changed this rule, albeit with important exceptions.

A. Exporting Components of a Patented Combination

In ordinary circumstances, a party supplying patented components along with instructions for their combination incurs liability for inducing infringement or contributory infringement under either § 271(b) or (c). But where the assembly of the components occurs outside the United States, there can be no direct infringement and thus no indirect infringement. When *Deepsouth* affirmed this principle, it opened a loophole for infringement. A potential infringer needed only to move the final assembly step abroad to avoid liability. A 1984 enactment closed the loophole:

(1) Whoever without authority supplies or causes to be supplied in or from the United States all or a substantial portion of the components of a patented invention, where such components are

uncombined in whole or in part, in such manner as to actively induce the combination of such components outside of the United States in a manner that would infringe the patent if such combination occurred within the United States, shall be liable as an infringer.

(2) Whoever without authority supplies or causes to be supplied in or from the United States any component of a patented invention that is especially made or especially adapted for use in the invention and not a staple article or commodity of commerce suitable for substantial noninfringing use, where such component is uncombined in whole or in part, knowing that such component is so made or adapted and intending that such component will be combined outside of the United States in a manner that would infringe the patent if such combination occurred within the United States, shall be liable as an infringer.

35 U.S.C. § 271(f). This subsection gave rise to a question of the scope of its extraterritorial rights when applied to software. In particular, does an entity that "supplies" a component abroad incur liability for copies made from that component in the foreign country?

The Supreme Court recently addressed this question in *Microsoft Corp. v. AT & T Corp.*, 127 S.Ct. 1746, 82 USPQ2d 1400 (2007). In this case, Microsoft included infringing voice recognition software in its software package. Microsoft then put this infringing software on a master "golden" disk and sent that abroad. Once abroad, Microsoft affiliates copied the master program onto thousands of other computers. A district court imposed liability on Microsoft under § 271(f) for all of those copies even though made abroad. After the Federal Circuit upheld that judgment because "the act of copying was subsumed in the act of 'supplying,'" the Supreme Court reversed. The Supreme Court instead determined that the statutory term "supplying" does not mean that Microsoft is liable in the U.S. for copying that occurs abroad. Instead the Supreme Court reiterated the territorial limitation on infringement: "As a principle of general application, moreover, we have stated that courts should assume that legislators take account of the legitimate sovereign interests of other nations when they write American laws.... Foreign conduct is generally the domain of foreign law, and in the area here involved, in particular, foreign law may embody different policy judgments about the relative rights of inventors, competitors, and the public in patented inventions." *Microsoft*, 82 USPQ2d at 1410 (quotations and citations omitted). Indeed, the Court firmly explained: "In short, foreign law alone, not United States law, currently governs the manufacture and sale of components of patented inventions in foreign countries. If AT & T desires to prevent copying in foreign countries, its remedy today lies in obtaining and enforcing foreign patents." *Id.*

B. Importation of Goods Manufactured by a Patented Process

In limited circumstances, a product made by a patented process extraterritorially infringes a United States patent. The statute, in particular, provides:

Whoever without authority imports into the United States or offers to sell, sells, or uses within the United States a product which is made by a process patented in the United States shall be liable as an infringer, if the importation, offer to sell, sale, or use of the product occurs during the term of such process patent. In an action for infringement of a process patent, no remedy may be granted for infringement on account of the noncommercial use or retail sale of a product unless there is no adequate remedy under this title for infringement on account of the importation or other use, offer to sell, or sale of that product. A product which is made by a patented process will, for purposes of this title, not be considered to be so made after—

(1) it is materially changed by subsequent processes; or

(2) it becomes a trivial and nonessential component of another product.

35 U.S.C. § 271(g). As a starting point, the imported physical article must have been produced by a patented process. Mere information generated by a patented process does not fall within the scope of the 1988 Act. *See Bayer AG v. Housey Pharms., Inc.*, 340 F.3d 1367 (Fed. Cir. 2003). Furthermore, the statute exempts any product "materially changed" after the patented process and any prod-

uct that is only a "trivial and nonessential component" of another product.

In the important pharmaceutical field, for instance, an importer can escape liability by either importing intermediates that need more processing before the market or that become insignificant components of a larger product. In one case, the Federal Circuit assessed the material change exception based on "the substantiality of the change between the product of the patented process and the product that is being imported." *Eli Lilly & Co. v. Am. Cyanamid Co.*, 82 F.3d 1568, 1573 (Fed. Cir. 1996).

V. INTERNATIONAL TRADE COMMISSION

While most patentees enforce their patents in federal court, the international marketplace has given considerable importance to another remedy. Often a patentee has the option of enforcing their patents by requesting the International Trade Commission (ITC) investigate an unfair importation under 19 U.S.C. § 1337, commonly known as Section 337.

The primary advantages to filing a complaint with the ITC include (i) faster resolution—it typically takes just over one year until the final determination (a distinct advantage for a petitioner who can prepare its case for months before placing the respondent under the pressure of time limits by filing a complaint)—and (ii) administrative law judges who are familiar with patent disputes. In addition, an ITC investigation does not preclude a patentee from concurrently filing a suit in district court over the same allegedly infringing acts. Thus, although an ITC action cannot award damages, it does not preclude a concurrent damages action in federal court. *Cf. In re Princo Corp.*, 478 F.3d 1345 (Fed. Cir. 2007).

Although these investigations are similar to cases brought in district court, they have important differences, for example, with respect to the parties involved, the elements for proof, and the available relief. Indeed, an ITC staff attorney represents the public in every investigation, thus interjecting a third party into the proceedings.

Moreover, the statute provides in part:

(1) Subject to paragraph (2), the following are unlawful, and when found by the Commission to exist shall be dealt with, in addition to any other provision of law, as provided in this section:

* * *

(B) The importation into the United States, the sale for importation, or the sale within the United States after importation by the owner, importer, or consignee, of articles that—

(i) infringe a valid and enforceable United States patent . . . ; or

(ii) are made, produced, processed, or mined under, or by means of, a process covered by the claims of a valid and enforceable United States patent.

19 U.S.C. § 1337(a). Accordingly, an ITC action requires an importation (or sale after importation)

of either an infringing good or a good produced, processed, or mined by a patented process. Although mimicking some provisions of 35 U.S.C. § 271, the infringement analyses are not identical. For example, the two statutory exceptions available in district court under § 271(g)—materially changed or trivial and nonessential component—are not available defenses for respondents before the ITC. *Kinik Co. v. Int'l Trade Comm'n*, 362 F.3d 1359 (Fed. Cir. 2004).

Beyond proving infringement, a patentee filing a complaint with the ITC must prove that a domestic industry exists or is in the process of being established. The statute, in particular, states:

(2) Subparagraphs (B) ... of paragraph (1) apply only if an industry in the United States, relating to the articles protected by the patent ... concerned, exists or is in the process of being established.

(3) For purposes of paragraph (2), an industry in the United States shall be considered to exist if there is in the United States, with respect to the articles protected by the patent ... concerned—

(A) significant investment in plant and equipment;

(B) significant employment of labor or capital; or

(C) substantial investment in its exploitation, including engineering, research and development, or licensing.

19 U.S.C. § 1337(a). Proving domestic industry has two prongs, both of which must occur in the United States. The first prong is technical—the patent must read on noninfringing goods of either the patentee or a licensee. *Cf., Corning Glass Works v. U.S. Int'l Trade Comm'n,* 799 F.2d 1559 (Fed. Cir. 1986). And the second prong is economic—the patentee must have significant investment in plant and equipment, significant employment of labor or capital, or substantial investment in the patent's exploitation. Notably, the patentee no longer needs to prove that the domestic industry is injured or threatened by the importation of infringing goods (or goods made by an infringing process). 19 U.S.C. § 1337(a)(1)(A); Pub. L. No. 100–418, 102 Stat. 1107 (1988). Once a patentee prevails before the ITC, he may seek both a cease-and-desist order and an exclusion order. A cease-and-desist order halts the sale and distribution of previously imported infringing goods, and an exclusion order directs U.S. Customs and Border Protection to halt the importation of the infringing goods. 19 U.S.C. §§ 1337(d) & (f). Notably, these are purely equitable remedies; a prevailing patentee may only seek monetary damages in federal court.

VI. EXCEPTIONS TO INFRINGEMENT

By tautology, authorized uses or sales of patented subject matter do not infringe. An express license authorizes use of the patented invention within the terms of the license. Each license agreement is a unique document tailored to the particular rights the patentee wishes to convey to the licensee. *See, e.g.*, *Intergraph Corp. v. Intel Corp.*, 241 F.3d 1353 (Fed. Cir. 2001).

In some cases, courts will imply a license as a matter of law to achieve some greater public objective. Beyond implied licenses, courts have also created some doctrines, like the first sale doctrine— sometimes called exhaustion—or the repair/reconstruction doctrine to authorize use of patented technology without liability. Furthermore, the activities of the infringer may be so minor or without commercial significance to except them from infringement. Furthermore, the Patent Act carves out particular behavior relating to pharmaceuticals.

A. Implied Licenses, First Sale & Exhaustion, and Repair & Reconstruction

Exhaustion bars enforcement of a patent where the patentee (or his licensee) has already made an unrestricted sale of the patented article and reaped the reward of the exclusive right. *Intel Corp. v. ULSI Sys. Tech., Inc.*, 995 F.2d 1566 (Fed. Cir. 1993). In other words, the patentee exhausts his patent rights—to both the article as well as the methods of using the article—with the first sale. Therefore, courts will imply a license, for instance, to sell components of a patented combination.

This doctrine, notably, is not limitless. In the first place, foreign sales generally do not exhaust the patentee's domestic patent rights nor create an implied license. *Jazz Photo Corp. v. Int'l Trade Comm'n*, 264 F.3d 1094 (Fed. Cir. 2001). And a patentee may restrict the use of a patented good at the time of sale, so long as the restriction is properly within the patent grant. For example, a patentee may restrict purchasers of his invention to a single (that is, disposable) use. *Mallinckrodt, Inc. v. Medipart, Inc.*, 976 F.2d 700 (Fed. Cir. 1992). In such a case, the restricted sale indicates only a relinquishment of patent rights that do not fall within the scope of the express constraint on use. *See Monsanto Co. v. McFarling*, 302 F.3d 1291 (Fed. Cir. 2002).

In the absence of an unauthorized (or, alternatively, restricted) sale, a purchaser of a patented good also has the right to repair it without incurring liability for infringement. But if the repairs are too extensive—that is, if the repairs entirely reconstruct the patented invention—the owner has in fact infringed. Despite the inherent difficulty in dividing permissible repair from impermissible reconstruction, case law has outlined guiding principles. If, for example, a patented item is entirely spent during use, rebuilding the item constitutes an impermissible reconstruction. But if, on the other hand, a patented item contains a replaceable part, replacing that part constitutes permissible repair, irrespective of whether the part is worn out. *Husky Injection Molding Sys., Ltd. v. R & D Tool & Eng'g Co.*, 291 F.3d 780 (Fed. Cir. 2002). In theory at least, the distinction between reconstruction and repair might depend on an analysis of the predictable life span of a patented invention. Repair would ensure the invention reaches its full useful life, while reconstruction might inordinately double or triple that predictable life. No court has adopted this formulation, however.

Instead, articulating a universally applicable distinction between reconstructing a spent part and repairing a replaceable part has proven elusive in practice, and the determination is necessarily fact-dependent. For example, in *Jazz Photo Corp. v. International Trade Commission*, 264 F.3d 1094 (Fed. Cir. 2001), the Federal Circuit held that, despite the patentee's unilateral intent that its lens-fitted film packages (colloquially known as "single-use" or "disposable" cameras) be used only once, reconstituting the packages with unexposed film, resetting the exposure counter, and resealing the broken case constituted permissible repair. Quixotically, the court further held that the patent rights to the claimed method of loading the packages with film was also exhausted by the unrestricted domestic sales of the packages. *Id.* at 1108–09. In other words, in this case at least, practicing each of the claimed steps did not incur liability because the patentee relinquished rights to that method by selling goods made by it.

B. Experimental Use

Despite the unqualified statutory language that unauthorized uses of patented technology constitute infringement, courts have excepted *de minimis* as well as experimental uses from infringement. A *de minimis* use occurs when there is merely a nominal infringement for which almost insignificant damages would arise. *See Deuterium Corp. v. United*

States, 19 Cl. Ct. 624 (1990). An experimental use, however, occurs when there is a noncommercial evaluation of patented subject matter. In 1813, for example, Justice Story commented that "it could never have been the intention of the legislature to punish a man, who constructed such a machine merely for philosophical experiments, or for the purpose of ascertaining the sufficiency of the machine to produce its effects." *Whittemore v. Cutter*, 29 F.Cas. 1120, 1121 (C.C. Mass. 1813) (No. 17,-600).

This common-law experimental use exception operates to protect alleged infringers in only the narrowest of circumstances: where the infringer acted "for amusement, to satisfy idle curiosity, or for strictly philosophical inquiry" without "definite, cognizable, and not insubstantial commercial purposes." *Embrex, Inc. v. Serv. Eng'g Corp.*, 216 F.3d 1343, 1349 (Fed. Cir. 2000) (quotations omitted). Indeed, even academic institutions engaged in research—irrespective of whether that research has a practical, real-world application—do not fall under the experimental use exception:

Our precedent clearly does not immunize use that is in any way commercial in nature. Similarly, our precedent does not immunize any conduct that is in keeping with the alleged infringer's legitimate business, regardless of commercial implications. For example, major research universities ... often sanction and fund research projects with arguably no commercial application whatsoever. However, these projects unmistakably further the institution's legitimate business objectives, including educating and enlightening students and faculty participating in these projects. These projects also serve, for example, to increase the status of the institution and lure lucrative research grants, students and faculty.

Madey v. Duke Univ., 307 F.3d 1351, 1362 (Fed. Cir. 2002).

As an example, this common law doctrine could not be invoked to protect a generic drug manufacturer that tests a patented pharmaceutical prior to the patent's expiration, even if those tests are necessary to obtain government approval. *See Roche Prods., Inc. v. Bolar Pharm. Co.*, 733 F.2d 858 (Fed. Cir. 1984). This decision resulted in a *de facto* extension of patent term, because a generic manufacturer may not begin proving the safety and efficacy of the drug until after the patent expires. To eliminate this practical extension of patent rights, a new comprehensive law overruled *Roche* and dramatically altered the relationship between research-based and generic pharmaceutical companies. *See* Drug Price Competition and Patent Term Restoration Act of 1984, Pub. L No. 98–417, 98 Stat. 1585. This Act, commonly known as the Hatch–Waxman Act, provided in part:

It shall not be an act of infringement to make, use, offer to sell, or sell within the United States or import into the United States a patented invention . . . solely for uses reasonably related to the development and submission of information under a Federal law which regulates the manufacture, use, or sale of drugs or veterinary biological products.

35 U.S.C. § 271(e)(1). Although only referencing drugs on its face, this provision also applies to experimentation with medical devices for submission of information showing safety and efficacy under the same statutory scheme that regulates the safety and efficacy of drugs. *Eli Lilly & Co. v. Medtronic, Inc.*, 496 U.S. 661 (1990). The Supreme Court has clarified that this provision has a very broad scope. Any research activity that may have even a remote link, this is, "uses reasonably related" to submissions for government approval, are exempt from infringement. Thus pre-clinical investigations and tests not even necessarily linked to a particular pharmaceutical composition may escape infringement liability. *Merck KGaA v. Integra Lifesciences I, Ltd.*, 545 U.S. 193 (2005).

VII. "ARTIFICIAL" INFRINGEMENT UNDER § 271(e)(2)

Like most patent law doctrines, infringement is by and large universally applicable across technological boundaries, with one notable exception. As an integral part of the Hatch–Waxman Act, which codified the experimental use exception for the development of generic drugs under § 271(e)(1), patents relating to pharmaceuticals receive special treatment under the patent statute. This nonexclusive infringement—meaning that pharmaceutically related patents may nonetheless be enforced under other subsections of § 271—relates to a generic manufacturer's submission of an Abbreviated New Drug Application (ANDA) that asserts bioequivalence to a previously approved drug. *See* 21 U.S.C. § 355(j)(2). In the most frequently litigated circumstance, the ANDA filer will also make a "paragraph IV" certification that any patent reading on the approved drug "is invalid or will not be infringed by the manufacture, use, or sale of the new drug." 21 U.S.C. § 355(j)(2)(A)(vii)(IV). The mere act of filing that ANDA is an infringement:

It shall be an act of infringement to submit—

an application under section 505(j) of the Federal Food, Drug, and Cosmetic Act or described in section 505(b)(2) of such Act for a drug claimed in a patent or the use of which is claimed in a patent ... , if the purpose of such submission is to obtain approval under such Act to engage in the commercial manufacture, use, or sale of a drug ... claimed in a patent or the use of which is claimed in a patent before the expiration of such patent.

35 U.S.C. § 271(e)(2). Because no generic drug may exist at the time the ANDA is filed (thus precluding a comparison of the claims to the accused product), this is an "artificial" act of infringement. *See generally Glaxo, Inc. v. Novopharm, Ltd.*, 110 F.3d 1562 (Fed. Cir. 1997). This artificial infringement, however, does not include indirect infringement. For example, where the approved use of a drug and the drug itself are unpatented, a method of unapproved

treatment comprising administering the unpatented drug does not constitute an artificial infringement under § 271(e)(2). *Warner-Lambert Co. v. Apotex Corp.*, 316 F.3d 1348 (Fed. Cir. 2003).

Once a patentee establishes artificial infringement, he does not receive the full range of remedies available under other types of infringement. Instead, the statute provides:

For an act of infringement described in paragraph (2)—

(A) the court shall order the effective date of any approval of the drug ... involved in the infringement to be a date which is not earlier than the date of the expiration of the patent which has been infringed,

(B) injunctive relief may be granted against an infringer to prevent the commercial manufacture, use, offer to sell, or sale within the United States or importation into the United States of an approved drug ..., and

(C) damages or other monetary relief may be awarded against an infringer only if there has been commercial manufacture, use, offer to sell, or sale within the United States or importation into the United States of an approved drug....

The remedies prescribed by subparagraphs (A), (B), and (C) are the only remedies which may be granted by a court for an act of infringement described in paragraph (2), except that a court may award attorney fees under section 285.

35 U.S.C. § 271(e)(2). Thus, the patentee may not receive monetary damages (unless the infringer has made the generic drug available to the public). Injunctive relief, which takes the form of both enjoining commercial activity as well as enjoining the approval of the ANDA, constitutes the primary award. In some circumstances—for instance, where there is litigation misconduct including vexatious or unjustified litigation or frivolous filings—attorneys fees may be awarded. *Yamanouchi Pharm. Co. v. Danbury Pharmacal, Inc.*, 231 F.3d 1339 (Fed. Cir. 2000). The artificial act of infringement, however, cannot constitute willful infringement. *Glaxo Group Ltd. v. Apotex, Inc.*, 376 F.3d 1339 (Fed. Cir. 2004). In sum, the Hatch–Waxman Act encourages litigation as a public policy tool to encourage early challenges to the validity of pharmaceutical patents.

VIII. INFRINGEMENT ABROAD

Currently, individual European countries issue patents, as does the European Patent Office. Notably, a single EPO patent may be enforced in each nation individually; in other words, the single patent is treated as multiple national patents. *See* European Patent Convention, Article 64(1). Indeed, "[a]ny infringement of a European patent shall be dealt with by national law." Article 64(3). For the most part, this does not cause problems, as most European nations have substantially harmonized patent laws. Claim construction, however, is not uniform throughout the member countries—which should come as no surprise given the inherently problematic nature of the inquiry. Germany and the United Kingdom, for example, construe claims broadly and narrowly, respectively. Due to this difference in claim interpretation, the European Patent Convention purports to set forth a proper methodology: "The extent of the protection conferred by a European patent or a European patent application shall be determined by the terms of the claims. Nevertheless, the description and drawings shall be used to interpret the claims." Article 69. Given the laconic nature of this methodology, the Protocol on the Interpretation of Article 69 provides additional guidance:

Article 69 should not be interpreted in the sense that the extent of the protection conferred by a European patent is to be understood as that defined by the strict, literal meaning of the wording used in the claims, the description and drawings being employed only for the purpose of resolving an ambiguity found in the claims. Neither should it be interpreted in the sense that the claims serve only as a guideline and that the actual protection conferred may extend to what, from a consideration of the description and drawings by a person skilled in the art, the patentee has contemplated. On the contrary, it is to be interpreted as defining a position between these extremes which combines a fair protection for the patentee with a reasonable degree of certainty for third parties.

Even though this purports to set forth a uniform standard, individual countries still have varying practices. Interestingly, each country may nonetheless achieve similar results through the doctrine of equivalents. Of course, this generalization, too, has difficulties because the United Kingdom professes to have no DOE. *Kirin-Amgen Inc. v Hoechst Marion Roussel Ltd.*, [2004] UKHL 46. Instead the United Kingdom employs a "purposive construction" doctrine that may occasionally recast claims to achieve the overarching purpose (as divined by the judges) of the invention.

CHAPTER 14

ADDITIONAL DEFENSES

I. INTRODUCTION

Aside from defenses of noninfringement, failure to comply with the substantive requirements for patentability under §§ 101, 102, 103, and 112, unenforceability for inequitable conduct, and double patenting (which are discussed in prior chapters), additional defenses—primarily equitable in nature—may also preclude a patentee from successfully enforcing a patent. These additional defenses—which include laches, estoppel, a peculiar type of implied license called a "shop right," misuse, temporary presence in the United States, and first inventorship—do not affect the patent's validity; rather, they affect whether the patent may be asserted against a particular party (with the exception of prosecution laches and patent misuse, which preclude enforcement against all parties). When successfully established, these defenses provide something akin to a limited license to practice the patentee's invention.

Courts and parties often address laches and estoppel concurrently, even though they entail different (yet nonetheless related) concepts. Even though they are not unique to patent law, patent-specific cases have recurring fact patterns that have generated a notable body of case law. Although infrequently occurring and heavily fact-dependant, these doctrines are well-defined.

The next three defenses, which are of course unique to patent law, occur with even less frequency than laches and estoppel. The first, "shop rights," is firmly entrenched, with a lengthy history, even if rare in the realities of modern corporate environments. An employer obtains a "shop right" to practice an invention that its employee created while in its employ. But this implied license is only the default rule, and employers may enter into contracts with their employees and independent contractors regarding ownership of inventions.

The second—the temporary presence defense under 35 U.S.C. § 272—excuses any transitory infringement by foreign-based vessels and vehicles engaged in international commerce. Under § 272, the temporary presence of a vessel, aircraft, or vehicle within the territory of the United States does not constitute infringement so long as limited solely to the operation of that craft and not sold, offered for sale, or involved in the manufacture of anything sold or exported from the United States.

Lastly, the third—the first inventor defense under 35 U.S.C. § 273—was enacted as a part of the American Inventors Protection Act of 1999. This defense permits a prior user of a business method to continue using that method if it is subsequently patented. In this respect, the defense is akin to prior invention under § 102(g), with a critical distinction being that a prior user of a business method need not have publicly disclosed the subject matter to evade liability for infringement. Furthermore, many foreign jurisdictions have similar prior-user provisions, although most are not limited to business methods.

The last defense addressed by this chapter is patent misuse, which borrows antitrust-like principles to preclude a patentee from enforcing his patent rights under some licensing agreements that extend beyond the literal terms of the exclusive right. Initially this doctrine was a defense limited to contributory infringers who sold unpatented components that were part of a patented combination or process. In other words, the defense originally belonged only to certain defendants. But the defense outgrew those confines. Now any defendant, regardless of whether it is merely a contributory infringer, may render a patent unenforceable for patent misuse.

II. LACHES AND ESTOPPEL

Even though not specifically identified in 35 U.S.C. § 282 as defenses to patent infringement, accused infringers may invoke laches or estoppel to avoid a judgment of liability. Laches resolves the inequity of a patentee attempting to enforce his patent rights too late. Estoppel, on the other hand, resolves the inequity of a patentee attempting to enforce his patent rights after inducing the defendant to reasonably believe that the patentee would not sue. Notably, the trial court has broad discretion to apply these defenses according to the equities of the situation. In *A.C. Aukerman Co. v. R. L. Chaides Construction Co.*, 960 F.2d 1020 (Fed. Cir. 1992), the Federal Circuit addressed these equitable defenses *en banc*, distinguishing them and setting forth their necessary elements of proof. The court, however, cautioned that the elements of these defenses are not immutable rules but guiding principles.

A. Laches

With respect to laches, the *Aukerman* court reaffirmed that two traditional elements apply in patent cases. The first element requires the alleged infringer to prove that the patentee's delay in bringing suit was unreasonable and inexcusable. This period of delay begins at the time the patentee knew or should have known of the allegedly infringing activities and ends when the patentee brings suit, although the clock cannot start before the asserted patent issues. Although the actual length of time that will be unreasonable varies with circumstances, a six-year period is presumptively too long.[12] Notably, this presumption only shifts the burden of going forward with evidence and does not shift the burden of persuasion. Furthermore, any

12. Although analogous to the six-year statute of limitations on damages under 35 U.S.C. § 286, the two periods of delay serve different purposes and have different effects. Indeed, § 286 is an statute-based arbitrary limitation on damages, whereas laches is a common-law-based discretionary limitation on liability. *Cf. Standard Oil Co. v. Nippon Shokubai Kagaku Kogyo Co.*, 754 F.2d 345 (Fed. Cir. 1985).

mitigating circumstances justifying the delay—for example, other litigation, negotiations with the defendant, poverty or illness, a national emergency, the extent of infringement and its evolution over the period of delay, or an ownership dispute—may influence the determination of inexcusability.

The second element requires the alleged infringer to prove a material prejudice caused by that delay. Such prejudice is typically available in two flavors: economic and evidentiary. Economic prejudice is not determined by the amount of damages that a defendant would pay if found to be infringing; instead, economic prejudice requires a detrimental change in the economic position of the defendant over the period of delay, such as the loss of monetary investments or incurrence of excessive damages. For instance, economic prejudice may occur where an infringer would have had an opportunity to switch to a noninfringing product had the patentee not been dilatory in asserting his patent. While economic prejudice is difficult to describe in the abstract because it attempts to prevent an excessive (and avoidable) punishment caused by the delay, evidentiary prejudice is much more straightforward. The defendant suffers evidentiary prejudice where the delay severely inhibits its ability to proffer a full and fair defense. That is, prejudice occurs upon loss of evidence such as critical records or documents, important witnesses, or simply diminished recollection of witnesses. The unobtainable evidence must significantly impede the court's ability to determine crucial facts in dispute, making the litigation intractable or perhaps even futile.

If a defendant successfully proves that the patentee's delay was unreasonable and that material prejudice resulted from that delay, the defendant escapes liability only for conduct before the filing date of the litigation. In other words, once the patentee files suit, that date triggers prospective liability even where laches precludes a defendant's liability for past infringement. Thus a patentee could still seek an injunction on continued infringement.

B. Equitable Estoppel

Similar to laches, the *Aukerman* court clarified the three-pronged test for equitable estoppel. First, the patentee must have misled the defendant into reasonably believing that the patentee does not intend to enforce its patent against that defendant. Unlike laches, delay is not essential to a successful invocation of estoppel, even if a relevant fact or circumstance. Rather, the first prong requires that a patentee's conduct support an inference that the patentee did not intend to assert an infringement claim against the alleged infringer. In most instances, this means that the alleged infringer has specific knowledge of the patent—an unnecessary requirement for laches. Furthermore, the alleged infringer typically knows (or has a reasonable belief) that the patentee knew of the allegedly infringing acts for an unduly long period of time. Frequently this occurs where the patentee notifies the defendant of the alleged infringement, lulls the alleged infringer into an expectation that the threat has lapsed, then springs into action once again to enforce the patent. But beyond affirmative conduct, a patentee's inaction coupled with a special relationship to the defendant may satisfy this first element. The instances of acquiescence or abandonment, however, are far less common than the cases involving affirmative misrepresentations.

The second element of estoppel requires the defendant to prove reliance on the patentee's misleading conduct. As the *Aukerman* court explained:

Reliance is not the same as prejudice or harm, although frequently confused. An infringer can build a plant being entirely unaware of the patent. As a result of infringement, the infringer may be unable to use the facility. Although harmed, the infringer could not show reliance on the patentee's conduct. To show reliance, the infringer must have had a relationship or communication with the plaintiff which lulls the infringer into a sense of security in going ahead with building the plant.

960 F.2d at 1043. Thus, the defendant must take an action—such as building a new facility, promoting and advertising accused products, or hiring additional employees—based on its reasonable belief that the patentee would not in fact assert the patent. Stated in other terms, the defendant must have confronted a decision that would be affected by potential liability for infringement and chosen a

route that would not have otherwise been taken in the face of a patent suit.

The third prong of equitable estoppel is similar to the second element of laches, namely, the defendant must suffer material prejudice. Again this prejudice may be either economic or evidentiary. Where the defendant has reasonably relied on the patentee's nonenforcement conduct, economic prejudice becomes easy to prove. Building a new facility or hiring additional employees, for example, would likely suffice.

If a defendant proves these factors and the court rules that it would be inequitable to allow the patentee to press the patent infringement claim any further, the patentee's entire claim is barred. In other words, unlike laches, a successful estoppel defense excuses past, present, and future behavior from liability.

C. Prosecution Laches

In addition to a delay in filing a suit for infringement, a patentee may forfeit rights to an invention as a result of a delay in prosecuting the applications that matured into the patent. *Woodbridge v. United States*, 263 U.S. 50 (1923); *Webster Elec. Co. v. Splitdorf Elec. Co.*, 264 U.S. 463 (1924). Although prosecution laches was recognized long ago, for many years it remained a forgotten defense to the problem of so-called "submarine patents." Although a patent's term now expires 20 years after the earliest effective filing date, it once expired 17 years after the date of issuance. Under that regime, an inventor could file an application to obtain an early date of priority, then, through the use of continuing applications permitted by the Patent Office's rules, prolong prosecution until the inventive technology matured in the marketplace. The cunning inventor would then amend the claims to cover products already on the market and sue the competition. *See, e.g.*, *State Indus., Inc. v. A.O. Smith Corp.*, 751 F.2d 1226 (Fed. Cir. 1985). The previously secret application—remember that the Patent Office began publishing pending applications for applications filed only after the American Inventors Protection Act of 1999—would "surface" as an issued patent only after the market had committed to the patented technology. Faced with the prospect of protracted and expensive litigation, the (now-beguiled) competitors oftentimes would simply license the submarine patent. Of course even if the application became a public document through issuance of a patent, continuations remained available for claims that avoided double patenting (either due to a mistake by the PTO or the operation of 35 U.S.C. § 121).

In 2002, however, the Federal Circuit reaffirmed the availability of prosecution laches as a defense, even if it provided no guidance on its application. *Symbol Techs., Inc. v. Lemelson Med., Educ. & Research Found.*, 277 F.3d 1361 (Fed. Cir. 2002). Instead, the court affirmatively ruled that laches may preclude enforcement of patent claims that issued after an unreasonable and unexplained delay in prosecution. This delay could occur even though the applicant complied with pertinent statutes and rules. In a subsequent case involving an appeal from the Patent Office, an applicant was barred from obtaining claims to an invention due to an unreasonably long eight-year prosecution process. *In re Bogese*, 303 F.3d 1362 (Fed. Cir. 2002). In filing a series of twelve continuation applications, the applicant, in particular, neither amended the pending claims nor addressed the outstanding rejections. The applicability of prosecution laches will, of course, winnow in light of the 20–years-from-filing term for patents as well as other Patent Office rules governing continuing prosecution, such as requests for continued examination under 37 C.F.R. § 1.114.

D. Licensee Estoppel

Although not directly related to patent enforcement, the related area of enforcing licenses on patents features another equitable doctrine, the doctrine of licensee estoppel. At one time, patentees often insisted on a clause in license agreements that prevented the licensee from challenging the validity or enforceability of the patent. *See, e.g.*, *Automatic Radio Mfg. Co. v. Hazeltine Research, Inc.*, 339 U.S. 827 (1950). These provisions could insulate weak, or even invalid, patents from attack. The Supreme Court, therefore, stepped in and ended that practice. In *Lear, Inc. v. Adkins*, 395 U.S. 653 (1969), the Court held that the public's interest in freely accessing ideas that belong in the public domain outweighed the interest in binding a party to a contractual promise not to sue. At the crux of its opinion, the Court explained: "Licensees may often be the only individuals with enough economic incentive to challenge the patentability of an inventor's discovery. If they are muzzled, the public may continually be required to pay tribute to would-be monopolists without need or justification." *Id.* at 670.

Although the reasoning of *Lear* would appear sweeping, its reach has been more limited. For example, a party entering into a consent decree in settlement of ongoing patent litigation that acknowledges the validity of a patent may not later challenge that patent's validity, due in part to res judicata, finality of judgments, and the public's interest in encouraging settlements of patent litigation. *Foster v. Hallco Mfg. Co.*, 947 F.2d 469 (Fed. Cir. 1991); *see also Hemstreet v. Spiegel, Inc.*, 851 F.2d 348 (Fed. Cir. 1988).

The Supreme Court, however, recently reinvigorated the *Lear* doctrine in *MedImmune, Inc. v. Genentech, Inc.*, 127 S.Ct. 764, 81 USPQ2d 1225 (2007). In that case, MedImmune promised to pay royalties to Genentech under a license agreement. At some point, however, MedImmune started to believe that the licensed patent was invalid and unenforceable and notified Genentech that it would be paying the contractual royalties "under protest and with reservation of all of its rights." 81 USPQ2d at 1227. Thereafter, MedImmune filed a suit under the Declaratory Judgment Act, all the while continuing to fulfill its obligations under the agreement. Without expressly discussing the precise contours of *Lear*, the Court held that there was a sufficient case or controversy to permit licensee to sue without surrendering the benefits of the license:

Respondents assert that the parties in effect settled this dispute when they entered into the 1997 license agreement. When a licensee enters such an agreement, they contend, it essentially purchases an insurance policy, immunizing it from suits for infringement so long as it continues to pay royalties and does not challenge the covered patents. Permitting it to challenge the validity of the patent without terminating or breaking the agreement alters the deal, allowing the licensee to continue enjoying its immunity while bringing a suit, the elimination of which was part of the patentee's quid pro quo. Of course even if it were valid, this argument would have no force with regard to petitioner's claim that the agreement does not call for royalties because their product does not infringe the patent. But even as to the patent invalidity claim, the point seems to us mistaken. To begin with, it is not clear where the prohibition against challenging the validity of the patents is to be found. It can hardly be implied from the mere promise to pay royalties on patents "which have neither expired nor been held invalid by a court or other body of competent jurisdiction from which no appeal has been or may be taken," App. 399. *Promising to pay royalties on patents that have not been held invalid does not amount to a promise not to seek a holding of their invalidity.*

Id. at 1233 (emphasis added). Earlier, the Supreme Court had similarly hinted that the *Lear* doctrine does not apply to a nonrepudiating licensee: "We express no opinion on whether a *nonrepudiating licensee* is similarly relieved of its contract obligation during a successful challenge to a patent's validity—that is, on the applicability of licensee estoppel under these circumstances." *Id.* at 1228. Therefore, while these circumstances may create a judiciable dispute, the parties may take that possibility into account in drafting and negotiating the license agreement.

Perhaps more importantly (and despite not being fully before the Court in the case), a footnote in *MedImmune* swept away well-established jurisprudence regarding the requisite showing to establish jurisdiction under the Declaratory Judgment Act. *Id.* at 1232 n.11. Following that footnote, the Federal Circuit ruled that any time a patentee offers to license its patent in light of specific, identified acts, there is a justiciable case or controversy giving rise to declaratory judgment jurisdiction. *SanDisk Corp. v. STMicroelectronics, Inc.*, 480 F.3d 1372 (Fed. Cir. 2007).

E. Assignor Estoppel

The *Lear* doctrine prohibits, in limited circumstances, a patentee from assigning the entire risk of an invalid patent to a licensee. That is, a license clause cannot prevent a licensee from challenging the validity of a licensed patent (absent additional circumstances). Assume, however, that the roles are reversed, and a patentee assigns his patent to an assignee. May the assignor—who received at least a modicum of consideration in return for the assignment—later attempt to invalidate the assigned patent? The Federal Circuit in *Diamond Scientific Co. v. Ambico, Inc.*, answered that question in the negative, because assignor estoppel "prevents one who has assigned the rights to a patent (or patent application) from later contending that what was assigned is a nullity." 848 F.2d 1220, 1224 (Fed. Cir. 1988). This equitable doctrine, the court went on to clarify, is rooted in the fundamental notion of fair dealing: "[I]t is the implicit representation by the assignor that the patent rights that he is assigning (presumably for value) are not worthless that sets the assignor apart from the rest of the world and can deprive him of the ability to challenge later the validity of the patent. To allow the assignor to make that representation at the time of the assignment (to his advantage) and later to repudiate it (again to his advantage) could work an injustice against the assignee." *Id.*

III. SHOP RIGHTS

Inventions often result from research within a corporate environment—a rational corporation, of course, willingly invests in research so long as it will profit from that research. To ensure that it owns the fruit of its employees' labor, a company oftentimes requires its employees to assign all rights to any inventions conceived of during their employment to that company. *See Univ. of W. Va. v.*

VanVoorhies, 342 F.3d 1290 (Fed. Cir. 2003). Cases involving the shop rights doctrine, however, arise because an employer has not placed such a condition in their employment contracts. Then, upon patenting technology, an employee may even seek to enforce that patent against his employer. The law provides that employer with limited rights to practice that invention, when the facts and circumstances surrounding the development of the invention equitably justify the employer's continued use of the invention.

For example, in *McElmurry v. Arkansas Power & Light Co.*, 995 F.2d 1576 (Fed. Cir. 1993), Arkansas Power & Light (AP & L) hired the inventor of the patent at issue, Bowman, as a consultant at one of AP & L's power plants. While a consultant, Bowman invented an improved method of measuring the level of fly ash in a hopper. AP & L eventually installed, at its own expense, this fly ash measurement system in all of its power plant hoppers. Bowman also assisted with the installation of the system at a different facility (again at AP & L's expense), but not before he filed an application that eventually matured into a patent on the system. When AP & L installed the system on more hoppers without Bowman's assistance, the patent holder filed suit. The power company raised the shop rights doctrine as its defense.

The Federal Circuit emphasized the fact-specific and equitable nature of the shop right rule. The court, in particular, adopted certain factors to evaluate the overall circumstances: whether the employer financed the employee's invention by providing wages, materials, tools, and working space; the contractual nature of the relationship between the employer and employee; whether the employee consented to the employer's use of the invention; and whether the employee induced, acquiesced in, or assisted in the use of the invention. Because the events compelled the conclusion that the employer retained rights to Bowman's invention, AP & L was not liable for the use of the invention.

Although common law principles of equity may create domestic shop rights, other jurisdictions have addressed employer-employee ownership and use rights by statute. For example, German law provides for mandatory compensation for inventions created through employment. Indeed, under the German Employed Inventor's Rights Law, an employer may only obtain rights to "tied" inventions, which result from the employee's assignments or the activities of the employer. For such "tied" inventions, the employee may demand reasonable compensation from the employer. By way of contrast, "free" inventions may not be used by the employer absent permission of the employee. Furthermore, German law disallows an employee from contracting away his right to compensation for any "tied" inventions.

IV.   TEMPORARY PRESENCE IN THE UNITED STATES

An infrequently applied, yet longstanding principle, relates to the noninfringement of shippers and transporters engaged in international commerce.

See Brown v. Duchesne, 60 U.S. (19 How.) 183 (1856). Enacted in part to implement the Paris Convention, the Patent Act currently provides:

The use of any invention in any vessel, aircraft or vehicle of any country which affords similar privileges to vessels, aircraft or vehicles of the United States, entering the United States temporarily or accidentally, shall not constitute infringement of any patent, if the invention is used exclusively for the needs of the vessel, aircraft or vehicle and is not offered for sale or sold in or used for the manufacture of anything to be sold in or exported from the United States.

35 U.S.C. § 272. The key to this provision is that the entry of the foreign vessel, aircraft, or vehicle must be "temporary." For example, in *National Steel Car, Ltd. v. Canadian Pacific Railway, Ltd.*, 357 F.3d 1319 (Fed. Cir. 2004), the court held that railway cars for hauling lumber from Canada that would be physically present in the United States for over fifty percent of their useful lifespans fell under the exception of § 272. In particular, the court explained that "a vehicle entering the United States 'temporarily' [is] a vehicle entering the United States for a limited period of time for the sole purpose of engaging in international commerce." *Id.* at 1329.

V. FIRST INVENTOR DEFENSE

As a part of the most recent substantial revision of the Patent Act, Congress enacted a new defense—the First Inventor Defense codified at 35

U.S.C. § 273—which although statutory (and thus by definition not equitable), arose from a perceived injustice to users of so-called business methods. As explained in Chapter 3, for years business methods were considered ineligible for patents. *State Street Bank & Trust Co. v. Signature Financial Group, Inc.*, 149 F.3d 1368 (Fed. Cir. 1998) changed that understanding. Even though that belief was misguided, *State Street Bank* was viewed as a dambursting event that threatened the financial services industry, which had by and large shunned patent protection in favor of trade secret protection for innovative products.

Section 273 remedies this perceived injustice in limited circumstances. To begin with, it only applies to patents claiming a "method of doing or conducting business," which is undefined by the statute and not yet subject to judicial interpretation. Nevertheless, this phrase likely corresponds, in general, to a computer-implemented method having an application in the financial or insurance industry. Furthermore, the invoking party must have reduced the subject matter to practice at least one year before the asserted patent's effective filing date. And the invoking party must have commercially used the infringing subject matter before the patent's effective filing date. Lastly, the invoking party must not have derived the subject matter from the patentee.

Although undeniably distinct, this defense is similar to the condition of patentability under § 102(g) in many respects, most notably with respect to attempting to resolve competing claims to first inventorship. *See* Chapter 7. In fact, § 102(g) all but renders § 273 superfluous, except in situations where the first user does not take steps to disclose publicly his invention in a patent application, an article, or otherwise. That is, § 273 fills the gap of the public disclosure requirement of first inventorship in limited circumstances. And in return, the patentee only loses his ability to enforce his patent against the first user without forfeiting his right to a patent altogether.

VI. PATENT MISUSE

Even if their intersection requires study unto itself, patent law and antitrust law both govern aspects of innovation, competition, and commerce. *Atari Games Corp. v. Nintendo of Am., Inc.*, 897 F.2d 1572 (Fed. Cir. 1990). At one of their intersections lies a defense available to any accused infringer: if a patentee misuses its patent rights by violating antitrust-like principles, that patentee may not assert its patent against any party. The violation need not rise to a full-fledged antitrust violation, even if most successful invocations of the misuse defense double as antitrust violations. This defense is particularly peculiar because it excuses potentially infringing behavior even if the victim of the patentee's misuse is a third party wholly distinct from the infringer. That is, this doctrine releases a wrongdoer (the infringer) and permits ongoing infringement because the victim (the patentee) may have wronged someone else through anticompetitive activity. Just like every other equitable defense, misuse is heavily fact dependent, hinging on the totality of circumstances that excuse the patentee's seemingly anticompetitive behavior. Furthermore, the statute and precedent, as clarified by the executive branch of the federal government, have severely limited its application to only a few, select instances.

The defense of patent misuse arose in a series of cases where the patent owner alleged contributory infringement by a manufacturer of unpatented components that were nonetheless covered by a patent license agreement. In these early cases, the party accused of contributory infringement raised this defense to escape infringement for sales of "unpatented" articles for use with a patented invention. *Motion Picture Patents Co. v. Universal Film Mfg. Co.*, 243 U.S. 502 (1917); *Mercoid Corp. v. Mid–Continent Inv. Co.*, 320 U.S. 661 (1944); *Mercoid Corp. v. Minneapolis–Honeywell Regulator Co.*, 320 U.S. 680 (1944). But the Supreme Court expanded the equitable defense's reach beyond those confines in *Morton Salt Co. v. G.S. Suppiger Co.*, 314 U.S. 488 (1942).

In *Morton Salt*, the patented technology related to a machine for depositing salt tablets into canned goods, which facilitated control over the amount of salt added to each can. Both the patentee and accused infringer made salt-deposition machines as well as the salt tablets themselves, although the Court noted that the competition in the sale of salt tablets was irrelevant. Rather than selling its patented machines, the patentee leased them on the condition that the lessees only purchase and use the patentee's salt tablets. The Court thus reasoned that the patentee was restraining trade in an unpatented article, the salt tablets, through its patent covering only a salt-deposition machine. In expanding patent misuse's application to noncompetitors, the Court explained: "It is the adverse effect upon the public interest of a successful infringement suit, in conjunction with the patentee's course of conduct, which disqualifies him to maintain the suit, regardless of whether the particular defendant has suffered misuse of the patent." *Id.* at 494. Under American law, it is highly unusual to allow a party completely unaffected by the alleged wrong to invoke that injustice as an equitable defense.

In 1952, Congress enacted 35 U.S.C. § 271(d)(1) through (3) and later added (4) and (5) so that the statute now carves out five separate behaviors that do not constitute patent misuse. Specifically, a patentee may:

(1) derive[ ] revenue from acts which if performed by another without his consent would constitute contributory infringement of the patent;

(2) license[ ] or authorize[ ] another to perform acts which if performed by another without his consent would constitute contributory infringement of the patent;

(3) [seek] to enforce his patent rights against infringement or contributory infringement;

(4) refuse[ ] to license or use any rights to the patent; or

(5) condition[ ] the license of any rights to the patent or the sale of the patented product on the acquisition of a license to rights in another patent or purchase of a separate product, unless, in view of the circumstances, the patent owner has market power in the relevant market for the patent or patented product on which the license or sale is conditioned.

35 U.S.C § 271(d). Therefore, a patentee who refuses to license others to sell a nonstaple article and insists that customers purchase a nonstaple good from him is not misusing his patent. *Dawson Chem. Co. v. Rohm & Haas Co.*, 448 U.S. 176 (1980).

Furthermore, the Federal Circuit now requires some anticompetitive effect, even if not rising to an antitrust violation, for a misuse violation. For example, in *Mallinckrodt Inc. v. Medipart Inc.*, 976 F.2d 700 (Fed. Cir. 1992), the court upheld, employing a rule of reason, a license agreement in which the patentee restricted purchasers of a medical device to use that device only once. In fact, current law appears to have cabined patent misuse to two limited instances: using the market power generated by a patent to restrain competition in an unpatented field and extending the term of a patent beyond its statutory term. *See, e.g., B. Braun Med., Inc. v. Abbott Labs.*, 124 F.3d 1419 (Fed. Cir. 1997).

More recent patent misuse cases from the Federal Circuit continue to cabin the doctrine as well. *Monsanto Co. v. McFarling*, 363 F.3d 1336 (Fed. Cir. 2004); *U.S. Philips Corp. v. Int'l Trade Comm'n*, 424 F.3d 1179 (Fed. Cir. 2005); and *Monsanto Co. v. Scruggs*, 459 F.3d 1328 (Fed. Cir. 2006).

CHAPTER 15

REMEDIES

I. INTRODUCTION

Once a court has determined that an enforceable patent claim is not invalid and infringed, the patentee is entitled to certain remedies under two statutory provisions: 35 U.S.C. §§ 283 & 284. At its very essence, the patent right naturally implies injunctive relief. In many instances, the most attractive or beneficial remedy for infringement is to make that infringer stop the infringing activity. The authority for granting injunctions, § 283, states:

> The several courts having jurisdiction of cases under this title may grant injunctions in accordance with the principles of equity to prevent the violation of any right secured by patent, on such terms as the court deems reasonable.

Beyond injunctions, a patentee may recover monetary compensation for the infringing activity. In one sense, damages measure the value of the invention. The authority for granting damages, § 284, states:

> Upon finding for the claimant the court shall award the claimant damages adequate to compensate for the infringement, but in no event less than a reasonable royalty for the use made of the

invention by the infringer, together with interest and costs as fixed by the court.

Beyond compensating a patent owner for infringement, however, damages theories also significantly influence substantive patent law. The availability and amount of damages informs not only an applicant's claiming strategy but also the administrative practices of the Patent and Trademark Office. Remedies also flesh out the interaction of patent law and other areas that regulate competition amongst corporations, such as antitrust and unfair competition. In short, the remedial aspects of domestic patent law also significantly affect the substance of the property rights.

II. INJUNCTIONS

An injunction is a critical part of patent law. In fact, one of the earliest pronouncements of the Federal Circuit related to its importance:

> The very nature of the patent right is the right to exclude others. Once the patentee's patents have been held to be valid and infringed, he should be entitled to the full enjoyment and protection of his patent rights. The infringer should not be allowed to continue his infringement in the face of such a holding. A court should not be reluctant to use its equity powers once a party has so clearly established his patent rights.

Smith Int'l, Inc. v. Hughes Tool Co., 718 F.2d 1573, 1581 (Fed. Cir. 1983). As the court recognized, injunctive relief is oftentimes a more valuable remedy than monetary relief. For example, a patentee would be foolish to squander its first-mover advantage or, perhaps more importantly, its market share. Foreign patent systems, particularly those emanating from the civil law tradition, reflect this truth: injunctive relief often is the only practical infringement remedy available in certain jurisdictions. Injunctive relief is available at three stages of litigation: preliminary to adjudication, accompanying a final judgment, and subsequent to enforcement of the injunction via contempt proceedings.

Although permanent injunctions are available to patentees once a court rules that the accused party infringed a valid and enforceable patent, litigation often spans a couple of years (or even the better part of a decade in some cases). Accordingly, a preliminary injunction can, in some situations, have tremendous value, particularly where the true damage caused by infringement would be difficult to assess. Before the Federal Circuit, patentees often faced formidable obstacles in obtaining preliminary injunctive relief. The equitable factors for injunctive relief were particularly hard to satisfy in patent cases. To begin with, injunctive relief required a showing of a likelihood of success in proving both validity and infringement at trial. When patentability standards were uncertain, the likelihood of sustaining the patent's validity was a difficult burden at a preliminary stage. In fact, a prior judgment of validity seemed to be the sole way of proving validity. Beyond a likelihood of success, equity also required no adequate legal remedy before imposing a preliminary injunction. Because damages would be available as a legal remedy, a patentee could almost never leap this hurdle. The Federal Circuit, however, reduced these obstacles substantially.

In *H.H. Robertson, Co. v. United Steel Deck, Inc.*, 820 F.2d 384 (Fed. Cir. 1987), the court reaffirmed that preliminary injunctions were available in patent cases, and the standards were neither higher nor lower than in other areas of the law. Rather, the four-factored test is the same: (1) a reasonable likelihood of success on the merits; (2) irreparable harm to the patentee without a preliminary injunction; (3) a balance of the parties' relative hardships; and (4) the public interest.

With respect to the first equitable factor, the patentee bears the burden of proving validity and infringement, keeping in mind the burdens and presumptions at trial. The Federal Circuit emphasized, for instance, that the patent enjoys a presumption of validity, which may only be overcome by clear and convincing evidence. Even so, the alleged infringer need only show a substantial question about the patent's validity.

On the second factor, irreparable harm—sometimes rephrased as a lack of an adequate remedy at law—the patentee enjoys a presumption of harm upon a showing of a likelihood of success on the merits. This presumption arises from the finite term of a patent, which of course runs as the litigation proceeds. The Federal Circuit observed that damage therefore necessarily results from a delay in excluding infringing goods from the marketplace. Importantly, this presumption is not irrebutable, and the alleged infringer may still show a lack of irreparable harm by certain activities of the patentee, such as licensing.

Even with irreparable harm, a court must still examine the third and fourth factors—the relative hardships between the patentee and infringer and the public interest. The fourth factor comes into play most frequently with respect to public health and safety concerns, such as cutting off the sole source of a life-saving technology. Although a lack of either a likely success on the merits or irreparable harm to the patentee in the absence of an injunction mandates a denial of a motion for a preliminary injunction, a court must consider all four factors.

Even if a court does not preliminarily enjoin the infringer's activities while the litigation is pending, it may permanently enjoin the infringer upon a final judgment of infringement. Indeed, until the Supreme Court stepped in recently to alter the general rule, *eBay, Inc. v. MercExchange, L.L.C.*, 126 S.Ct. 1837, 78 USPQ2d 1577 (2006), the Federal Circuit favored a permanent injunction upon a judgment of infringement in almost every instance. The decision in *eBay* was influenced by the era of concern about "patent trolls." Indeed MercExchange, the patent owner, had some of the characteristics attributed to "trolls," such as a predominant licensing practice and no production of the patented invention. The Supreme Court interpreted the language of § 283 (above) and emphasized that the use of the term "may" makes an injunction optional under the standard four-factor equity test even after a finding of willful infringement.

The more interesting aspect of the Supreme Court's decision was the competing concurrences. Three justices, including Chief Justice Roberts, wrote that "a page of history is worth a volume of logic," apparently advocating a continued adherence to a general rule in favor of permanent injunctions after a finding of infringement. Three other justices, including Justice Kennedy, wrote that a segment of the patent "industry" (apparently a reference to trolls) warrants a change in the past permanent injunction rules. In any event, *eBay* will require additional proof justifying a permanent injunction even after a finding of infringement.

In one circumstance, threats to public health, the fourth element of the equitable test is likely to defeat a permanent injunction. The most famous case on this principle, even if over a half-century old, is *City of Milwaukee v. Activated Sludge, Inc.*, 69 F.2d 577 (7th Cir. 1934). In that case, the appellate court vacated a permanent injunction that would have prevented the city of Milwaukee from using an infringing system of sewage treatment. If enjoined, the city would have dumped its sewage into Lake Michigan. Accordingly, an injunction would have caused great harm to the public health and welfare without a substantial benefit to the patentee, who did not practice the claimed invention.

After a permanent injunction issues, parties occasionally dispute the precise contours of its scope. For the most part, such a dispute arises when the patentee brings a contempt proceeding based on a reengineered product that is similar, though not identical, to the infringing product. The infringer naturally asserts that the differences take the modified good outside the scope of the patent (and thus of the injunction), while the patentee asserts the opposite through a contempt proceeding. Alternatively, the patentee could bring a separate infringement action. In addressing the relative merits of a contempt proceeding or a separate infringement suit, the Federal Circuit stated:

> In sum, the initial question to be answered in ruling on a motion for contempt is whether contempt proceedings are appropriate. That question is answered by the trial court's judging whether substantial disputed issues must be litigated. The second question, whether an injunction has been violated, requires, at a minimum, a finding that the accused device is an infringement.

KSM Fastening Sys., Inc. v. H.A. Jones Co., 776 F.2d 1522, 1532 (Fed. Cir. 1985).

III. DAMAGES

Although equitable relief can hold tremendous value for the patentee, legal relief is also essential to compensate for infringement. The statute instructs that a court must "award the claimant damages adequate to compensate for the infringement." 35 U.S.C. § 284. These damages are sometimes called "but-for" damages, because a court attempts to reconstruct the pecuniary benefit that the patentee would have obtained without infringement. A court has wide discretion to use any economically viable theory to achieve these compensatory damages. In other words, a patentee is not subject to a one-size-fits-all theory of damages. The only mandatory part of the equation is that the award cannot be "less than a reasonable royalty." Typically damages not classified as a reasonable royalty fall under the rubric of lost profits, which although usually more lucrative are also more speculative and more difficult to prove. Nevertheless, case law has developed a rough framework for proof of lost profits.

A. Lost Profits

The lost profits method of damages calculation attempts to restore to the patentee the profits lost due to sales diverted to the infringer. To acquire lost profits damages, a patentee must first show that the infringement caused the profit loss. In other words, the "but for" causation test requires the patentee to show that it would have made each of the infringer's sales of the invention if infringement had not occurred. With Chief Judge Markey of the Court of Customs and Patent Appeals as author, the Sixth Circuit set forth a key test for showing causation. This lost profits test, occasional-

ly called the DAMP test or the *Panduit* test, relies
on four factors:

> To obtain as damages the profits on sales he
> would have made absent the infringement, i.e.,
> the sales made by the infringer, a patent owner
> must prove: (1) demand for the patented product,
> (2) absence of acceptable noninfringing substi-
> tutes, (3) his manufacturing and marketing capa-
> bility to exploit the demand, and (4) the amount
> of the profit he would have made.

Panduit Corp. v. Stahlin Bros. Fibre Works, Inc.,
575 F.2d 1152, 1156 (6th Cir. 1978). This test
operates most reliably in a two-supplier market,
where the patentee and the infringer are the only
players. In that setting, the DAMP test implements
the presumption that the patentee would have
made every sale that the infringer made. *See, e.g.*,
Kaufman Co. v. Lantech, Inc., 926 F.2d 1136 (Fed.
Cir. 1991); *Micro Chem., Inc. v. Lextron, Inc.*, 318
F.3d 1119 (Fed. Cir. 2003). The DAMP test, of
course, still requires identification of the relevant
market, excluding alternatives to the patented product with disparately different prices or significantly
different characteristics. In economic terms, this
identification roughly equates to differentiating the
perfect from the imperfect substitutes for the patented good. After defining the market and showing
only two suppliers, the patentee need only show
that it had the capability to produce and market the
additional infringing goods at a profit.

Importantly, with market conditions often varying widely, courts have not exclusively employed this test for proving lost profits. Other complimentary theories have emerged as ways to compensate the patentee for profits lost due to the infringement. For example, the leading Federal Circuit case on proof of lost profits, *Rite-Hite Corp. v. Kelley Co.*, 56 F.3d 1538 (Fed. Cir. 1995) (*en banc*), held that a patentee may sometimes recover lost profits for product sales in direct competition with the infringing goods, even though those products are not even covered by the patent. In other words, the product replaced by the infringer's goods need not itself be patented. Rather, the product need only be in direct competition with the infringing goods. The key is that the infringer's product must substitute for the patentee's product. If the patentee can show that consumers would have bought its product if the infringing product were not on the market (even if the goods are different in some respects), the patentee can recover the profits it would have made on the sales that instead went to the infringer. *See, e.g., King Instruments Corp. v. Perego*, 65 F.3d 941 (Fed. Cir. 1995). Permitting recovery of lost profits on competitive goods eliminates the need for a second "reverse" infringement investigation into whether the patentee's goods embody the claimed invention. Furthermore, permitting recovery even where the patentee does not commercialize the claimed invention eliminates a potential for inadequate compensation—and a windfall to the infringer.

Similarly, the Federal Circuit has expanded the DAMP test to allow recovery of lost profits in a market with many competing products. *See State Indus., Inc. v. Mor–Flo Industries, Inc.*, 883 F.2d 1573 (Fed. Cir. 1989). With many substitutes in the market, the patentee has great difficulty showing it would have made each of the infringer's sales. Nonetheless, under a market share approach, the patentee can recover lost profits according to its proportional share of the market. The market share rule, in a common sense fashion, divvies up the customers that bought the infringing good amongst the noninfringing substitutes and the patentee according to their market share. Of course, these noninfringing substitutes must still be sufficiently similar in price and characteristics to qualify as substitutes in the same market.

In *BIC Leisure Products, Inc. v. Windsurfing International, Inc.*, 1 F.3d 1214 (Fed. Cir. 1993), for instance, the patentee had exclusive rights to sailboard technology that encompassed both large, expensive sailboards and small, inexpensive funboards. In other words, the claim embraced at least two separate markets. The patentee, Windsurfing International, a manufacturer of large sailboards, could not show that it would have made each of the infringer's sales because BIC sold only funboards.

To illustrate the market share methodology, imagine the same sailboard market but now the infringing good A, the third-party good B, and the patentee good C are all large interchangeable sailboards with comparable prices (usually the ultimate measure of substitutability and market definition). Assuming that goods A, B, and C each enjoy 33⅓% of the market, the market share rule would split the sales of A evenly between the third party and the patentee. The patentee would thus receive lost profits calculated on 50% of the infringing sales. In fact, the two-supplier market rule can be understood as a simplification of the more generally applicable market share rule. That is, imagine a market comprising infringing good A and patentee good B. No matter the market share of each good, the patentee will always capture the sales of infringing good A, thus receiving lost profits based on 100% of the infringing sales.

Of course, the infringer may always attempt to rebut the second prong of the DAMP test by showing the availability of a noninfringing substitute. In *Panduit*, the court reasoned that a "product lacking the advantages of that patented can hardly be termed a substitute 'acceptable' to the customer who wants those advantages." 575 F.2d at 1162. This phrase emphasizes that the claimed invention will rarely have substitutes unless they encompass all the same advantages. In other words, this articulation of the test for noninfringing substitutes is rather strict. The marketplace, on the other hand, very often supplies several substitutes for every product—each with its own advantages and trade-offs. Thus, as the emphasis in damages law has shifted towards a compensation model, the requirements for "noninfringing substitutes" have reflected economic reasoning.

In *Grain Processing Corp. v. American Maize–Products*, 185 F.3d 1341 (Fed. Cir. 1999), for example, the court held that a product not under production or on sale anywhere can serve as a noninfringing substitute. In that case, the accused infringer could have easily made and sold the substitute but had instead sold the cheaper infringing product. The Federal Circuit, however, recognized that in the absence of infringement, the infringer would have simply switched to the alternative:

Reconstructing the market, by definition a hypothetical enterprise, requires the patentee to project economic results that did not occur. To prevent the hypothetical from lapsing into pure speculation, this court requires sound economic proof of the nature of the market and likely outcomes with infringement factored out of the economic picture.

By the same token, a fair and accurate reconstruction of the "but for" market must also take into account, where relevant, alternative actions the infringer foreseeably would have undertaken had he not infringed. Without the infringing product, a rational would-be infringer is likely to offer an acceptable noninfringing alternative, if available, to compete with the patent owner rather than leave the market altogether ... Thus, an accurate reconstruction of the hypothetical "but for" market takes into account any alternatives available to the infringer.

Grain Processing, 185 F.3d at 1350–51.

In a subsequent case, *Micro Chemical, Inc. v. Lextron, Inc.*, 318 F.3d 1119 (Fed. Cir. 2003), however, the Federal Circuit clarified and limited the *Grain Processing* holding. In that later case, the court emphasized that the noninfringing substitute must be readily available, meaning easy access to equipment, know-how, and experience for the substitution. In *Micro Chemical*, a development period of four months coupled with multiple design changes showed that the purported substitute was not readily available.

Based on these cases, the Federal Circuit seems to be directing damages proof towards a unified theory of lost profits. Under this unified theory, entitlement to lost profits would entail four steps. First, the patentee would define the relevant marketplace to include the infringing good and its consumer-recognized substitutes, taking into consideration varying prices and characteristics. The analysis continues to the remaining steps only if the patentee sells a substitute for the infringing good, even if that substitute does not embody the invention. Second, the patentee would determine a presumptive market share of the patentee's goods without infringement—that is, a hypothetical reconstruction of the relevant market based solely on market shares of noninfringing goods. *See, e.g.*, *Ericsson, Inc. v. Harris Corp.*, 352 F.3d 1369 (Fed. Cir. 2003). Third, the infringer would rebut or reduce (perhaps to zero) this market share, either by demonstrating that the infringing good and the patentee's good are imperfect substitutes, *see King*

Instruments Corp. v. Perego, 65 F.3d 941 (Fed. Cir. 1995), or by demonstrating that noninfringing alternatives were readily available, even if not on the market, *see Micro Chemical, Inc. v. Lextron, Inc.*, 318 F.3d 1119 (Fed. Cir. 2003). Fourth, the patentee's lost profits would equal the profit margin indicated by an economic analysis of the likely price in the post-reduction market multiplied by the number of infringing sales. At this point, the model probably requires some economic expertise to determine the elasticity of demand (the market's sensitivity to price changes). This model would apply as well to a market with multiple infringing goods competing with many patentee and third-party goods.

B. Price Erosion

A patentee may use theories other than lost profits to obtain full compensation for the infringement. Price erosion damages—separate yet related to lost profits—attempt to correct for the cross-elasticity of demand between the infringing good and the patentee's good. In other words, if an infringing good is a reasonable substitute for the patentee's good, the price of the infringing good will likely depress the price of the patentee's good. An infringer may often enter the patentee's market at a lower price. After all, the infringer has far less research and development costs. The cheaper infringing good will likely force the patentee to reduce prices to retain sales. Thus, the patentee would not only lose sales to the infringer but also earn fewer profits due to the depressed price. Price erosion thus assumes that, without infringing competition, the patentee could have sustained a higher price and allows damages to compensate for the difference.

Once again, proof of price erosion requires some economic sophistication:

> Moreover, in a credible economic analysis, the patentee cannot show entitlement to a higher price divorced from the effect of that higher price on demand for the product. In other words, the patentee must also present evidence of the (presumably reduced) amount of product the patentee would have sold at the higher price.... "[B]ut for" infringement, Crystal would have tried to charge at least 89 cents more per CODEC.

* * *

> Most of the CODECs Crystal sold were priced at under $10 per unit. A minimum 89 cents price increase would have translated to an approximate 10% increase in selling price. Because Crystal was competing in a competitive market, a 10% price increase would have likely caused customers to substitute the CODECs of other manufacturers for Crystal's CODECs. Crystal, however, presented no evidence of the elasticity of demand of the PC sound card CODEC market. Nor did Crystal make any estimates as to the number of sales it would have lost or kept had it increased its prices by 89 cents per unit. Thus, Crystal did not make a showing of "but for" causation of price erosion.

* * *

Without economic evidence of the resulting market for higher priced CODECs, Crystal cannot have both lost profits and price erosion damages on each of those lost sales. The district court correctly denied Crystal's price erosion damages for lack of adequate record support.

Crystal Semiconductor Corp. v. TriTech Microelectronics Int'l Inc., 246 F.3d 1336, 1359–60 (Fed. Cir. 2001).

C. Reasonable Royalty

As a fallback position, a patentee may seek damages that amount to a reasonable royalty. Thus, a patentee may try to prove that it deserves lost profits for each of the infringer's sales. If unable to show it would have made each of those sales, the patentee still receives reasonable royalties on each of the infringer's uncompensated sales. Courts define a reasonable royalty as the amount likely to have come from a hypothetical negotiation between a willing patentee and infringer at the time when the infringement began. The best way to prove this hypothetical negotiation amount is to produce evidence of licenses the patentee in fact entered with other parties similarly situated to the infringer. But even if the patentee has not licensed the patent, established royalty rates on comparable patents can ground this hypothetical analysis in economic reality. *Mahurkar v. C.R. Bard, Inc.*, 79 F.3d 1572 (Fed. Cir. 1996). Importantly, however, a hypothetical reasonable royalty may exceed an established royalty in many cases, such as when widespread infringement artificially depressed the value of the license. *Nickson Indus., Inc. v. Rol Mfg. Co.*, 847 F.2d 795

(Fed. Cir. 1988). Courts often use a multi-factored list—often called the *Georgia-Pacific* factors—to guide the hypothetical negotiation and prevent it from lapsing into unconstrained speculation. Some of those factors include:

1. The royalties received by the patentee for the licensing of the patent in suit, proving or tending to prove an established royalty.

2. The rates paid by the licensee for the use of other patents comparable to the patent in suit.

6. The effect of selling the patented specialty in promoting sales of other products of the licensee; the existing value of the invention to the licensor as a generator of sales of his non-patented items; and the extent of such derivative or convoyed sales.

8. The established profitability of the product made under the patent; its commercial success; and its current popularity.

9. The utility and advantages of the patent property over the old modes or devices, if any, that had been used for working out similar results.

12. The portion of the profit or of the selling price that may be customary in the particular business or in comparable businesses to allow for the use of the invention or analogous inventions.

13. The portion of the realizable profit that should be credited to the invention as distinguished from non-patented elements, the manufacturing process, business risks,

> or significant features or improvements added by the infringer.

15. The amount that a licensor (such as the patentee) and a licensee (such as the infringer) would have agreed upon (at the time the infringement began) if both had been reasonably and voluntarily trying to reach an agreement; that is, the amount which a prudent licensee—who desired, as a business proposition, to obtain a license to manufacture and sell a particular article embodying the patented invention— would have been willing to pay as a royalty and yet be able to make a reasonable profit and which amount would have been acceptable by a prudent patentee who was willing to grant a license.

Georgia-Pacific Corp. v. United States Plywood Corp., 318 F. Supp. 1116, 1120 (S.D.N.Y. 1970), *modified* 446 F.2d 295 (2d Cir. 1971); *e.g., Smith-Kline Diagnostics, Inc. v. Helena Labs. Corp.*, 926 F.2d 1161 (Fed. Cir. 1991). While the first fourteen *Georgia-Pacific* factors round out the economic picture, the last factor uses that economic picture to reconstruct a hypothetical negotiation that yields the reasonable royalty.

Although the hypothetical negotiation purportedly requires some analytical rigor, a so-called rule of thumb is that a reasonable royalty is oftentimes roughly ¼ to ⅓ of the infringer's profits. While certainly not a foolproof model, the rule of thumb can be helpful in approximating damages without a complete economic analysis.

Because a reasonable royalty serves as a floor for the damage award and because lost profits are typically larger than reasonable royalties, patentees often seek to maximize the damage award by splitting it between the two. For example, imagine an evenly divided market of perfect substitutes, with five goods—infringing good A, third-party goods B, C, and D, and patentee good E—each enjoying a 20% market share. Under the market share rule, 25% of the infringing sales would be captured by the patentee, who would thus be entitled to recover lost profits on that portion. The patentee would therefore be entitled to a reasonable royalty on the sales of A comprising the market share captured by goods not made by the patentee: 75%. Assume further that the patentee's profit margin is approximately equal to the infringer's profit margin (which is typically true in a competitive market). In this situation, the size of the award for a reasonable royalty (using the rule of thumb as a guide) is roughly equivalent to the size of the award for lost profits.

D. The Entire Market Value Rule

As suggested in the *Georgia-Pacific* factors, a patentee may recover lost profits for unpatented components that it would have sold without infringement. To use a simple illustration, if the patented technology was a new kind of tennis racquet frame, the patentee might also seek damages for strings and racquet covers—items sold along with the invention. In *Rite-Hite*, the Federal Circuit explained:

When a patentee seeks damages on unpatented components sold with a patented apparatus,

courts have applied a formulation known as the
"entire market value rule" to determine whether
such components should be included in the damage computation, whether for reasonable royalty
purposes, or for lost profits purposes. Early cases
invoking the entire market value rule required
that for a patentee owning an "improvement
patent" to recover damages calculated on sales of
a larger machine incorporating that improvement, the patentee was required to show that the
entire value of the whole machine, as a market-
able article, was "properly and legally attribut-
able" to the patented feature ... We have held
that the entire market value rule permits recovery of damages based on the value of a patentee's
entire apparatus containing several features
when the patent-related feature is the "basis for
customer demand."

The entire market value rule has typically been
applied to include in the compensation base unpatented components of a device when the unpatented and patented components are physically
part of the same machine. The rule has been
extended to allow inclusion of physically separate
unpatented components normally sold with the
patented components. However, in such cases, the
unpatented and patented components together
were considered to be components of a single
assembly or parts of a complete machine, or they
together constituted a functional unit.

Rite-Hite, 56 F.3d at 1549–50. Thus, under the
Federal Circuit rule for convoyed sales, the unpatented component must form a functional unit with
the patented device.

In the tennis racquet illustration, this rule would probably permit the patentee to recover the profits on strings, because they function as a single unit with the racquet. The racquet cover, however, might not qualify under the rule because the cover has little to do with striking a tennis ball. As a theoretical matter as this illustration shows, the "functional unit" test seems at odds with the rest of the *Rite-Hite* reasoning that allowed lost profits based on the reasonable expectation that the patentee would have made the sale "but for" infringement. Indeed foreign courts often follow this more sound economic reasoning. See, e.g., *Gerber Garment Tech. Inc. v. Lectra Sys. Ltd.*, [1995] RPC 383.

E. Marking

Even though infringement is a strict liability tort, the statute places a key limitation on the ability to recover for past infringement. In particular, a patentee must provide notice of its patent rights by marking its product. The marking provision, § 287(a), states:

Patentees, and persons making, offering for sale, or selling within the United States any patented article for or under them, or importing any patented article into the United States, may give notice to the public that the same is patented, either by fixing thereon the word "patent" or the abbreviation "pat.", together with the number of the patent, or when, from the character of the article, this can not be done, by fixing to it, or to the package wherein one or more of them is contained, a label containing a like notice. In the event of failure so to mark, no damages shall be recovered by the patentee in any action for infringement, except on proof that the infringer was notified of the infringement and continued to infringe thereafter, in which event damages may be recovered only for infringement occurring after such notice. Filing of an action for infringement shall constitute such notice.

Oftentimes, a patentee does not itself make, offer for sale, sell, or import a product embodying the invention and instead chooses to license, either impliedly or expressly, the patent. In such a case, the marking statute still applies—the statute recites "for or under"—and precludes a damage award to the patentee, unless its licensees mark the patented goods. *Amsted Indus. Inc. v. Buckeye Steel Castings Co.*, 24 F.3d 178 (Fed. Cir. 1994).

Furthermore, without adequate marking, the statute precludes recovery of any damages until actual notice to the infringer. This actual notice requires an affirmative act by the patentee which informs the infringer of the infringement. *Dunlap v. Schofield*, 152 U.S. 244 (1894). This means that the notice cannot merely advise the infringer of the patent's existence or ownership; rather, the patentee must identify the allegedly infringing device with a specific charge of infringement. Furthermore, the focus is on the patentee's actions. It is irrelevant that the infringer knew of the infringement independent of the actual notice from the patentee. While a generalized notification does not suffice, filing an infringement lawsuit satisfies the requirement. In any event, without the constructive notice supplied by marking a patented article with the patent number, the patentee may not recover any damages before giving the infringer actual notice.

A party, however, cannot mark an article without a good-faith belief that the patent actually covers the article. In fact, 35 U.S.C. § 292 allows any private party to bring a *qui tam* action against entities who mark an article with a patent number "with the intent of counterfeiting or imitating the mark of the patentee, or of deceiving the public." If successful, the fine of up to $500 per falsely marked article is split between the private party who brought the *qui tam* action and the United States.

Not all patents claim products or devices, of course. In cases where the patent claims only a method, the patentee has nothing physical or tangible to mark. In such a case, the marking statute does not apply; the patentee may recover damages without supplying actual notice to the infringer. But where the patent claims (and the patentee asserts) both product and process claims, the law has reached varied results. For example, *American Medical Systems, Inc. v. Medical Engineering Corp.*, 6 F.3d 1523, 1538 (Fed. Cir. 1993), states:

> The purpose behind the marking statute is to encourage the patentee to give notice to the public of the patent. The reason that the marking statute does not apply to method claims is that, ordinarily, where the patent claims are directed to only a method or process there is nothing to mark. Where the patent contains both apparatus and method claims, however, to the extent that there is a tangible item to mark by which notice

of the asserted method claims can be given, a party is obliged to do so if it intends to avail itself of the constructive notice provisions of section 287(a).

On the other hand, in *Hanson v. Alpine Valley Ski Area, Inc.*, 718 F.2d 1075 (Fed. Cir. 1983), and *Crystal Semiconductor Corp. v. TriTech Microelectronics Int'l, Inc.*, 246 F.3d 1336 (Fed. Cir. 2001), the court sustained damages on an unmarked process when the patentee could have marked an apparatus that performed the process.

IV. WILLFUL INFRINGEMENT: ENHANCED DAMAGES AND ATTORNEY FEES

No matter the size of the compensatory award and no matter whether the patentee establishes it by lost profits, a reasonable royalty, or a combination of both, the statute allows a court to enhance the damages as well as award attorney fees to the prevailing party. Enhanced damages are authorized by § 284:

[T]he court may increase the damages up to three times the amount found or assessed.

Attorney fees are authorized by § 285:

The court in exceptional cases may award reasonable attorney fees to the prevailing party.

Under these sections, the court has discretion to treble the damages and to award attorney fees in cases of "willful infringement." Under § 285, the court has additional discretion to award attorney fees in cases of bad faith litigation or inequitable conduct. Nevertheless, willful infringement forms a substantial portion of the case law on enhanced damages.

Much like a reasonable royalty, willfulness requires an assessment of the totality of the circumstances surrounding the infringement. These factors traditionally include:

1. Whether the infringer deliberately copied the ideas or design of another.

2. Whether the infringer, when he knew of the other's patent protection, investigated the scope of the patent and formed a good-faith belief that it was invalid or that it was not infringed.

3. The infringer's behavior as a party to the litigation.

4. The infringer's size and financial condition.

5. The closeness of the case.

6. The duration of the defendant's misconduct.

7. Remedial action by the defendant.

8. The defendant's motivation for harm.

9. Whether the defendant attempted to conceal its misconduct.

See Read Corp. v. Portec, Inc., 970 F.2d 816 (Fed. Cir. 1992). Because willful infringement depends on the totality of the circumstances—a fact-based inquiry—the factfinder will determine whether the infringer willfully infringed the patent. But even if the jury concludes that the infringer acted willfully, the court retains the discretion to decline to award enhanced damages or attorney fees.

Until recently, the *Read* factors compelled putative infringers to obtain opinion letters to satisfy the duty to avoid infringing another's patent rights. Although providing a steady source of employment, that compulsion became problematic during a trial on infringement. For example, the opinion letter might provide opposing counsel insight into the infringer's litigation strategy, might make the opinion drafter a witness (thus disqualifying her and possibly her firm), might force waiver of the attorney-client privilege, might compel disclosure of the putative infringer's trade secrets, and most importantly might impair the opinion drafter's ability to provide an alleged infringer with a full and frank assessment of the chances of avoiding liability. To resolve some of these concerns, the Federal Circuit took up the issue of willful infringement generally in *Knorr-Bremse Systeme fuer Nutzfahrzeuge Gmbh v. Dana Corp.*, 383 F.3d 1337 (Fed. Cir. 2004). To prevent some of the friction between the attorney-client privilege and the necessity of opinion letters to avoid willfulness, the court decided that the trial court shall not draw any adverse inference when a party invokes the attorney-client or work product privilege to shield an opinion letter. Nevertheless, the court maintained that "there continues to be an affirmative duty of due care to avoid infringement of the known patent rights of others." *Id.* at 1345 (quotation omitted).

This last holding, however, led to another examination of the willfulness rules. Because trial courts occasionally applied a blanket waiver to attorney communications whenever a party relied on an opinion letter, the Federal Circuit took up another case to consider the scope of its *Knorr-Bremse* holding.

The case that the Federal Circuit chose to reconsider *en banc, In re Seagate*, 497 F.3d 1360 (Fed. Cir. 2007), caused a sea of change in the law of willfulness. The Circuit overruled the long-standing duty of due care to avoid infringement and substituted instead a test of objective recklessness for willfulness. The Federal Circuit reasoned that the due care standard was "akin to negligence" and out of sync with willfulness standards used in other intellectual property disciplines (particularly copyright). Without a duty of due care, the Federal Circuit pointed out, potential defendants also have no affirmative obligation to obtain opinion of counsel to protect against willfulness findings. At the same time, the court ruled that defendants who introduce opinions of counsel to rebut willfulness will not risk waiver of attorney-client or work product privileges claimed for the separate work of the trial attorney.

These holdings will have many implications. For example, without a duty of due care, defendants may often succeed in disposing of willfulness charges in a preliminary summary judgment decision. Patentees, on the other hand, may have an incentive to provide more information about the patent to the marketplace at an earlier time to build a case for reckless disregard of infringement warnings. Of course, a patentee who undertakes these pre-suit communications also increases the risk of a declaratory judgment action that allows the defendant to choose the district court for adjudication. In addition, potential defendants no longer need to obtain an opinion of counsel. Nonetheless these opinions will still yield important advantages at and before trial. Indeed, those opinions will undoubtedly contain more candid assessments of infringement and validity because they are no longer the linchpin of a willfulness defense. Finally, and perhaps most important, major manufacturers and researchers can actually consult patents in their design work (particularly during efforts to design around protected technology) without fearing that mere knowledge of the patent will trigger charges of willfulness. The objective standard annunciated in *Seagate* thus encourages prompt, frank communications regarding potential infringement issues and minimizes incentives to fashion a record with an eye to potential future litigation.

V. **INTERNATIONAL REMEDIES**

Preliminary and permanent injunctions are typically available in legal regimes outside the United States. In fact, in some jurisdictions—particularly those emanating from a civil law tradition—injunctions often are the sole practical remedy available. Preliminary injunctions take many forms. Some, such as Italian precautionary measures and Austrian interim injunctions, are roughly analogous to United States preliminary injunctions. Others are different, such as *ex parte* orders like the British "Anton Piller" order and the French saisie-contrefaçon. Such orders do not aim to allow patentees to confiscate infringing technologies, but are in a sense a form of discovery, allowing patentees to establish the origin and extent of the infringement.

The effectiveness of such proceedings varies considerably. In Japan, a patentee's application for a preliminary injunction occurs in a separate proceeding from the primary lawsuit, although the same judges may decide both matters. Because the duration of the preliminary injunction suit may not be considerably shorter than that of the primary suit, experienced litigants often do not seek a preliminary injunction at all. In contrast, the most potent preliminary measure is the Dutch *kort geding*, or short proceeding, which typically only lasts weeks between the initiation of the proceeding and written opinion.

Aside from equitable relief, foreign jurisdictions also award damages to compensate for infringement, recently moving towards a greater acceptance of a reconstruction of the but-for world, similar to the United States methodologies. *See Gerber Garment Tech. Inc. v. Lectra Sys. Ltd.*, [1995] RPC 383. In Japan, for example, remedies such as lost profits are now available in contrast to the historically limited monetary relief. Similarly, the scope and size of potential damage awards in Germany has increased recently, allowing damages to be determined under more generous unfair competition principles.

CHAPTER 16

INTERNATIONAL PATENT LAW

I. MAJOR INTERNATIONAL AGREEMENTS

This Nutshell focuses primarily on the patent laws of the United States, but draws upon experience of other national patent systems as well. This comparative approach applies with particular force for patents because technology, of course, knows no borders. Adequate protection for inventions in an international market will require protection in many different nations. Normally the reach of patent law in each individual nation extends only to acts carried out in the territory of that state. As a general rule each nation has its own laws and institutions to enforce patents. This general rule, however, turns out to be only approximately true as further explained in Chapter 13.

To obtain adequate protection for inventions in a global market, inventors must seek patent protection beyond their own national boundaries. Due to different filing requirements for patent applications including critical timing issues, protection in many nations presents significant burdens. The international community drafted the first great commercial treaty, now known colloquially as the Paris Convention, to alleviate this burden. The latest version of

427

this treaty occurred in Stockholm in 1967. The World Intellectual Property Organization (WIPO) explains the intricacies of this international treaty on its website:

http://www.wipo.int/about-ip/en/iprm/pdf/ch5.
pdf#paris.

A. Paris Convention

The Paris Convention, administered by WIPO, contains three notable principles that bind all signatories: national treatment; patent independence; and international priority. Because over 150 countries are now signatories to the Paris Convention, these principles are nearly universal. The first, national treatment, requires that a signatory refrain from discriminating against foreign inventors. In other words, foreign inventors may not be treated any different than domestic inventors. Paris Convention, Art. 2. Patent independence, the second principle, ensures that each patent functions independent of its foreign counterparts. Art. 4bis. For example, a domestic patent expires on its own terms without regard to the status of counterpart patents in other nations, thus permitting a patentee to allow individual patents to lapse or expire without relinquishing counterpart patent rights in other jurisdictions. At the same time, however, the independence principle requires an inventor to enforce each patent individually in each country, which raises the specter of inconsistent judgments of claim scope and validity. Finally, the most important principle, international priority, protects an inventor's priority dates when filing patents in different nations. Art 4. The first three paragraphs of Article 4 create this protection:

A.—

(1) Any person who has duly filed an application for a patent, or for the registration of a utility model, or of an industrial design, or of a trademark, in one of the countries of the Union, or his successor in title, shall enjoy, for the purpose of filing in the other countries, a right of priority during the periods hereinafter fixed.

(2) Any filing that is equivalent to a regular national filing under the domestic legislation of any country of the Union or under bilateral or multilateral treaties concluded between countries of the Union shall be recognized as giving rise to the right of priority....

B.—

Consequently, any subsequent filing in any of the other countries of the Union before the expiration of the periods referred to above shall not be invalidated by reason of any acts accomplished in the interval ...

C.—

(1) The periods of priority referred to above shall be twelve months for patents and utility models, and six months for industrial designs and trademarks.

(2) These periods shall start from the date of filing of the first application; the day of filing shall not be included in the period....

In its most fundamental aspect, the Paris Convention permits an inventor to secure a priority date by filing an application in any member country (typically, the inventor's home country). With that initial filing, the inventor then has up to one year to file an application on the same subject matter in any other member country. If filed in any member country within the year, the initial filing date becomes the effective filing date for priority. An applicant for a United States patent may take advantage of this procedure, which is authorized by Article 4 of the Paris Convention, under 35 U.S.C. § 119, which states:

(a) An application for patent for an invention filed in this country by any person who has, or whose legal representatives or assigns have, previously regularly filed an application for a patent for the same invention in a foreign country which affords similar privileges in the case of applications filed in the United States or to citizens of the United States, or in a WTO member country, *shall have the same effect* as the same application would have if filed in this country on the date on which the application for patent for the same invention was first filed in such foreign country, if the application in this country is filed within twelve months from the earliest date on which such foreign application was filed....

Section 119 requires a few critical elements: (1) both the foreign and domestic applications must have a common owner; (2) both the foreign and domestic applications must claim the same invention; (3) the foreign application must be for a patent; (4) the foreign application must have been in a country that provides reciprocal rights to United States' citizens or in a country that is a WTO member; (5) the domestic filing must come within one year of the foreign filing; and (6) the statutory bars under § 102(b) remain in effect.

Of these, most problems involve verifying that the foreign application describes the same invention claimed in the domestic application. For example, in *In re Gosteli*, 872 F.2d 1008 (Fed. Cir. 1989), the court refused to grant priority under § 119 to a patent application filed in Luxembourg. The United States application was rejected in light of a patent filed in the United States after the Luxembourg application. This § 102(e) prior art anticipated the claimed genus because it disclosed a species within that scope. If the applicant could claim priority back to its Luxembourg filing, of course, the § 102(e) reference would not be prior art. Unfortunately when transferring the Luxembourg application to the United States, the applicant supplemented the United States application with additional disclosure not appearing in the prior foreign application. Thus, the United States application claimed that broader subject matter or new matter with respect to the Luxembourg filing.

The court first explained that the written description requirement under § 112, which is described in Chapter 9, applied to a claim to priority under § 119, much like a claim to a priority of a domestic application under § 120. Under that new matter doctrine, the foreign application must evince possession of the subject matter claimed in the domestic application. Because the Luxembourg filing did not sufficiently describe the claimed genus, the broad claims could not claim priority back to the foreign filing and thus were invalid for anticipation under § 102(e). *Gosteli* was decided in 1989. The court based its judgment on the principle that the Paris Convention only protects the same invention taught in the foreign application. "Same Invention," G2/98, 2001 Official Journal EPO 413. However, since 1995 foreign acts themselves can be used to show prior invention by the inventor and hence arguably the intermediate reference in *Gosteli* could have been eliminated under § 102(a) using a Rule 131 affidavit antedating the reference. *See* Chapter 7.

Notably, claiming priority to a foreign application under § 119 to avoid an intervening reference does not alter the date of a domestic patent for prior art purposes under either § 102(e) or § 102(g). In other words, the date of a domestic patent for prior art is the domestic filing date, not the foreign priority date. *In re Hilmer*, 359 F.2d 859 (CCPA 1966); *In re Hilmer*, 424 F.2d 1108 (CCPA 1970). In *Hilmer*, the PTO conducted an interference between Hilmer and Habicht over their claims to the same invention. Because of an earlier filing date in the U.S., Habicht prevailed. Hilmer did not give up, but drafted a new set of claims that were slightly different from the interference count. The PTO examiner imposed a rejection based on Habicht as § 102(e) prior art.

Hilmer responded that its priority date related back to a prior German filing that antedated the Habicht filing in the U.S. The PTO sought to rely on Habicht's filing date in Switzerland that was prior to Hilmer's German filing.

The Court of Customs and Patent Appeals, however, denied the PTO that earlier date as the basis for the prior art. Although § 119 purports to give the foreign filing the "same effect" as a domestic filing, the CCPA declared that this provision is only a defensive provision, meaning it only permits a claim of priority to preserve the validity of a claimed invention. The CCPA prevented the PTO from using § 119 to give the Habicht reference the offensive capability to act as prior art beyond its U.S. filing date. The CCPA relied on the language of § 102(e) that limited this prior art category to filings "in the United States." Similarly § 102(g), the prior invention section, limits prior art to filings "in this country."

The patent laws of most other countries permit rejection of an application on the basis of another unpublished application from an earlier Paris Convention application. However, such unpublished applications can usually only apply for novelty rejections, not obviousness or inventive step rejections. In any event, for this purpose the unpublished application used as prior art is given its Paris Convention filing date instead of its actual filing date as is the case in the United States under § 102(e). Whether the Paris Convention actually requires this result is a matter of some dispute.

B. Patent Cooperation Treaty

By its own terms, the Paris Convention is not an exclusive agreement. In fact, the PCT complements the Paris Convention well. Without the PCT, international applicants would have to file an application in each separate country within a year of their first national filing. With the PCT in place, those applicants can instead file a single PCT application. The PCT filing, in turn, designates additional nations where the applicant intends to seek patent rights. At its most basic, the PCT defers nation-by-nation prosecution—also known as entry into the "national phase"—until many months after the priority date. With these additional months, a patent applicant can defer the costs of international prosecution, which can be substantial with translation and foreign counsel fees.

To take advantage of the fee-deferring and time-shifting effect, an applicant files a PCT application with a PCT "Receiving Office." This application is automatically published 18 months after the earliest priority date, which may be the filing date of an application to which the PCT application claims priority. The Receiving Office also automatically performs a prior art search and issues a perfunctory search report without substantive examination. A PCT applicant, however, may request (for an additional fee) a preliminary examination of the claims. This request is also called a "demand" for preliminary examination. Even though this may superficially seem like substantive examination, the preliminary examination report is in fact a nonbinding opinion on the patentability of the claimed invention.

In essence, the PCT facilitates a patent filing system, not a patent granting system. The PCT does not create an "international patent" of any kind. To get patents, applicants still need to apply to each national office. Under the Paris Convention alone, a patent applicant would need to file those multiple applications in other nations within 12 months of the first filing. That process would entail multiple different formality requirements, translations, amendment and publication procedures, and fees. This timeline illustrates the traditional Paris Convention filing system:

Under the PCT system, the applicant can file a single international application which can then undergo a single preliminary examination. This filing process permits the applicant to postpone entry into multiple nations for up to 30 months from the original filing. The following illustration shows the contrast from the traditional Paris Convention system and highlights the advantages of the PCT filing system. As this shows, the applicant can amend a single application in response to prior art and likely streamline the process of acquiring a patent from the various national patent offices at the end of 30 months:

In sum, the PCT can reduce the burden and expense of seeking worldwide protection for an invention. In the long run, the PCT affords extra time beyond the 12 months granted by the Paris Convention. This additional delay in prosecution often gives time for an accurate evaluation of the value of the patent rights eventually obtained. The extra time may also allow applicants to identify potential licensees or other parties interested in the technology before incurring filing fees and costs at the national phase.

C.   Regional Agreements

1.   European Patent Convention and the European Union

In Europe, a patent applicant has the option of filing a single application for multinational rights and prosecuting that single application in pursuit of a single patent under the European Patent Convention (EPC). The EPC establishes a single office—the European Patent Office (EPO)—for substantive examination and also creates a single period of opposition (9 months) before an application matures into a patent. The inventor, however, must enforce the single EPC patent on a country-by-country basis. Hence, the process of obtaining a patent in Europe is complex. Each country that has joined the EPC maintains its own local patent system, but also acknowledges patents obtained through the EPO.

Members of the European Union have retained the power to make patent law for themselves subject to the powers granted to European Union institutions to create patent laws for the entire Union. Thus, when the EPO institutions reach a consensus, those rules bind the signatories. Under this procedure, the Union created the biotechnology directive, an order from the European Commission to each of the member states to conform their patent law to those requirements. The European Commission itself enforces the directive to ensure that each signatory complies. The Commission has attempted to create a uniform rule for software patents, but has not as yet been able to enact either a software directive or regulation. The current status of the efforts of the Commission in the field of patents appears on its industrial property website: http://ec. europa.eu/internal_market/indprop/index_en.htm.

2.   TRIPS and Bilateral Free Trade Agreements

The World Trade Organization has really assumed a leadership role in harmonizing intellectual property rights under its TRIPS—Trade–Related Aspects of Intellectual Property—agreement. TRIPS harmonizes international regimes by establishing minimum legal standards for patentable subject matter, patentability, infringement, enforcement, patent terms, compulsory licensing, and more. In one important respect, TRIPS is not just an ordinary treaty that relies on each signatory to implement and enforce its provisions. Instead the TRIPS agreement includes a method for determining violations and an enforcement system to impose trade sanctions on any country found to violate its provisions. This agreement revolutionized the treatment of intellectual property in signatory countries, particularly those countries with weak protections for intellectual property. For example, to comply with the terms of this agreement, India recently enacted laws that made pharmaceuticals eligible for patenting.

TRIPS is a landmark treaty for many reasons, but one section is of particular importance. Part III of the agreement sets minimum standards for enforcement of the rights of individual owners of intellectual property. This unique part requires nations to provide "fair and equitable" enforcement procedures, TRIPS, Art. 41.2. The agreement requires decisions "preferably in writing" and "without undue delay." TRIPS Art. 41.3. The agreement also mandates some form of discovery. In fact, Article 43 empowers judges to "order that this evidence be provided by the opposing party, subject to ... protection of confidential information." TRIPS, Art. 43.1. The agreement also provides injunctions, TRIPS, Art. 44, adequate damages, TRIPS Art. 45, and powers to seize goods to prevent infringing goods from entering the market or to preserve evidence. TRIPS, Art. 50. Thus, TRIPS has set standards for the performance of judicial officers in nations wishing to join the WTO.

TRIPS also set minimum standards for patent protection in WTO nations. Thus, those nations must offer patents, "whether products or processes, in all fields of technology." TRIPS, Art. 27.1. Article 27 also establishes three substantive criteria for patentability: novelty, inventive step (or obviousness), and industrial application (or utility).

Another important provision of TRIPS governs compulsory licensing. Compulsory licensing is the disfavored process wherein a government forces a patent owner to license its technology. Article 31 of TRIPS limits that practice. Perhaps the most important limit is that a patent owner has a right to "adequate compensation" for any technology subject to the government-compelled license. TRIPS, Art. 31 (h).

Many nations have responded to the challenges of enforcing IP rights by creating special courts with the expertise to handle these complex adjudications. TRIPS, by its terms, does not require these special courts. TRIPS, Art. 41.5. Nonetheless Japan, China, Thailand, Korea, and many European nations (e.g., U.K., Germany), to name just a few, have created special IP courts. Some of these nations, like Japan and China, have special IP courts at both the trial and appellate levels. Others, like the U.K., have special IP courts only at the trial level. Then, of course, the U.S. is the prime example of a system with judges having IP expertise only at the appellate phase. These courts of expertise testify to the importance of intellectual property in the modern world economy.

In addition to the landmark multinational TRIPS agreement, numerous free trade agreements (often bilateral agreements between the U.S. and Jordan or Korea or another nation) contain provisions ensuring adequate patent protections. Some of these treaties go beyond TRIPS to provide "TRIPS plus" requirements. Again, these treaties encourage compliance with the threat of trade sanctions for violations.

II.　INTERNATIONAL ENFORCEMENT

Patents are generally territorial, meaning each state enforces its own patents in its own territory. However, occasionally the patent laws of one state take into account activities in another state. For example courts in both the United States and the U.K. have enforced patents against systems that used computers located in another state. *NTP, Inc. v. Research In Motion, Ltd.*, 418 F.3d 1282 (Fed. Cir. 2005); *Menashe Bus. Mercantile Ltd. v. William Hill Org. Ltd.*, [2003] 1 All E.R. 279. Moreover as discussed in Chapter 13, the United States has a special provision that covers some foreign acts, 35 U.S.C. § 271(f).

Finally, to streamline the process of enforcing patents in several nations, litigants have occasionally asked a court in one nation to consider a claim of patent infringement that took place in another state. That request asks the court to apply under conflict of law principles the law of the nation in which the infringement occurred. In the United

States, for instance, the Federal Circuit has declined invitations to use supplemental jurisdiction to consider foreign infringement under foreign law. *Mars Inc. v. Kabushiki–Kaisha Nippon Conlux*, 24 F.3d 1368 (Fed. Cir. 1994); *Voda v. Cordis Corp.*, 476 F.3d 887 (Fed. Cir. 2007).

*

INDEX

443

†